AF560152

INDIGENOUS PEOPLE
ISSUES AND EMPOWERING STRATEGIES

INDIGENOUS PEOPLE

ISSUES AND EMPOWERING STRATEGIES

Editors

Dr. P. Viswanadha Gupta

Assistant Professor

Dept. of Adult, Continuing Education & Extension

University of Pune

Pune (India)

&

Prof. Dhananjay Lokhande

Professor

Director and Head

Pune University Bulletin

DPH

DISCOVERY PUBLISHING HOUSE PVT. LTD.

NEW DELHI-110 002

Published by:
Tilak Wasan

DISCOVERY PUBLISHING HOUSE PVT. LTD.
4383/4B, Ansari Road, Darya Ganj
New Delhi-110 002 (India)
Phone : +91-11-23279245, 43596064-65
Fax : +91-11-23253475
E-mail : discoverypublishinghouse@gmail.com
sales@discoverypublishinggroup.com
parul.wasan@gmail.com
web : www.discoverypublishinggroup.com

***First Edition:* 2014**

ISBN: 978-93-5056-483-7

Indigenous People: *Issues and Empowering Strategies*

Printed at:
Dynamic Printers
Delhi

Preface

Education in every cultural setting is an instrument for survival, adaptation and change. Tribal society which is segregated in social, economic and geographic entities requires a lot of inputs among which education has a pivotal role to play. Adult education emphasises upon three main components namely: literacy, functionality and awareness. Literacy which is supposed to be a stepping stone for education includes the three rudimentary skills of reading, writing and numeracy and is considered as a minimum need for every human being to have a better life in the society. Functional literacy implies self-reliance in literacy and numeracy; become aware of the causes for their deprivation and moving towards amelioration of their conditions through organization and participation in the process of development, acquiring skills to improve the economic status and general well-being; imbibing the values of national integration, conservation of the environment, women's equality, observance of small family norms, etc. Functionality more or less is concerned with making the individual to function well individually, socially, culturally and economically.

Education enables the scheduled tribes who happen to be backward to acquire knowledge about the individual's environment, development avenues, and programmes being implemented for their well-being. Adult education in India does not end with providing literacy, functionality and awareness. It extends further leading to life-long education and continuing education. The scope of adult education extends to all sections of the community and adult education is a pre-condition to accelerate the pace and magnitude of development especially among the scheduled tribes.

Recognising the special needs of Scheduled Tribes, the Constitution of India made certain special safeguards to protect these communities from all the possible exploitation and thus ensure social justice. While Article 14 confers equal rights and opportunities to all, Article 15 prohibits discrimination against any citizen on the grounds of sex, religion, race, caste, etc., Article 15(4) enjoins upon the State to make special provisions for the advancement of any socially and educationally backward classes; Article 16(4) empowers the State to make provisions for reservation in appointments or posts in favour of any backward class of citizens, which in the opinion of the State, is not adequately represented in the services under the State; Article 46 enjoins upon the State to promote with special care the educational and economic interests of the weaker sections of the people and, in particular, the STs and promises to protect them from social injustice and all forms of exploitation.

We hope this book will be useful for researchers of tribal development, activists, planners, research scholars and all the sympathizers of this national cause in terms of tribes. Our regards to the authors who is accepted the invitation and contributed papers. We are extremely thankful to Discovery Publishing House Pvt. Ltd., for bring out this book in reasonable time. We thank all those who have helped us directly and indirectly to bring out this volume.

P. Viswanadha Gupta
Dhananjay Lokhande

Contents

1

Impact of ICT – An Innovative Approach for Promotion of Education of Adolescent Tribal Girls Children Under SSA

Dr. Sujata Pattanaik*

INTRODUCTION

ICT plays a vital role in the present scenario with its multi-dimension approach under SSA. Major responsibilities of ICT are to promote quality elementary education through distance mode without transmission loss, reaching at the un-reached and remote areas without geographical barriers. Use of ICT brings various innovative approaches which have been reflected in many of the interventions of SSA. This is also an innovative as well as challengeable task for mainstreaming of tribal girls through Bridge course camp.

ICT has a vibrant effect in Quality improvement and is the potential promise in the context of Innovative approach at Elementary Education. It has potentialities with value based experimental segments by using distance learning materials (print, audio, video, etc.,) in regular interval of time. Collection

* Assistant Director, Odisha Madhyamika Siksha Mission Rastriya Maedhyamika Sksha Abhiyan, 18, Forest Park, Bhubaneswar.

of feedback, remedial teaching, motivational camp through Video shows, Parental counseling, Door to door survey by using electronic media are some of the flexible activities associated with this package.

Through this paper Impact of ICT have been analysed during the course of time to meet the challenge as to bring back the non-starter/drop-out girl children to school and to mainstream them.

Rationale of the Study

In order to enhance quality education and mainstream the SC/ST adolescent girls one has to:

- Identify the socio-cultural barriers in education of the non-starters.
- Study the attitude of the parents towards education of their girls in the camp.
- Study the attitude and reaction of never enrolled girls towards the schooling system.
- Study the rate of achievement of individual child in scholastic and mostly on co-scholastic areas.
- Study the various practices undertaken for life skill and vocational education.
- Identify the minimum level of competencies acquired by each child.

SSA is a community based programme, and the role of Community has been considered quite central in the elementary education. Different Activities taken up during the Bridge Course has its own effort and potentialities to make the success in particular and mobilize the community in general. Ultimately this enhances quality Education by promoting girls education.

National Curriculum Framework (2005) strongly recommended for substantial improvement in QEE. It is therefore decided to undertake this study for "Impact of ICT gets back the tribal girls children enrolled in Schooling but also continue and complete the Schooling System".

Activities under Quality Improvement

- A systematic and logical method.
- Association of stimuli, treatment, environmental conditions and observations.
- Effective application without class room but in residential camps where variables can be controlled to some degree.
- To predict events in the experimental setting.

The most dynamic and inventory activities organized in this study are as follows. One diagrammatical representation is also given.

Three Dimensional Module and Quality Initiative

Quality Improvement has 3 Major Dimensions

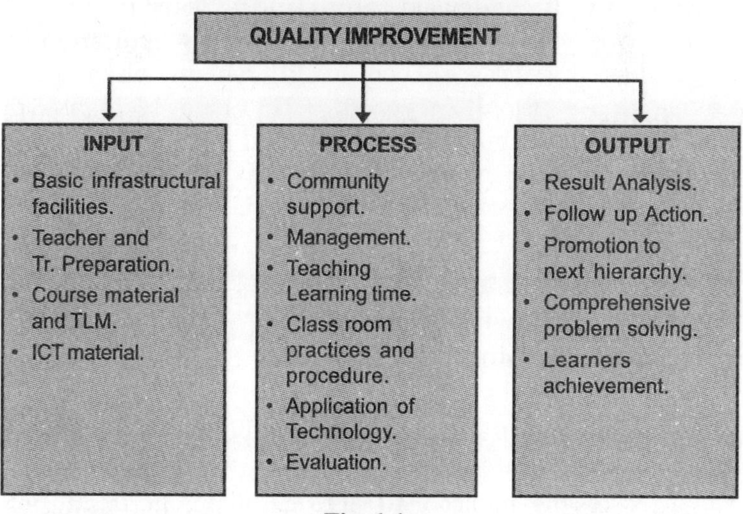

Fig. 1.1:

(The entire 3 dimensional figure involves in the Experimental Approach for completion of the course successfully).

Regular and vibrating activities through this module promote girls education and ultimately promotes QEE. Quality improvement relates with sustainability, stimulus-response in teaching learning process, providing support material, new method, LATS, achievements in series, result analysis, main streaming etc., are the activities in adolescent girls camp.

ICT in Adolescent Girls Camp

Facilities and a series of activities relating to ICT, Audio-Video Programme, Dance, Songs, Music, follow up actions, monitoring, evaluation etc., are furnished from beginning to the end of this camp in a regular basis with an intension to bring the level of competencies of each child for main streaming.

Bridge Course Material

The bridge course module 'Sanjukta' has been designed for preparing out of school children to join formal school. This Bridge course or Back to school strategy enables the learners to achieve the competencies in appropriate for their age in a short period, during which the children are allowed to learn at their own pace. The curriculum transacted to the learners is in a condensed form and the learners achieve equivalence with their peers in the formal school and join them in appropriate class. There are different models of Bridge Course for 5-8 yrs old, 7-9 yrs old, 9-11 yrs old, 12-14 yrs old, 9-14 yrs old, which are Residential and Non-residential in nature. Sometimes the girls can go on to directly attend the camp rather than going from a residential centre.

Objectives in View

Keeping in view the above matters the present paper based on the following objectives.

- To promote education of adolescent non starter/drop-out SC/ST girls.
- To enhance quality education in both scholastic and co-scholastic areas.
- To assess the impact of distance learning materials during the course.
- To orient the girls through distance education mode (print, audio, video and multi-media).
- To provide basic education through Bridge Course.

(Sanjukta Module)

- To impart life skill and vocational education.
- Empowerment of girls for future building and capacity building.

- To provide modalities like continuous and comprehensive evaluation.

Background of the Study

Tribal Education in Odisha SSA:

1. Tribal literacy rate 27 per cent less than the overall Female literacy rate and widening over decade.
2. Tribal children Drop-out rate at primary (31%) elementary (49%) level.

It is a fact; Tribal children are fond up of music, songs, dance, stories, Pictures etc., and in order to promote their education. The tribal adolescent girls need to be monitored closely and separately. The Audio-Video Materials has taken major role to motivate them by arrangement of community sensitization programme. To ensure cent per cent retention and zero per cent drop-out of 6-14 age group, all type of support have been provided to a group of adolescent girls.

Implementation of quality education with full experimental in remote tribal pocket and several attempts has been taken at the initial stage to bring the children to the camp.

For this, elaborate data base of Orissa child census-2005 has been followed to locate out of school children in the age group of 6-14 yrs in Rayagada bock of dst. Rayagada. Total 261641 (CTS-06) children within this age are out of school children these children either did not join the school system or they left the school before completing their schooling.

Design of the Study

Thirty (30) SC/ST girl children of 9-14 yrs age group from different villages of Rayagada block, Dist. Rayagada, Odisha, SSA have been selected and provided with reading writing materials, Bridge Course module Sanjukta, Boarding and Lodging facilities, sports materials, materials for Life skill Training, Audio Video, multi-media material, full time trained EV, Life skill instructor for this six months course. Different stages were taken up which are as below:

(i) One motivational camp has been held up where all the parents of the children were invited, and Sarapanch, VEC, DPG, DIs, BRCC, CRCC, State level Officers, GC, Zonal coordinator of NPEGEL etc., attended the meeting. The VEC president has given speech in local language.

(ii) One Video show was organized with the success stories developed by DEP, IGNOU and Opepa, Jhumpara Jeed (received National award), and Asha, Banamallira Mahak, Nua Suruj, Abe Bujhili and others.

(iii) Questionnaire both for parents and children (newly admitted) were administered and data collected, which were compiled latter.

(iv) A continuous and comprehensive evaluation tools have been designed and used to study the fruitfulness of the camp in relation to scholastic and co-scholastic achievement of the children for mainstreaming after completion of their course successfully.

(v) Remedial teachings are also provided for increasing the competency level of the low achievers.

(vi) The case history of each child has been maintained. A progress card with grade, learning competency, personal and social attitude/behaviour, co-curricular activities, etc., has been maintained regularly.

(vii) Regular use of Audio-Video materials was recorded before use and after use.

Scope and Limitation

- The study is delimited to only 30 girls child of SC/ST category of Rayagada block, Dist. Rayagada, Orissa, enrolled in the six month bridge course camp 'Sanjukta' located at Matikana Primary school.
- Except one they are all non-starters and from low socio-economic background.
- One child is physically handicapped.
- The analysis and comparison of data has to been made through percentage analysis method.
- Mainstreaming is the major scope behind the study.

Method of Study

Sampling

Sample of the study constitute the students of adolescent girls camp located at Matikana, Rayagada block, Rayagada district. The most important concern of the sampling is that they are all non-starters and belong to SC/ST group.

Organization of Sample

Regular assessments of the samples (total 30) were made at the teaching centre by the EV and BRCC in different formats provided to them. Sample of the study has been selected from the target children of non starter and drop-out of the following age group.

Table 1.1: Shows the number of out of school children of different age group

Description	Age Group 5-8	Age Group 9-11 yrs	Age Group 12-14 yrs	Age Group 9-14
Total No. of the Children	1	13	16	29

Tools

For impartial collection of data the researcher has used the pre-term, mid-term and final term examination tools during this six month bridge course camp.

Collection of Data

Pre-term, mid-term and final term examination tools have been distributed in due time *i.e.,* before commencement of this camp, after three months and lastly after six months or completion of course.

Analysis and Interpretation

Pre-test Analysis

The Pre test was supported by 20 numbers of questions and administered among each girl of the camp by face to face interaction before entering into the camp. It is used as a self-reporting technique to record the responses of the girls. The main aim is to the back ground information of the out of school children, difficulties faced by them, exceptional behaviour, special attitude of their personal and social qualities.

Table 1.2: Achievement contour of the adolescent girls in 1st unit test of scholastic area

Sl. No.	Subject	N	Mean	Mean Percentage
1.	Language	366/29	12.62	50.48
2.	Math	453/29	15.62	62.48
3.	EVS	330/29	11.37	45.52

(Table 1.2 shows the mean percentage in achievement of 1st unit test).

Table 1.2 data reveals that, the children those who were not even speak and afraid to come to front they have appeared the test and achieved to a greater extent. There is significant improvement in the performance of each child.

Table 1.3: Mean and mean percentage of mid-term test in scholastic areas

Sl. No.	Subject	N	Mean	Mean Percentage
1.	Language	382/30	12.73	50.93
2.	Math	410/30	13.66	54.64
3.	EVS	454/30	15.13	62.52

After the completion of 3 months camp with Sanjukta Bridge Course Module, mid term test has conducted. The subjects were considered in 17 items (attached in Annexure 4). It has interpreted from Table 1.3, that, there is no doubt a significant effect in systematic testing followed by remedial teaching and by use of audio video material.

(Table 1.3 and 1.4 exhibits the percentage of effectiveness by application of DL materials).

It can be explained here that the achievements of the adolescent girls are significant. Though 96.66 per cent of girls are non-starters they were achieved a lot during these 3 months.

Table 1.4: Mean and mean percentage of final-term test in scholastic areas

Sl. No.	Subject	N	Mean	Mean %
1.	Language	1204/30	40.13	57.33
2.	Math	604/28	20.96	30.66
3.	Social studies	1073/29	37.00	52.85
4.	Science	1122/29	40.00	57.14

Table 1.5: Achievement status in co-scholastic areas both in 1st, mid and final test

Area	Girls Secured A Grade % in Mid and Final Test		Girls Secured B Grade % in Mid and Final Test		Girls Secured C Grade % in Mid and Final Test	
Art and Craft	20.00	30.00	49.99	65.66	40.00	20.00
General knowledge	20 .00	20.00	40.00	60.00	26.66	—
Music and dance	66.66	83.63	16.66	16.66	6.85	—
Personality status	56.66	93.33	27.33	6.66	28.65	—
Vocational status	54.33	66.60	50.00	33.33	50.00	—
Health status	83.33	95.00	16.66	—	—	—

(Table 1.5 exhibits co-scholastic achievement status in percentage).

Table 1.5 co-scholastic achievement status has revealed that the girls have achieved an extraordinary success in these areas which are the key personality development of the children.

* Detail descriptions of various data are given in annexures.

Findings of the Study

- Advances in ICT through Child Census-2005 have increased our reach to pick up 30 out of tribal adolescent girl children in the age group of 9-14 yrs.
- Awareness of the parents, motivation, counseling, are the various strategies made tangible inputs to achieve this success.

- Enhancement of girl's achievement in relation to scholastic and co-scholastic areas is quite significant.
- Active partition of the girls in all sorts of activities is note worthy.
- Maximum use of TLM and DL Materials made the entire course lively and interesting.
- Supplementary teaching materials in shape of ICT and Remedial teaching provided during the course are highly attractive and participatory in nature.
- Education in Informal setting has proved the most challenging. As per the performance report of girls 23 out of 30 were achieved the competency level of class V and has been main streamed in nearby KGBV Schools of Rayagada for further study. At the same time the other 7 girls were also admitted in the formal schools as per the instruction of DI of schools.

Effectiveness of ICT Materials

The intensive mobilization of the community, Education of drop-out girls in an experimental situation, regular monitoring, regular use of DL Materials and ICT, provision of vocational education, life skill in making personality building of these children.

Educational Implications

- Improves quality education.
- Promotes education and Capacity building of tribal girls.
- A great support to present education system.

Great success is Champi Saraka disabled girl who will be one great example to promote CWSN under SSA.

REFERENCES

Report of Lab area activities by DEP of Orissa.

ICT Initiatives Quality Improvement Elementary.

Education DEP-IGNOU New Delhi.

Original Scripts of Action Research.

One video DVD/VCD has been shown at the time of Presentation (25 mnts of time) where entire Programme has been documented.

ANNEXURE – I

Name	Level 4 Assessment Test Co Curricular Activities:				
	(GK)	(Art and Craft)	(Music and Dance)	(Personality Development)	(Health Status)
1	2	3	4	5	6
Subhadra Ganta	A	A	A	A	A
Gouri Kand	A	A	A	A	A
Manika Saraka	B	B	A	A	A
Gouri Himirika	B	A	A	A	A
Kumati Piribaka	C	C	A	A	A
Ambika Puala	B	A	A	A	A
Sandhe Madangi	B	B	A	A	A
Chumalu Saraka	B	B	A	A	A
Lalmani Kalaka	A	A	A	A	A
Radhika Mandingi	B	B	A	A	A
Sanju Mandingi	B	B	A	A	A
Sukanti Batriya	B	B	A	A	A
Basanti Minaka	C	B	A	A	A
Rosy Mandingi	B	A	A	A	A
Chuni Mandingi	A	B	A	A	A
Buchi Tadingi	B	B	A	A	A
Sesi Tadingi	B	A	A	A	A
Ajanti Piribaka	B	B	B	A	A
Lalita Garadia	B	B	B	B	A
Champi Saraka	B	B	A	B	A
Pratima Mandangi	B	B	A	A	A
Senkeri Mandangi	C	B	B	A	A
Mamy Mandangi	A	B	A	A	A
Sindi Mandangi	B	B	A	A	A
Dambai Mandangi	B	B	A	A	A

(Contd...)

1	2	3	4	5	6
Aasimi Mandangi	A	A	A	A	A
Champa Bidika	B	A	A	A	A
Chandrabati Bidika	C	B	A	A	A
Rajmani Benia	C	B	B	A	A
Jatini Saraka	C	B	B	A	A
Grade – A (above 80%)					
Grade – B (above 60%)					
Grade – C (above 50%)					

ANNEXURE – II

Name	Mid-Term Assessment Test Co-Curricular Activities:				
	(GK)	(Art and Craft)	(Music and Dance)	(Personality Development)	(Health Status)
1	**2**	**3**	**4**	**5**	**6**
Subhadra Ganta	A	A	A	A	A
Gouri Kand	A	A	A	A	A
Manika Saraka	A	A	A	A	A
Gouri Himirika	A	A	A	A	A
Kumati Piribaka	C	C	A	B	B
Ambika Puala	B	A	C	A	A
Sandhe Madangi	C	A	A	C	A
Chumalu Saraka	C	B	A	A	A
Lalmani Kalaka	B	B	A	A	B
Radhika Mandingi	B	B	C	C	A
Sanju Mandingi	C	B	A	A	A
Sukanti Batriya	A	C	A	A	A
Basanti Minaka	B	B	A	A	A
Rosy Mandingi	B	B	B	C	A
Chuni Mandingi	A	B	A	A	A

(Contd...)

1	2	3	4	5	6
Buchi Tadingi	C	B	A	A	A
Sesi Tadingi	B	C	B	B	A
Ajanti Piribaka	C	B	C	A	A
Lalita Garadia	C	C	C	A	A
Champi Saraka	C	B	B	B	A
Pratima Mandangi	B	B	C	B	B
Senkeri Mandangi	B	C	B	B	A
Mamy Mandangi	C	B	A	B	A
Sindi Mandangi	C	C	A	A	B
Dambai Mandangi	B	B	A	A	A
Aasimi Mandangi	B	B	C	C	A
Champa Bidika	B	C	A	A	B
Chandrabati Bidika	C	B	C	C	A
Rajmani Benia	B	C	B	B	A
Jatini Saraka	C	C	C	C	A
Grade – A (above 80%)					
Grade – B (above 60%)					
Grade – C (above 50%)					

ANNEXURE – III

Description on Progress Made in Mid-Term Test

Name	Mid-Term Language	Assessment Test Math	F.M. - 25 EVS
1	2	3	4
Subhadra Ganta	22	21	24
Gouri Kand	20	19	22
Manika Saraka	21	20	23
Gouri Himirika	20	18	23
Kumati Piribaka	16	15	19
Ambika Puala	23	17	20

(Contd...)

1	2	3	4
Sandhe Madangi	17	20	21
Chumalu Saraka	17	18	22
Lalmani Kalaka	14	15	16
Radhika Mandingi	17	15	20
Sanju Mandingi	18	19	21
Sukanti Batriya	8	14	18
Basanti Minaka	15	14	18
Rosy Mandingi	17	15	18
Chuni Mandingi	8	12	9
Buchi Tadingi	7	8	9
Sesi Tadingi	9	10	12
Ajanti Piribaka	12	15	16
Lalita Garadia	12	14	16
Champi Saraka	10	12	12
Pratima Mandangi	12	10	12
Senkeri Mandangi	15	10	7
Mamy Mandangi	7	10	9
Sindi Mandangi	12	14	15
Dambai Mandangi	6	12	8
Aasimi Mandangi	12	8	9
Champa Bidika	9	8	10
Chandrabati Bidika	7	8	9
Rajmani Benia	7	5	8
Jatini Saraka	10	14	8

2

Tribal Education and Development

An Over View of Programmes, Policies and Perspectives

Pradeep Kumar Mishra*
Dr. Rashmirekha Sethy**

INTRODUCTION

Indian is a pluralistic country, with reach diversity, reflected in the multitude of culture, religions, languages and racial stocks. The Indian population includes different castes, communities and social groups. The prevalence of such pluralism has made the social fabric, stratified and hierarchical, consequently, social and economic opportunities are differently distributed on the lines of caste and class affiliation. At the geographical level also, India has equally has pervasive and diverse feature. Apart from a minuscule minority the rest live in the rural areas of India. India is such a country where the real reflection of life comes from the core of rural areas.

Rural India is characterised by lack of infrastructural facilities, poverty and indebtedness, which has led to the perpetuation of layers of inequalities and disparities at various

* Ph.D Scholar, RIE (NCERT), Bhubaneswar. Mob. 09090785455. E-mail: pradeepmshr05@gmail.com

** Assistant Professor, RIE (NCERT), Bhubaneswar. Mob. 8763666527. E-mail: rasna_rosnara@yahoo.co.in

levels. As a result, not only have certain deprived group and section of population been unable to partake in the process of development but also affected the very pace of India's socio-economic development. This is particularly severe in the case of scheduled tribe as they not only live in hinterland, bereft of basic amenities of modern life, but also socially and economically marginalised. Their social deprivation is aptly reflected in their educational backwardness. In this context it can be said that tribal India is the least developed area and the tribals are the worst sufferers as they are doubly disadvantageous.

From the time immemorial, the tribal of the country have been neglected in different fields. They have been devoid of their right and basic amenities. They used to live in a society where there was hardly any scope for freedom and open expression of thought and feeling. This issue was addressed after the independence when the constitutional framers came with some of the immediate measures to mainstream the tribal into the current of educational and socialisation process. In order to protect their right, the constitution of India came with some of the non fixable provisions which might help them to recognise their own capacity and wisdom. In this connection, some of the provisions of the Indian constitution have been cited below which takes care of the educational issues of the disadvantaged groups.

Constitutional Provision on Education for the Disadvantaged Group

Art. 21A: The State shall provide free and compulsory education to all children of the age of six to fourteen years in such manner as the State may, by law, determine. (Eighty-Sixth Amendment Act, 2002).

Art. 41: Right to work, to education and to public assistance in certain cases.

The State shall, within the limits of its economic capacity and development, make effective provision for securing the right to work, to education and to public assistance in cases of unemployment, old age, sickness and disablement, and in other cases of undeserved want.

Art. 45: Provision for free and compulsory education for children.

1. The State shall endeavour to provide, within a period of ten years from the commencement of this Constitution, for free and compulsory education for all children until they complete the age of fourteen years.
2. The State shall endeavour to provide early childhood care and education for all children until they complete the age of six years. (Eighty-Sixth Amendment Act, 2002).

Art. 46: Promotion of educational and economic interests of Scheduled Castes, Scheduled Tribes and other weaker sections.

The State shall promote with special care the educational and economic interests of the weaker sections of the people, and, in particular, of the Scheduled Castes and the Scheduled Tribes, and shall protect them from social injustice and all forms of exploitation.

Minorities

Art. 29: Protection of interests of minorities.

1. Any section of the citizens residing in the territory of India or any part thereof having a distinct language, script or culture of its own shall have the right to conserve the same.
2. No citizen shall be denied admission into any educational institution maintained by the State or receiving aid out of State funds on grounds only of religion, race, caste, language or any of them.

Art. 30: Right of minorities to establish and administer educational institutions.

1. All minorities, whether based on religion or language, shall have the right to establish and administer educational institutions of their choice.

(1A) In making any law providing for the compulsory acquisition of any property of an educational institution established and administered by a minority, referred to in clause.

1. The State shall ensure that the amount fixed by or determined under such law for the acquisition of such property is such as would not restrict or abrogate the right guaranteed under that clause.
2. The State shall not, in granting aid to educational institutions, discriminate against any educational institution on the ground that it is under the management of a minority, whether based on religion or language.

Equality

Art. 15: Prohibition of discrimination on grounds of religion, race, caste, sex or place of birth.

1. The State shall not discriminate against any citizen on grounds only of religion, race, caste, sex, and place of birth or any of them.
2. No citizen shall, on grounds only of religion, race, caste, sex, place of birth or any of them, be subject to any disability, liability, restriction or condition with regard to:
   (a) access to shops, public restaurants, hotels and places of public entertainment; or
   (b) the use of wells, tanks, bathing ghats, roads and places of public resort maintained wholly or partly out of State funds or dedicated to the use of the general public.
3. Nothing in this article shall prevent the State from making any special provision for women and children.
4. Nothing in this article or in clause (2) of article 29 shall prevent the State from making any special provision for the advancement of any socially and educationally backward classes of citizens or for the Scheduled Castes and the Scheduled Tribes.

Art. 17: Abolition of Untouchability.

'Untouchability' is abolished and its practice in any form is forbidden. The enforcement of any disability arising out of 'Untouchability' shall be an offence punishable in accordance with law.

Art. 24: Prohibition of employment of children in factories, etc.

No child below the age of fourteen years shall be employed to work in any factory or mine or engaged in any other hazardous employment

Gender and Vulnerable Groups

Art. 39: Certain principles of policy to be followed by the State.

The State shall, in particular, direct its policy towards securing:

(a) That the citizens, men and women equally, have the right to an adequate means of livelihood.

(b) That the health and strength of workers, men and women, and the tender age of children are not abused and that citizens are not forced by economic necessity to enter avocations unsuited to their age or strength.

(c) That children are given opportunities and facilities to develop in a healthy manner and in conditions of freedom and dignity and that childhood and youth are protected against exploitation and against moral and material abandonment.

In addition to the educational provisions, the government has taken several initiatives in order to improve the status of the tribal people who are being considered as the underprivileged group of Indian society. Constant effort has been made by the government to mainstream the tribal people by devising various policies and special programmes under different annual and five year plans. Here accounts of all annual and five years plans have been given in order to create a consensus regarding the different developmental issues of the tribal people.

The First Five-year Plan (1951-56)

The First Five-year Plan outlined a positive policy for assisting the tribals as under:

(*i*) Assisting them to develop their natural resources and to evoke a productive economic life wherein they will enjoy the fruits of their own labour and will not be exploited by more organized economic forces from outside.

(*ii*) It is not desirable to bring about changes in their religions and social life, except at the initiative of the tribal people themselves and with their willing consent.

(*iii*) It is accepted that there are many features in tribal life which should not only be retained but also developed.

(*iv*) The qualities of their dialects, and the rich content of their arts and crafts also need to be appreciated and preserved.

Taking into consideration the conditions of the tribal people, The First Planning Commission quoted that "There may be a good deal of justification for such (isolation) a policy of non-interference; but it is not easily practicable when tribal life has been influenced by social forces from without, and tribal communities have reached a certain degree of acculturation accompanied by the penetration of communications in the tribal areas, and of social services for the betterment of their lives".

In the First Five-year Plan, Community Development Projects for all round development of rural areas especially the weaker sections were started.

Third Five-year Plan (1961-66)

Towards the end of the second plan, *i.e.*, in 1959, the government of India appointed a committee under the chairmanship of Verrier Elwin to review the SMPT Blocks. According to the recommendations of this committee, during the Third Plan period, SMPT Blocks were renamed as Tribal Development Blocks (TDB) and suggested it to be opened in all areas where over 60 per cent of the populations are tribals. In addition to the normal allotment of Rs. 12 lakhs to a community development block, a provision of Rs. 10 lakhs for 1st stage, and Rs. 5 lakhs for 2nd stage for TDB was also made.

Three Annual Plans (1966-69)

During this period no special funds were provided for tribal development. However in 1969-70 a decision was taken to extent the total life of TDBs to 15 years by incorporating a new stage three. During the 3rd stage each TDB was given Rs. 10 lakhs.

Fourth Five-year Plan (1969-74)

During the Fourth Five-year Plan, a series of programmes were conceived and addressed to specific target groups. The Small Farmers Development Agencies (SFDA) and Marginal Farmers and Agricultural Labourers Development Agencies (MFAL) were the first two in the series. In these cases, attention was shifted from area development to development of identified individuals who qualified for special attention according to certain objective criteria.

The Drought Prone Area Programme (DPAP) was another measure in the same direction but with a difference. Here the attention is given to the problem faced by an entire region which is depressed because of its agro-climatic situation. The specific target-group approach, however, was adopted to cater attention on the weaker sections of the society. In the wake of establishment of these area specific and weaker-group oriented projects, the programme for tribal areas were also on a pilot basis. Tribal Development Agencies (TDA's) were established on the pattern of SFDA which addressed themselves to the problems of the tribal population. The level of investment in the new programme was much higher compared to TD Block. Six tribal development agencies were started during the Fourth Plan. Each Tribal Development Agency covered a group of TD Blocks. Tribal Development Agencies were expected to comprise elements of educational development, social services and prospective measures.

By the time of Fourth Plan, one of the drawbacks of the functioning of TDBS became clear that their activities were not properly integrated with the general development plans for the region. The Fourth Plan tried to rectify this drawback by adopting the integrated area development approach. Sectoral outlays for tribal development during the First Five-year Plan to the Fourth Five-year Plan are shown in the Table 2.1 below.

Table 2.1: Sector-wise outlays for tribal development

(Rs. in crores)

Plan Period	Education	Economic Upliftment	Health, Housing etc.	Total
Ist plan	5.10	8.46	3.81	17.37
IInd plan	8.05	22.70	9.76	40.51
IIIrd plan	13.23	30.72	7.10	51.05
1966-69	9.32	24.07	1.93	35.32
IVth Plan	3 1.50	42.25	10.45	84.20

Source: Fourth Five-year Plan Approach Paper.

Table 2.1 shows that the investments in (sector-wise) successive Five Plan period have progressively increased and the sector-wise out lay on education has increased sharply. Sectoral outlay of economic upliftment was given the highest priority in different plans.

Fifth Five-year Plan (1974-79)

During the middle of the Fourth Five-year Plan, *i.e.*, in the year 1972, the Planning Commission set up a 'Task force on Development of Tribal Areas' with L.P. Vidyarthi as the Chairman. In their appraisal, the task force observed that in spite of various kinds of investment by the State and Central governments for tribal development in successive plans, the problem of the tribals reflected in primitive methods of agriculture, land alienation, indebtedness, adverse effects of industrialization, low rate of literacy, poor health of nutrition etc., had not been solved. The committee opined that one of the important factors for the lack of impact so far was that development of Scheduled Tribes and tribal areas had been looked upon as a problem of 'welfare' as distinguished from 'development'.

Taking into account of the recommendations of the task force and other previous committees, during the Fifth Five-year Plan, an altogether new approach was adopted towards tribal development. This was termed as Tribal Sub-plan. It envisaged the total development of the tribal areas and provided the mechanism for integrating the developmental activities of the government and the semi government organizations by financing through the Integrated Tribal Development Project (ITDP). The Sub-Plan aimed at narrowing the gap between the levels of development of tribal and other areas, and to improve the quality of life of the tribal communities in general.

Table 2.2: The investment in the tribal areas from the first plan to the fifth plan

(Rs. in crores)

Plan	Total Plan Outlay	Tribal Development	Percentage
First plan	1,960	19.93	1.0
Second plan	7,672	42,92	0.9
Third plan	8,577	50.53	0.6
Annual plans (1966-67)	6,756	32.32	0.6
Fourth plan	15,902	75.00	0.5
Fifth Plan (1974-79)	39,322	1,182.00	3.01

Source: The Sixth Five-year Plan Approach Paper.

The Tribal Sub-Plan 1974-79 basically represented disaggregation of sectoral programmes and the total out lay was a derived figure from this sector-wise qualification. The First Sub-Plan 1974-79 accorded the highest priority to elimination of exploitation.

During the Fifth Plan, agricultural and allied sectors claimed the highest investment amounting 26 per cent followed by education and health services which accounted for about 21 per cent. Co-operation has been given a very high step up during this plan period with a total investment of Rs. 60 crores largely meant for marketing of agricultural and minor forest produces. Transport and communication had been kept at a low key claiming only about 8 per cent of the total investment.

For each Integrated Tribal Development Project (ITDP), an Integrated Area Development Plan focusing attention on the specific problems of the area and the tribal people has been formulated. The Sub-Plan areas in each state thus comprised a number of viable projects.

Sixth Five-year Plan (1980-85)

The Sixth Plan continued the Sub-Plan approach of the Fifth Plan. This was to be supplemented by target beneficiary approach with the objective of narrowing the gap between the level of development of the tribals and other developed communities and bringing about a qualitative change in the life of a tribal community.

The broad objectives of the Sixth Plan were:

(i) A progressive reduction in the incidents of poverty and unemployment.

(ii) Improving the quality of life through minimum needs programme.

(iii) A reduction in inequalities of income and wealth.

(iv) Infrastructural development for further exploitation of potential of the tribal region.

The strategy of development lays emphasis on consolidation of the gains of protective measures, programmes of full employment, education and health services. The programmes under different sectors of development are required to be intensified with suitable modifications to remove the present inadequacies in implementation. The States have to give due importance to the integration of programmes in the field and effective delegation of powers to the Project Authorities in ITDPs. The approach in the Sixth Plan for the development of backward areas in general was to rely, to a greater extent, on the development of agriculture, village and small-scale industries subsidiary occupations and related services and also the Minimum Need Programmes and Area Development Programmes. Improvement of economic status of the tribals should be the first concern and suitable programmes of horticulture, cattle development, poultry and piggery etc., were carried out.

Emphasis was placed more on family-oriented programmes than on infrastructure development unlike in the previous Plans.

Seventh Five-year Plan (1985-90)

The basic premises of the Tribal Sub-Plan continued in the Seventh Plan also. During the Seventh Plan, the Tribal Sub-Plan strategy comprised the following:

(a) Identification of the Development Blocks where tribal population is in majority and their constitution into ITDPs with a view to adopt there an integrated and project-based approach for development.

(b) Marking of funds for the Tribal Sub-Plan and ensuring the flow of funds from the control of State plan, sectoral outlays and from financial institutions.

(c) Creation of appropriate administrative structures in tribal areas and adoption of appropriate personnel policies.

The programme of tribal development with ITDP pattern was continued in the Seventh Plan also without any basic or major changes in the approach, Pattern or structure, but better co-ordination was sought between various agencies, and social services were given priority. LAMPS (Large Agriculture Marketing Societies) were to be strengthened through broadening their popular base. Seventh Plan paid attention towards the rehabilitation of poor tribals and the removal of tribal women's backwardness.

Expenditure in different plan periods for development of Scheduled Tribes were shown in the Table 2.3. The following Table 2.3 shows that funds from State Plan is higher than the funds from the Special Central Assistance (SCA). SCA was low during the Fifth Five-year Plan and high during the Seventh Five-year Plan. The total expenditure for tribals development has been increasing sharply. The seventh Plan's investment was highest with 795 1.82 crores. During the Seventh Plan the funds from the state Plan is high with 7100.57, crores.

Table 2.3: Expenditure in different plan periods for tribal development

(Rs. in crores)

Plan	Funds From State Plan	Funds from Special Central Assistance	Total
Fifth plan	759.44	186.76	946.20
1979-80 (Actual)	382.45	59.45	44 1.90
Sixth plan	3387.89	486.1 1	3874.00
Seventh plan	7100.57	85 1,25	795 1.82

Source: A Note on Review of Programmes during the Seventh Plan, Planning Commission, New Delhi.

Eighth Five-year Plan (1992-97)

In the Eighth Plan, taking in view of the problem related to the implementation of schemes for tribal development, the planning commission tried to be more realistic. The Plan largely emphasises the re-orientation of administrative structure at all levels for functional co-ordination and effective delivery of services. The strategy of Eighth Plan also specifically aimed at improving the living environment of the tribals by giving them better social and civic amenities and facilities. The working group has recommended that the objective of the Seventh Plan would continue for the eighth plan period.

The objectives for the Eighth Plan are detailed below:

(a) Progressive reduction in poverty and creation of employment thereby providing reduction in income inequalities.

(b) Improving the quality of life through a minimum needs programme.

(c) Development and strengthening of infrastructure for further economic exploitation of the Tribal Sub-Plan area.

(d) Development of confidence of tribals along the desired lines through intensive educational efforts.

In the Eighth Five-year Plan, Tribal Sub-Plan (TSP) area, MADA (Modified Area Development Approach), Scattered Development Plans, and Primitive Tribe Development Plans for the tribal development approach have been stressed". Despite the effects to diversify economic activities in non-formal sectors, the predominant source of livelihood in TSP area continuous to be agriculture. The main thrust would be on the development of fisheries, sericulture, horticulture, plantation on waste land and growing vegetables. During the Eighth Plan these areas would provide supplemental income and new avenues of employment to the tribals. Human resources development through education, vocational/ craftman training would be taken up to improve the skills of the tribals. Expansion of irrigation facilities and electrification of tribal settlements, expansion of irrigation wells, fertilizers, improvement of cattle breed and mining activities have also been given. In this plan, family oriented schemes have been also stressed to uplift the tribal families. The comnlunity development programmes are given second priority.

Educational Status of Tribals

Literacy Status

Despite the fact that there has been an increase in the literacy rates of SCs/STs since independence, the present position is still far from satisfactory. The overall increase in literacy rate in the country during the period 1961-2001 was 36.54 against which increase in literacy rate for SCs and STs during the same period was 44.42 and 38.57 respectively. The female literacy rates among STs continue to remain a serious cause of concern, as it is only 34.76 per cent as against the total fcmale literacy rate of 53.67 per cent.

However, in overall terms, the female literacy rate has increased significantly since independence; the female literacy rate was only 8.86 per cent in 1951. The literacy rate of females is 53.67 per cent as compared to 75.26 per cent among males in 2001. The female literacy rate has risen by 14.38 per cent compared to a corresponding increase of 11.13 per cent in the case of male literacy during the period 1991-2001, which indicates a meaningful narrowing of the gender gap in education.

Enrolment in Elementary Education

(a) Primary (I-V)

There has been over all increase in the enrolment of children belonging to Scheduled Castes and Scheduled Tribes at all levels after independence. At primary stage, the Scheduled Castes enrolment has increased from 1.1 crore accounting for 14.88 per cent in 1980-81 to 2.31 crore, accounting for 18.03 per cent of the total enrolment at primary stage in 2003-04. The enrolment of Scheduled Caste girls has increased from 13.2 per cent in 1980-81 to 17.3 per cent in 2003-04 while enrolment of Scheduled Caste boys increased from 15.92 per cent in 1980-81 to 18.66 per cent in 2003-04.

The Scheduled Tribes enrolment has increased from 46.60 lakhs in 1980-81 to 125.17 lakhs in 2003-04. The enrolment of Scheduled Tribe girls considerably increased from 15.27 lakhs in 1980-81 to 57.41 lakhs in 2003-04 while the enrolment of Scheduled Tribe boys increased from 31.33 lakhs in 1980-81 to 67.76 lakhs in 2003-04.

(b) Upper Primary (VI-VIII)

About 22 lakhs Scheduled Caste students were enrolled at Upper Primary stage in 1980-81, which increased to 80.77 lakhs in 2003-04 accounting for 10.7 per cent in 1980-81 and 16.58 per cent in 2003-04 of the total enrolment at Upper Primary stage. Percentage enrolment of Scheduled Caste boys and girls accounting for 11.66 per cent and 8.85 per cent in 1980-81 increased to 17.40 per cent and 15.55 per cent in 2003-04 respectively. The enrolment of Scheduled Tribes at Upper Primary stage increased from 7.42 lakhs in 1980-81 to 36.62 lakhs in 2003-04 accounting for 3.58 per cent in 1980-81 and 7.51 per cent in 2003-04 of the total enrolment.

While the total enrolment at Primary stage has increased by 6.68 times between 1950-51 and 2003-04, for girls it has shown an increase of about 11 times. The relative share of girls' enrolment in total enrolment at primary level has increased from 28.12 per cent in 1950-51 to 46.68 per cent in 2003-04.

Similarly, at the upper primary level, the relative share of girls' enrolment to total enrolment has gone upto 44.15 per cent in 2003-04 from 16.13 per cent in 1950-51.

(c) High/Higher Secondary (IX-XII)

About 11.52 lakhs Scheduled Caste students were enrolled at High/Higher Secondary stage in 1980-81, which increased to 47.60 lakhs in 2003-04 accounting for 10.47 per cent in 1980-81 and 13.6 per cent in 2003-04 of the total enrolment at High/Higher Secondary stage.

Percentage enrolment of Scheduled Caste boys and girls accounting for 11.92 per cent and 7.23 per cent respectively in 1980-81 increased to 14.26 per cent and 12.65 per cent in 2003-04. The enrolment of Scheduled Tribes at High/Higher Secondary stage increased from 3.29 lakhs in 1980-81 to 19.51 lakhs in 2003-04 accounting for 2.99 per cent in 1980-81 and 5.57 per cent in 2003-04 of the total enrolment.

While the total enrolment at High/Higher Secondary stage has increased by about 23 times from 1950-51 to 2003-04, the relative share of girls' enrolment in total enrolment at High/Higher Secondary stage has increased by about four times only during the same period.

Gross Enrolment Ratio

Primary (I-V)

The Gross Enrolment Ratio of all categories has increased from 80.5 per cent in 1980-81 to 98.2 per cent in 2003-04 registering an increase of 17.7 per cent at the Primary stage over a period of 24 years. The comparative Gross Enrolment Ratio of Scheduled Castes is 82.2 per cent in 1980-81 and 88.3 per cent in 2003-04 registering an increase of 6.1 per cent and that of Scheduled Tribes from 70 per cent in 1980-81 to 91.3 per cent in 2003-04 registering an increase of 21.3 per cent. There is thus a significant achievement in the Gross Enrolment Ratio of the Scheduled Castes and Scheduled Tribes.

Similarly, the Gross Enrolment Ratio of girls at the primary stage has increased from 24.8 per cent in 1950-51 to 95.6 per cent in 2003-04.

Upper Primary (VI-VIII)

The Gross Enrolment Ratio of all communities has increased from 41.9 per cent in 1980-81 to 62.4 per cent in 2003-04 registering an absolute increase of 20.5 per cent at the Upper Primary stage whereas the Gross Enrolment Ratio of Scheduled Castes has increased from 29.1 per cent in 1980-81 to 71.8 per cent in 2003-04 registering an increase of 42.7 per cent and that of Scheduled Tribes from 19.5 per cent in 1980-81 to 75.7 per cent in 2003-04 registering an increase of 56.2 per cent. The rate of increase of Gross Enrolment Ratio of Scheduled Castes and Scheduled Tribes in a preceding period of 24 years is higher than that for the general categories, though these communities and particularly the Scheduled Tribes are still far behind in terms of literacy.

At the Upper Primary level, the GER of girls has gone up from 4.6 per cent in 1950-51 to 57.6 per cent in 2003-04. However, large disparities exist between the States having lower GER than the all India averages.

Drop-out Rates

At the Primary level, the drop-out rate among the Scheduled Castes in 1990-91 was 49.4 per cent, which reduced to 36.6 per cent in 2003-04. At the Upper Primary level the drop-out rates have reduced from 67.8 per cent in 1990-91 to 59.4 per cent in 2003-04.

At the Primary level, the drop-out rate among Scheduled Tribes in 1990-91 was 62.5 per cent, which reduced to 48.9 per cent in 2003-04. At the Upper Primary level the drop-out rates, which was 78.6 per cent in 1990-91 reduced to 70.1 per cent in 2003-04.

The drop-out rates of girls have decreased year after year, in the Primary classes from 64.9 per cent in 1960-61 to 31.47 per cent in 2003-04. Similarly in the Upper Primary classes, the drop-out rates have decreased from 78.3 per cent in 1960-61 to 52.3 per cent in 2003-04.

Conclusion

All the developmental programmes, exclusively designed for the welfare of the tribal people, are hardly meeting the field demands. The unrealistic planning coupled with unsystematic execution has left the government astray and probably it is one of the potent causes of policy logjam. The flow of resources from the central government is mischennalised in different way in the name of tribal welfare. The official report on tribal welfare with reference to literacy and enrollment ratio is far from reality. The rate of wastage and stagnation especially in the tribal dominated inhabitants is still high even if after the 10 years of execution of Sarva Shiksha Abhiyan (SSA). The deteriorating health status with poor economical condition of tribal people is the clear reflection of the executional drawbacks of government machinery.

Therefore, in order to bring real change in the educational, economical and health status of the tribal people, the government needs to focus the execution part at the grassroot level. All the planning related the tribal development, should be done after rigorous field visit and open deliberation with the locals for whom the scheme is meant for.

Recommendation

Education is the single most important means by which individuals and society can improve personal endowments, build capacity levels, overcome barriers, and expand opportunities for a sustained improvement in their well-being.

In the context of tribal education, finding a balance between preserving tribal cultural identity and mainstreaming for economic prosperity means building education programmes that ensure a tribal child's success in mainstream schools. Recognising that the education system is currently designed for the dominant group, there needs to be investment in creating support mechanisms that supplement the integration of tribal children into the formal education system.

The support within the education system includes:

- Sing both tribal and state languages during the pre-primary and primary levels.
- Creating supplemental tribal relevant learning materials.
- Introducing monetary/non-monetary incentives for teachers in tribal areas.

- Addressing the health and nutritional needs of tribal children.
- Improving community participation by training tribal teachers and youth as peer educators.
- Establishing and strengthening transitional education centres which focus on mainstreaming tribal children.
- Creating seasonal hostels and residential schools for children of migratory parents.
- Training female teachers for single sex classrooms.

This would provide a solid foundation that leverages the tribal assets and develops stronger individual potential that can transcend the barriers experienced by tribals in mainstream society.

REFERENCES

Census Report, Government of India, 1991.

Census Report, Government of India, 2001.

Eight Five-year Plan (1992-97).

M. Kunharnan, "Tribal Development in India. Retrospect and Prospect", Budgeting for Whom. Update Quarterly No. 1, April-June 1997.

Mishra, M. 2007, "Status of Elementary Education in Tribal Areas of Orissa". Department of Tribal Education, Orissa.

P. D Kulkami, "Tribal Welfare some Problems of Implementation", Published in Souvenir: National Seminar on We (lhre of Tribes and Denotified Communities with Reference to Fourth Plan, Bhopal, 1 964, pp. 44-122.

Planning Commission, Government of India, Approach Paper for Planning Commission, Government of India, First Five-year Plan, (1951-56) New Delhi, pp. 524-640.

R. N. Thakur, "Tribal Development Need for a Fresh Perspective"; Kurukshethra, March-April 1997, p. 92.

3

Culture, Language, Art and Lifestyle of Tribes

Pushplata Chaturvedi*

INTRODUCTION

As a country as whole, the tribal regions and thereby the tribal people are the poorest segment of our society. The situation in Gujarat in respect of the tribal regions and tribal people is no way much different than the overall situation of the tribal regions and people in the whole country. As per the census report 1991, the tribal population in Gujarat was around 15 per cent of the State population. This in itself is not a small percentage. The tribal belt in Gujarat consists of the districts of Danga, Surat, Broach, Baroda, Panchmahals, Sabarkantha and Banaskantha. Tribes such as the Siddhis, Rabari's, Padhar, Mer's and Bharwads live in the coastal Saurashtra districts of Junagarh, Jamnagar and Kutch. Tribes with Bhil features account for more than 50 per cent of the Gujarat's Adivasi population.. The tribal people of Gujarat are religious and are animistic in religion. The tribes of Gujarat are engaged in

* I-103, Anand Vihaar, Tragad-IOC Road, Behind Nirma University, Ahmedabad - 382 470. E-mail: history3376@rediffmail.com

different occupations. In olden days the Bhils depended on the slash-and-burn cultivation system under which they cleared thick forests by cutting trees or burning them and cultivated crops in this land for a few years until the natural fertility of the soil was exhausted. They then moved on to new forests, leaving the land fallow for it to recover its fertility. They also lived by gathering forest produce and hunting wild beasts or fishing. Some tribes work as casual labourers, cattle breeders and find employment in the ports. The social set up of the tribes in Gujarat is quite different from that of a usual Hindu community. The women in these communities have more freedom than their Hindu counterparts in matters of marriage, divorce and remarriage. Besides this the customs and lifestyle of the tribes vary as well. The colourful costumes of the tribal people of Gujarat add charm to the eyes of the beholder. Moreover the tribal people celebrate various fairs and festivals with great gaiety and tribal folk songs and dances. In this paper I would like to present Culture, Language, Art and Lifestyle of the tribals of Gujarat.

Tribes of Gujarat have an interesting history. The Ramayana and the Mahabharata make several references to the hill tribes. The reference to the Bhil hunter mistakenly slaying Lord Krishna at Prabhas Patan shows that the tribe had freedom in this region. In the character of Shabri, Valmiki's Ramayana portrays the simple and hospitable nature of the Bhil women. Bhil tribes ruled over the Chhota Udaipur, Rajpipla and Sagbara region of Ratanmal in the Panchamahals district, the Danta region in the Banaskantha district and over principalities around Idar.

In the 11th century, Karnadeo (son of Bhimadeo, the Chalukya king who ruled over North Gujarat) marched against Asha Bhil of Asha Palli and vanquished him. He then established Karnavati, a new kingdom near Palai, in the southern suburb of Ahmedabad.

The composition and distribution of tribal population in Gujarat today is interesting. Out of total population of 1, 61, 49,036 covering the eighteen districts of Gujarat, the tribal's account for 20, 64,522 *i.e.* 12.78 per cent of the total. The tribal population is concentrated in the. South-eastern region of Gujarat. The important tribes may be noted Bhil, Charan, Dhanka, Dhodia, Dubla, Bharwad, Gamit, Kali, Kolcha, Parashi, Rabari, Siddi, Vasava, Vagari and Wari, etc. Tribal Life in Gujarat reveals two distinct pattern of life.

Firstly, purely primitive age, who live in the mountain region and *secondly*, a cultured communities, those who live in plain region. It is in the fastness of the hills and forest that we still meet with the early strata of tribal population.

The majority of the population is of Indo-Aryan origin. Nearly 20 per cent of the people are tribal and the Bhils, Kolis, Dhubla, Naikda and Macchi-Kharwa are some of the tribes which can be still found in Gujarat. The Aryans were the first people to come from the north who either conquered or drove away the Bhils, the traditional rulers of Gujarat. Kolis are also equally important and occupy an intermediate social position between the Aryans and the Bhils. Aryans are now commonly recognised as Hindus. The immigration during the medieval period brought Islam and Zoroastrianism to Gujarat and initiated the growth of a multi-religious society. The peninsula of Kathiawar is named after the Kathis who came to Saurashtra at the close of the fourteenth century.

Location of Tribes of Gujrat

Tribes of Gujrat inhabit the rugged terrain adjoining the Aravallis, the western ridges of the Vindhya and Satpura mountain Range and the northern slopes of the Sahyadri Ranges.

The tribal belt in Gujarat consists of the districts of Danga, Surat, Broach, Baroda, Panchmahals, Sabarkantha and Banaskantha. Various sects of adivasis, mainly of Bhil tribe and Konkan origin reside in this region. Tribes such as the Siddhis, Rabari, Padhar, Mers and Bharwads live in the coastal Saurashtra districts of Junagarh, Jamnagar and Kutch.

The Siddhis are known to have come to India from East Africa and have distinct Negroid features. The Rabaris and the Mers seem to have come from the Mediterranean in early times. The Australoid Adivasis (who have Australoid features) live in two tracts. They have Konkan features. The other group lives in the hill tracts along the state's eastern border and comprise of the Bhil Garasias, Dungri Bhils, Ratwas, Naikas and others. They have Bhil features.

In the plains of the Surat, Broach and Bulbar Districts, there are also other tribes, such as, the Dublas, who seem to have a foreign origin, the Dhodias, who might have migrated from the Dhulia region of Maharashtra and the Choudhuris, who may have come from Orissa or West Bengal.

Demographics of Tribes of Gujrat

There are over 5 million Adivasis or tribal communities in Gujarat. Tribes with Bhil features account for more than 50 per cent of the Gujrat's Adivasi population. Most of the Adivasi sects claim descent from clans, such as, the Rathod, Solanki, Chauhan, Parmar and Makwana. The colourful ghagra, the jhulki, the sallo and the jewellery worn by the Bhil Garasia women reveal Rajput influence as well.

The Bhils near Akkalkavu in West Khandesh and those living in Ratnapur, came under the influence of the Muslims and though they adopted the Muslim faith, their women neither accepted the practice of wearing veils.

Culture of Tribes of Gujrat

The tribal people of Gujarat are religious and are animistic in religion. They worship animals, such as the tiger, crocodile and snake as Gods and also worship some plant Gods and a hill God (Thumbi Dev). They also have many Gods in common with the Hindus such as Chaminda, Kalka, Amba, Lord Hanuman and Lord Krishna. Their greatest festival is Holi.

It is said that this and other festivals such as Diwali, which it is said originally belonged to these aborigines, were in due course of time adopted by the Hindus. Scholars are also of the opinion that the concept of the Mother Goddess, Parvati (daughter of the hill king) and that of the LordShiva has been borrowed by the Hindus from the Adivasis. The tribes also worship their dead ancestors.

Dangs Darbar is a colourful festival that is celebrated in the Dang district, located in the Saputara Hills in Gujarat. The festival is a three-day annual cultural show corresponding with the Holifestivities. The Dangs Darbar fair exhibits the interesting art and culture of the local tribes of the Dang area which is located in the Satpura hills. Dang Darbar is celebrated just few days before Holi.

The festival is exactly celebrated in Ahwa near Saputara. The name of the festival has been derived from the Ahwa Darbar, an old assembly (Darbar) venue for English ministers and mandarins during the Raj era. Now, the name has been changed to Jamabandi Durbar and the District Collector officiates at it. The Dang area still bears the fragrance of the British era.

A large number of tribal inhabitants and tourists come from distant places to attend one of the most colourful and attractive festivals of the Dangs. A galore of men and women adorn themselves in different colours of attires and are seen agog with festivities during the Darbar. Nomad tribes carry different types of instruments like shehnai with them while coming to attend the festival.

All the men put on lion clothes which are complimented with a waistcoat and coloured turban. Women adorn thenselves in saree and blouses. They also wear heavy silver jewellery. The carnival ground can be seen buzz with activities and merchants who come to sell their products. Dangs Darbar at Gujarat displays a panorama of musical programmes, dances and folk arts. The three day festival, witnesses many activities like folk dances, Raas, Garba programmes, songs and dramas. The fair also provides a platform to search for brides and grooms. Visitors can enjoy the folk music from the tribal instruments like Kahalia and Tadpur accompanied by the folk dances. Tribal dances of the region are spectacular to watch. People move in concentric circles holding each other by the waist, dancing to the beat of percussion and wind instruments.

Dangs Darbar fair is the perfect venue to witness the cultural and social life of the local tribes of Gujarat.

An exhibition of local culture, tribal development schemes and forest environment is also inaugurated on the occasion during the festival. During the festival, the customs instituted earlier still continues like giving pensions to the Tribals such as Daher, Gadhvi, Linga, Pimpri and Vasurna were awarded pensions in 2009). The Dangs Darbar in Gujarat thus attracts thousands of tourists every year from all across the globe.

Occupation of Tribes of Gujrat

The tribes of Gujarat are engaged in different occupations. In olden days the Bhils depended on the slash-and-burn cultivation system under which they cleared thick forests by cutting trees or burning them and cultivated crops in this land for a few years until the natural fertility of the soil was exhausted. They then moved on to new forests, leaving the land fallow for it to recover its fertility. They also lived by gathering forest produce and hunting wild beasts or fishing. Some tribes work as casual labourers, cattle breeders and find employment in the ports.

Even today the tribal groups, such as, the Koknas, Gamits, Dhodias, Vasawas, Garasias and some other Bhils generally lived on agriculture. Most of the Adivasis depend on agriculture either as landowners or as farm workers.

The social set up of the tribes in Gujarat is quite different from that of a usual Hindu community. The women in these communities have more freedom than their Hindu counterparts in matters of marriage, divorce and remarriage. Besides this the customs and lifestyle of the tribes vary as well. The colourful costumes of the tribal people of Gujarat add charm to the eyes of the beholder. Moreover the tribal people celebrate various fairs and festivals with great gaiety and tribal folk songs and dances.

There are 29 cultured tribal communities in Gujarat. It is difficult to describe all of them. However we are mentioning a brief profile of these main tribes:

Rathawa Tribe

Most of them are found in Chotta Udaipur taluka of Baroda district and Panchamahal district. The history of Rathawa tribals says they are migrated from central India.

Dhanka Tribe

They are .mainly found in Baroda, Bharuch and Surat districts. They work as agriculturist and agriculture labour also. Worship Hindu God and Goddess.

Dublas

The second largest tribal community of Gujarat is Dublas. They are found in plains of Surat and Valsad district. They are dark in complexion and short in stature. Basically agricultural labour.

Chaudhary

They are found in Surat district. They have their own dialect mainly agriculturist and having of Hindu religion.

Kathodis

They are minor tribal group, scattered over Surat, Dang, Bharuch and Sabarkantha district. They are essentially forest tribe and livelihood is dependent on the labour work.

Kolghas

They are mainly inhabited the Dharampur, Beads, Chikli talukas in Valsad district. They work as farm labour and live with other tribal group. Kotwallas. They are scattered in the district of Surat and Bharuch, their main livelihood is basket making and bamboo work.

Gracia

· They are mainly found in Sabarkantha district of Gujarat, they are farm labourer. They are different from other tribe; their origin is from Rajasthan or Rajputs. They have whitish face, sharp nose and glittering eyes.

Dangs is a gift, which is sent by nature to Gujarat. It is a small district and it has much wealth of forest. Dangs is colonized by original tribes like Kunbis, Bhils which are called as Kukanas, it is situated in the area of Dharampur. Gamits and Warlis are rooted here from a long time. Ahwa is located on Saputara and on plateau; these two places are famous for tourists.

Warli Tribe

Warlis, Bhils and Kunbis captured the Dangs before the eighth century to the tenth century; Naikas and Gamits came here later. All these tribes are part of the population of Dangis in today's date. It is a contracted blend of many tribes. Even if Dangi has so many tribes, still their cultural development carries the common ethos, through these Dangi tribe personality causes a typical way of feeling, thinking, behaving with mutual sentiments, ideas and beliefs. Warli tribe usually live in a forested area. Warlis live in Vansda taluka, Umargaon, Dharampur, Dang district all these locations are situated near the border of Maharashtra. As per the Enthoven, Warli tribe is a sub tribe of the Bhil with 3 sub groups and several Gotras such as Murday, Davar, Nehri. Most of the Davars are located in Gujarat. Kunbi and Warli tribe speaks Gujarati language. The villages, in which this tribe lives, are undeveloped or remote that's why they are unknown from the other tribes that time villages plays the role of a binding force. They live unknown from the other people in the hilly area, and have no connection with the major population, helping them to sustain their typical traditional lifestyle. Patel accede play an important role in managing the social, individual and religious customs. During weddings, Pagri tying is the custom of the Patel. Burning the slashing the cultivation begins during the start of April and May. They do cultivation during the monsoon season. After that to earn money, they migrate from there to search the occupation. They started collecting honey, Mahuwa, gum, Timroo leaves, Doli, Ambla and sell these forest items in the market. For Warlis, nature is very important, more than cultivation or agriculture. They were known as nature's children. Till now they live independent because of nature.

Kunbi Tribe

The combination of Warli, Gamit, Bhil and Kunbi, can be found in the Singana village; it is situated in the Ahwa Taluka, district Dangs. In Singana village, there are eighty five houses, five hundred people live there. Their house is called as, Pucca house; they decorate it by painting the wooden pillars which are carved. Aged people of this tribe wear khameez and dhoti. Women commonly wear sari in Maharashtrian style in the colour of green or red with the designs of flowers. In ornaments, they like to wear silver Bali, Baju Bandh, Kada, golden Kata Nath, Asura necklace and Kada.

Kunbi tribe generally have 3 joint weddings. Mangla Sutra, Jhanhar anklets, Cupboard, Dhorlu necklace consists of the Trousseau on the family side. The bride's in laws usually give Kundala earrings and Teak Nath in the wedding. In the wedding ceremony, bride generally wears the sari in Maharashtrian way and choli. They also wear Odhni which is called as Farki, they also have silver rings in their toes all these ornaments have essential position in the wedding occasion. Kunbi tribe celebrates the festivals like Dangs durbar in the month of March and Holi. They perfom the Waghdev Barasa Puja, in the jungle which is near Sakarpatar. They have a traditional or typical dance forms on the occasions such as Dholak, Sambre, Banjo and Basuri.

Kukna Tribe

The name Kukna comes from the Kankan armlet, it is worn by this tribe and also because they migrated to Gujarat from some of the Konkan part in the earlier times. This tribe is situated in Valsad, Kuknas, Vansad, Dharampur. They are also known as Kokna or Kokni. People of Kuknas living in Dharampur and Dangs are very similar. The languages they use are Gujarati, Marathi and Hindi. The tribe is divided in the clans and Kuls. This tribe people believe in unity among the community and family; that's why they travel in groups outside the village.

Kuknas build the walls of houses by using whitewash and mud, their houses usually don't have windows and the roof of the houses is covered by grass. Kuknas tribe eat natural things like: plants, roots, honey and wild animals. Among the all tribes, Kuknas earned a high position because of the improving literacy rate. They make vegetable by using sweet oil, but they don't use spice and Ghee. Kadmai village; where all three tribes Kukna, Warlu and Nayak are living communally. Villagers don't allow young generation to learn art like stone carving, wall painting from the old generation people. They celebrate Diwali festival in bamboo made temple. In the Kuknas tribe, people believe in big or joint families but because of the occupation they also shift to the nuclear family system. For them wedding is very important, even if wedding rituals take place after 1 or 2 children's birth. Festivals like Navaratri, Shivratri, Diwali and Dussera are celebrated by the Kuknas.

Gamit tribes are known as one of the major tribal communities of Gujarat and they are widely distributed in the mountainous terrains and also in some of the plains of Surat, Valsad, Dang and Bahruch districts. The Gamit tribes are also popular as Vasava, Gamta, Gmit, Gavit, Mavchi, Pandvi etc.

The etymological significance of the term Gamit signifies a villager. The research of the some of the eminent anthropologists has traced the history of the origin of this Gamit tribal community. In the year 1920, the British ethnographer, Enthoven had rightly claimed that this Gamit tribal community was immigrated to Gujarat from various other places. It is also assumed that these Gamit tribes belong to the famous proto-Australoid family thereby it becomes obvious that this Gamit tribes have made their arrival in the country some what fifty to sixty thousand years ago. The Gamit tribal community is the fourth leading tribal community of Gujarat.

The language of the Gamit tribes is Konkani Language and for writing most of these Gamit tribal community make use of the Devanagari script. They also speak in their local dialect named as Gamit language. With the time, due to the influence of the external world, most of these Gamit tribes have adapted some of the trends and languages of the modern day world. The amalgamation they create with their own culture admixtured with a modernzing adds a different flavour to their tribal culture. The Gamit tribes celebrate different festivals together flaunting their tribal cultural ethics. Among them, the festival of colour, Holi is celebrated with lots of merry making and tribal songs and dance.

Their knowledge about numerous herbal plants with high medicinal values have made their names popular amongst people who are residing in the other parts of the Indian territory. For curing health hazards they have set up their unique mode of treatment using these local plants and herbs. Although much of the indigenous customs have been lost in to oblivion, this practice is still prevalent and even passed to the next generation of people.

Siddhi Tribe

Siddi tribe is one of the major tribal communities of Gujarat and this tribe is also known by the names of Siddhi, Sheedi and Habshi. This tribal community has occupied a considerable portion of the state of Gujarat. Especially in Junagarh district of Gujarat, these Siddi tribes have got a major concentration. Although Siddi tribes have adopted the native customs of the region, some African traditions and practices have also been preserved. The tribal community of Siddi is one of the primitive tribes, which have got the heritage of almost three hundred years. However, with the passage of time their ancient tradition and culture have also got a modernised shade. Various cultural forms, namely: dance, music, folklores, etc., are quit Apart from working as labourers many of these Siddi tribes have taken up the occupation of farming and lead a more settled life. With all the restrictions and prohibitions, the Siddi tribes maintain a uniqueness that is apparent and that distinguish them separately from the other tribal groups.

Bhil Tribe

In their society, marriage within the same clan is prohibited. Marriage within first cousins is also not allowed. Sacrifices are also made during several occasions. Widow-remarriage is allowed in their society. They also allow polygamy. The eastern Bhils reside in the mountains of central western India particularly in northern Gujarat, southern Rajasthan and northern Maharashtra. The gallantry of the Bhils has also been mentioned in the Indian legends like Mahabharata and Ramayana. The previous history of the Bhils is unknown but according to some scholars they inhabited India before the arrival of the Dravidians. It has also been assumed that they are amongst the earliest group of people in the sub-continent.

The Bhil people are generally medium-sized with dark skin and thick hair. The Bhils are strong and brave people maintaining simple lifestyle and habits. Though they are excellent warriors, to earn their livelihood they mainly work as peasant farmers, field labourers, and village watchmen. Bhili is their dialect which is an Indo-Aryan Language. Their dialect also includes Rajasthani, Gujarati, Hindi, Marathi words, and also some unique words without any non-Sanskrit elements in it. They are the worshippers of numerous Hindu deities, chiefly a deity by the name of Raja Pantha. Bhils also worship crops, fields, water, the forest and the mountains. The Bhils are highly religious by nature and they worship several Hindu deities. They are superstitious too and wear charms and amulets for keeping off all kinds of evil spirits. They usually bury the dead and also observe some funeral rites. Bhils do not accept any outsider into their community. They eat all kinds of flesh and drink liquor. They are mainly engaged in farming and cultivation.

The Bhil people have a rich indigenous culture. Ghoomar dance is one of the popular aspects of Bhil culture. Sawang is a popular form of entertainment among the Bhil tribes. This form consists of storytelling combined with dancing and music with an abundance of drinking. They celebrate their festivals in honour of their departed ancestors. One of the most famous and important festival of the Bhils is the Gavri. This is considered as an honour and a duty to participate in a roving group of performers who enact Hindu stories in village squares throughout their district. Gavri is enjoyed by the participants and audience alike. As this festival restricts the female participation in the dramas and programmes enacted in the festival, so the part of the females is played by the men. The performers are dressed in colourful and showy costumes. Moreover, a series of acts based on the Hindu epics, tales of the heroes and villains of Hindu scriptures are played in Gavri and due to this reason this festival is considered as a religious, even holy event to the people of Bhil tribe. Popular enactments include the legends of the great goddess Amba Mata, the story of one of the aspects of Lord Shiva and his wife Parvati. Apart from these they celebrate births, betrothals, marriages, Holi, Dussehra, Baneshwar fair and hunting expeditions with great fervour.

The costumes of the Bhil tribes display a distinct characteristic that goes well with the rustic but ethnic lifestyle. The Bhil woman wears an upper garment called the kapada, a ghaghra and an odhna. The kapada is a short-sleeved cotton blouse, which is held by cloth ties at the back around the neck and the waist. The ghaghra is ankle-length and is ingeniously turned into a pair of trousers, while working in the fields. Bhil women also prefer to wear the bor and jhela on their forehead. Ornaments are a part of their dressing. Their ear-ornaments include the dhimmna and oganiya. The hansli, haar and tagli are the neck-ornaments that the Bhil women wear. The muthia are a set of bangles worn on the forearms and comprise the kasla and the kamkada. Kaslas are bangles made of coconut shells embellished with silver bands and the latter are plain bands of brass or lacquer worn around the wrist. Finger rings called beenti, and bidi are made of brass or copper. Married women wear brass anklets called 'pejania'. Toe rings are called 'bichiya' and are made of silver, brass or white metal. Tattoos are very popular and have acquired a certain social and religious significance. The people of Bhil community use patterns like birds, flowers and scorpions for tattooing. The usual areas tattooed are the forearms, wrists, forehead, chin, calves and feet. The women of this community wear an intricate and complicated hairstyle. Their hair is combed forward, to hang on the forehead and is pleated into an ornamental network that falls over the eyebrows.

The costume of a Bhil man comprises a turban or 'feto', an angi, tunic and a lower garment called 'potario'. The turban is made of a white handspun, hand-woven fabric. The tunic is made of course, hand spun, unbleached cotton. It is a full-sleeved, hip-length garment and has an asymmetrical front with a yoke. It is fastened with cloth ties at the shoulder and centre front. It has slits on the sides, with a bias edging. The lower garment is knotted around the waist and the entire length is drawn between the legs and tucked in at the back. Bhil men also keep a pacheri or shawl on their person. The dresses of the young Bhil boys are different from the mature men of this community. At the time of marriage, the groom wears an 'ango', a shin length tunic, which is worn with a turban and a dhoti.

Gujarat - Art and Craft, Literature

Tribal art is not aesthetic but mainly utilitarian. Apart from satisfying a deep rooted want, art has helped to integrate the people and enrich their life. It has filled in certain gaps in their life of a mental and spiritual nature. It is a medium through which the vitality, zest and exuberance of their life have been expressed. In other words, the tribal art is intimately related to their life.

The artistic activities may be divided into: *(i)* plastic and graphic art. *(ii)* Music and dance *(iii)* oral literature. Perhaps the oldest form ofart in which primitive man first expressed himself is dramatic art. Mimic art still exist in the optic or acoustic form. Fortunately this art along with the time honored tribaldances still survives in Gujarat.

Adornment of the body is another aspect in which the artistic impulse of the tribal people has found expression. It is in a way the exclusive art of the woman.

Another important aspect in which their artistic talent can be seen is their works in clay, wood and stone.

They are naturalistic in their conception and execution. The cult objects in clay and the funerary pillars in stone are positive examples of their artistic impulse and expression of their way of life.

Gujarat has successfully preserved its rich tradition of song, dance and drama. Most of the art traditions trace back their origin to the ancient period of Lord Krishna. The most popular amongst these are the Ras and Garba. Other popular forms of folk dances in Gujarat are Tippani Nritya, Siddi dance, Padhar Nritya, Dangi Nritya and other local tribal dances. Folk drama in Gujarat is known as Bhavai.

Ras

The Ras dance is considered a form of Ras Leela, which Lord Krishna used to perform at Gokul and Vrindavan. The Ras is simple and is generally performed by a group of youthful people who move in measured steps around a circle, accompanied by a singing chorus and a host of musical instruments like: the dhol, cymbals, zanz, shehnai (flute). The typical folk costume for this dance is a small coat called kedia, with tight sleeves and pleated frills at the waist with highly embroidered borders, tight trousers, colourfully embroidered cap or coloured turban and colourful kamarbandha (cummerbund).

Dandia - Ras

Also known as the 'stick' dance, this is another form of dance that is also a feature of Navratri. Here, men and women join the dance circle, holding small polished sticks or dandias. As they whirl to the intoxicating rhythm of the dance, men and women strike the dandiyas together, adding to the joyous atmosphere. The best Ras dancers are the Kathiawari Ras dancers, who hail from the Saurashtra region.

Garba

Just as Lord Krishna popularized the Ras dance, Usha, the grand daughter-in-law of Lord Krishna gets the credit for popularizing the Lasya Nritya, which came to be known as Garba Dance. It is a circular dance performed by women around an earthenware pot called a garbo, filled with water. A betel nut and a silver coin are placed within the pot, called a kumbh, on top of which a coconut is placed. As the dancers whirl around the pot, a singer and a drummer provide the musical accompaniment. The participants clap in a steady rhythm.

Literature

"The adivasi has always been described as a figure of pity by mainstream writers. But there is a group of tribal writers, who, through their literature, are giving an answer to the questions raised on their identity. This is a phase of revolt for tribal writers, who are trying to showcase the tribes in the same light. It is only after this that the tribal writers can write about the beauty of their world". Jitendra Vasava, a lecturer at Adivasi Academy, Tejgadh.

Purva Prakash, the publication wing of Bhasha Research and Publication Centre documents and publishes books, children's magazine, glossaries and small magazines on adivasi literature and culture. A not-for-profit publishing house, Purva Prakash is dedicated to providing voice and space to adivasi expression.

In a first of its kind attempt, Veer Narmad South Gujarat University (VNSGU) will compile literary creations of various tribal languages and details of litterateur of the languages. The project has been conceptualized to preserve the tribal culture through its languages. The project to be implemented by the newly formed department of Gujarati aims to preserve the literature in tribal languages like Vasavi, Dangi, Kukni, Bhili, Rathvi and others. So far attempts have been made to develop audio compilation of the tribal literature.

Tribal society of Gujarat is unified and the subtle differences that are observed are because for the economical and modern administrative system of the tribal communities. There is a sense of oneness among the members of the tribal communities.

The tribal people give equal respect and freedom to the women of the community. The women of the tribal communities of Gujarat mix freely with men in all spheres of life. They are free to take up any occupation like the men of the community and even in the matter of marriage, the consent of the bride is given importance and they are given the freedom to take necessary decisions of their personal lives.

Though marriages arranged by parents are customary among the tribal communities, the more popular forms seem to be marriages of love preferably those made by elopement with the eloped lovers returning home after a few days spent in hiding. Their parents then complete the formalities and celebrate the wedding.

The custom of levirate is common among the Bhil tribes, the Dhankas and many other tribes in Gujarat. Literacy among the Adivasis has spread with the opening of hundreds of schools (Ashram Shalas) in the tribal belt by social reformers.

The influence of the Christian Missionaries activities in Broach, Surat and Bulsar and of the Arya Samajists in Surat has had a considerable impact on Adivasi thinking. The enactment of the prohibition law has, to a large extent, helped in improving the tribal way of life.

The tribal communities of Gujarat have produced ministers and legislators in Gujarat from among the Choudhury, Vasawa, Bhil, and Dhodia groups. They are also to be found as doctors, professors, journalists, government officers, contractors, businessmen, lawyers and magistrates.

Among the arts and crafts of the tribal communities of Gujarat, the most interesting are textiles, wood and ivory carving, horn, bamboo and cane work and the making of a variety of archetypal bronzes used for ritual and domestic purposes. It is surprising how the technique of bronze casting practiced in India from the proto historic age survives today in the tribal craftsman's method of bronze casting.

The cult of the totem is an important feature in the tribal culture, which has conditioned the life and thought of thc people and their arts and crafts. The totem is deeply revered in each clan and many of the significant forms and colours used by them bear an intimate relationship with their life. Totems are propitiated through rituals and magic.

Dance, with all its intricacies, is a salient feature of the social expression of the tribal communities and constitutes an important part of ceremonies connected with marriage, harvesting and funeral rites. The aesthetic awareness is also revealed in their personal adornments and belongings.

Conclusion

When we take into account the culture, art, language and lifestyle it is difficult to understand the backwardness of these tribal regions. With the available natural resources as above, these regions should not have been backward, and yet, they are the most backward. Who is responsible for such paradoxical situation? Fate? Irony? Apathy of everyone?

When we talk of apathy of the State or the Government, it is not that the efforts have not been made to improve the conditions of the tribals. Infact, there have been serious efforts to improve the conditions of the tribals and huge amount have been spent on such efforts all these years. However, the impact of such efforts and investments are not visible and most of the tribal regions, with some exceptions here and there, have remained more or less at the same level as they were few decades ago. The proof of this statement is, to repeat, in the fact that the 10 most backward talukas in the State are the tribals and other tribal talukas also fall in the bottom portion of the development ladder.

Our national picture, in which many of our well-planned and well-intentioned schemes have failed at the implementation level, is more true in case of the tribal regions. Look at various schemes and the investments in the tribal developments since the introduction of Tribal Sub Plan approach and one finds that the success rate between 25-50 per cent of any such schemes and investments would have made tremendous impact on the lives of the tribals.

Last not the least, the development of extremely backward tribal regions requires holistic approach in which, all types of activities need to be incorporated and integrated. But, a strong focus on above three sectors is very vital for the tribal regions, if we want to witness fast and tangible progress in our tribal regions.

REFERENCES

http://www.indianetzone.com/27/tribes_gujarat_sudras.htm

http://www.indianetzone.com/42/bhil_tribe.htm

http://www.nmsadguru.org/Article_TribalOfGujarat.htm

http://www.indianexpress.com/news/symposium-held-on-gujarat-tribal-literature-culture/585310

http://www.indiantribalheritage.org/?p=6873

http://articles.timesofindia.indiatimes.com/keyword/tribal-culture/recent/4

4

Status of Tribal in Uttar Pradesh
An Overview

Dr. Vinod Kumar Pandey*

INTRODUCTION

The term tribe does not necessarily pertain to a specific group or community as such. It rather denotes a particular stage in the historical evolution of human community marking the era of food producing economy. As such there are some indicators or markers of uniqueness by which it can be said that this tribe differs from the other and vice-versa. But these indicators are not only superfluous but also misleading when one strikes to understand at what stage of development a tribe is. The traditional identification marks such as language, culture, race religion; physical traits etc., are no longer held valid. A more rational basis for identification can be whole range of tribal modes of life, *i.e.*, language, customs, traditions, religious beliefs, arts and crafts, archaic traits portraying occupational pattern, economy, etc., and lack of educational and economic development. India can proudly be called the

* Assistant Professor, Department of Social Work, Teerthanker Mahaveer University, Moradabad, (UP).

largest 'tribal' population in the world. The scheduled tribes in India constituted 8.2 per cent of India's population according to 2001 census (the figures for Scheduled Tribes as per Census 2011 are not yet available). Northeast India is the homeland of a large number of tribes. There are about 145 tribal communities of which 78 are large each with a population of more than 5000. They constitute around 12 per cent of the total tribal population of India and 25.81 per cent of the total population of North-East India.

Uttar Pradesh has been one of the most highly populated states in India for a long time now. The census over the years has put the state at the pinnacle in terms of population. Located in the northern region of the country, the state shares its borders with states like Rajasthan, Madhya Pradesh, Bihar and Haryana. The state also borders the capital of India New Delhi along with the newly formed state of Uttarakhand. Uttar Pradesh has been one of the oldest states in the country and in every single way reflects the life and culture of India as a whole. The state has a population of about 190 million according to the Uttar Pradesh Census 2011. The tribal population of Uttar Pradesh comprises only a small percentage (0.07% According to 2001 census) of the entire population of the state and is also one of the weakest communities in the entire state. The growth rate of the population of Uttar Pradesh is about 20 per cent which is alarming among the highest growth rates in the country. Spread over an approximate area of 240928 Sq. Km., the state has many places of strategic and cultural significance. The state has some of the most important educational institutions in the country and boasts of some of the biggest tourist destinations in the country. Uttar Pradesh is the second best state in terms of economy in the country and a large part of the revenue of the state comes from the Agriculture and the services sector. A new state Uttarakhand was carved out of the state of Uttar Pradesh in 2000 and it now covers about 7 per cent of India's total area. According to the Uttar Pradesh Census 2011, the density of population in Uttar Pradesh is about 828 people per sq km which is way above the national average of about

380 and a major cause of concern. The literacy rate in the state has gone up in recent years and yet continues to linger at about 70 per cent which is below the national average of 74 per cent. The sex ratio is almost at par with the national average and stands at about 908.

The five major tribes found in Uttar Pradesh are: *(i)* Tharu, *(ii)* Jaunsari, *(iii)* Raji, *(iv)* Bhotia and *(v)* Buksa. They are mainly found in the present state of Uttarakhand comprising areas like Uttarkashi, Pauri Garhwal, Tehri Garhwal, Haridwar, Nainital, Chamoli, Bageswar, Udham Singh Nagar, Pithoragarh, Champawat, Almora, Dehradun and Rudraprayag. The tribal population of Uttar Pradesh mostly hails from the hilly regions of Uttar Pradesh and belongs to the Jat or the Gujjar race. These tribal people are concentrated in the districts bordering Nepal and owe their lineage to the Indo-Aryan and Indo-Scythian tribes. Interestingly the tribals of Uttar Pradesh have physical features that are very different from those residing in either Oudh or Eastern Uttar Pradesh. They have distinctive cultural characteristic which can easily be differentiated from the rest of the state. The culturally distinct and ethnic population is divided mainly within three regions like the terai-bhabhar area near Bahraich district, the Vindhyan tracts near the frontiers and the marginal mountain tracts of Garhwal, Kumaon and Uttarakhand.

The greatest challenge that the Government of India has been facing since independence is the proper provision of social justice to the scheduled tribe people, by ameliorating their socio-economic conditions. Scheduled Tribes, Scheduled Castes and denotified tribes constitute the weakest section of India's population, from the ecological, economic and educational angles. They constitute the matrix of India's poverty. Though the tribals are the sons of the same soil and the citizens of the same country, they born and grow as the children of the nature. From the historical point of view, they have been subjected to the worst type of exploitation social. They are practically deprived of many civic facilities and isolated from modern and civilized way of living since so many centuries.

What is a 'Tribe'?

Before discussing the demographic composition of scheduled tribes, need and compulsions for their development, it is relevant highlight briefly what a tribe is and what precisely the term 'tribe' connotes. The English term 'tribe' is derived from the Latin word 'tribeus' designating a particular kind of social and political organization existing in all these societies. Originally, it was used to imply three divisions among the early Romans. Later on it was used to mean the 'poor' or the 'masses'. In English languages, the word appeared in the sixteenth century and denoted a community of persons claiming descent from a common ancestor. In India the term 'tribe' has legal and administrative connotation. British census officials-cum-anthropologists first used the term 'tribe' for the purpose of enumerating social groups in India and the term was used from 1881 to 1931 censuses. The government of India Act, 1935 used the term 'backward tribe'. The Indian constitution has retained the terminology with slight modification does not contain a precise definition of the term. The dictionary of anthropology mentions a tribe as social groups, usually with a definite area, dialect cultural homogeneity and unifying social origination. The term 'tribe' in that sense refers to a type of society and designates a stage of evolution in human society. As a type of society, the term of signifies a set of characteristic features and as a stage of evolution. It con not a specific mode of social organization. Anthropologists define tribe as a collection of groups of people who share patterns of speech, basic cultural characteristic and in the traditional sense, a common territory.

According to G.S. Ghurye, the common features possessed by all tribal groups are as follows:

1. They live away from the civilized of world in the inaccessible parts in the forests and hills.
2. They speak the same tribal dialect.
3. They belong either to one of the three stocks – Negritos, Austroloid or mongoloid.

4. They profess primitive religion known as animism in which worship of ghost and sprits is the most important element.
5. They follow primitive occupation such as gleaning, hunting and gathering of forest products.
6. They are largely carnivorous.
7. They live either naked or semi-naked.
8. They have nomadic habits and love for drink and dance..

However, there is no particular definition, which is universally accepted. There are diversities of views of each anthropologist. Nevertheless, curtain characteristic features as discuss of above, have been put forward for determining a 'tribe' or a 'tribal' community.

Population Status of Tribes

The population of STs in India stood at 84.33 million (about 835.80 lakh) as per the Census of 2001. STs constitute 8.2 per cent of the total population of the country with 91.7 per cent of them living in rural areas and 8.3 per cent in urban areas. The sex ratio of ST population in 2001 was 978, which was much higher than the national average of 933. The Scheduled Tribe (ST) population of Uttar Pradesh is 107,963 at 2001 census; constituting a small percentage (0.07%) of the total population (166,197,921) of the State (the figures for Scheduled Tribes as per Census 2011 are not yet available). The decennial growth of ST population has been 42 per cent, which is 16.2 per cent higher than the growth of total population (25.8%) during 1991-2001. The five major tribes found in Uttar Pradesh are Tharu, Jaunsari, Raji, Bhotia and Buksa. They are mainly found in the present state of Uttarakhand. The tribal population of Uttar Pradesh mostly hails from the hilly regions of Uttar Pradesh and belongs to the Jat or the Gujjar race. These tribal people are concentrated in the districts bordering Nepal and owe their lineage to the Indo-Aryan and Indo-Scythian tribes. Interestingly the tribals of Uttar Pradesh have physical features that are very different from those residing in either Oudh or Eastern Uttar Pradesh.

The tribal population of the State is predominantly rural with 88.8 per cent of them residing in villages.

District-wise distribution of ST population shows that Kheri district has the highest proportion of STs (1.2%), followed by Balrampur (1.1%), Shrawasti and Bahraich (each 0.4%) districts. Whereas some districts have negligible proportion of ST population like Gond, Dhuria, Nayak, Ojha, Pathari, Raj Gond (in the districts of Mehrajganj, Sidharth Nagar, Basti, Gorakhpur, Deoria, Mau, Azamgarh, Jonpur, Balia, Gazipur, Varanasi, Mirzapur and Sonbhadra) Kharwar, Khairwar (in the districts of Deoria, Balia, Ghazipur, Varanasi and Sonbhadra) Saharya (in the district of Lalitpur). Parahiya (in the district of Sonbhadra), Baiga (in the district of Sonbhadra), Pankha, Panika (in the districts of Sonbhadra and Mirzapur), Agariya (in the district of Sonbhadra), Patari (in the district of Sonbhadra), Chero (in the districts of Sonbhadra and Varanasi), Bhuiya, Bhuinya (in the district of Sonbhadra).

Tribes wise description is given as under:

- *Tharu:* Out of five major STs, Tharu is the most populous tribe, having a population of 83,544; they constitute 77.4 per cent of the total tribal population of the State. At the level of individual tribe, Tharu are primarily concentrated in Kheri, Balrampur and Bahraich districts.
- *Buksa:* Buksa is the second major tribe, having a number of 4,367; Buksa have the highest concentration in Bijnor followed by Farrukhabad districts. Other three major STs, Bhotia, Jaunsari and Raji have returned maximum population in Agra, Kheri and Gorakhpur districts respectively. Among the five major STs, Buksa and Raji tribes have been recognised as Primitive tribes. Together, they constitute 5 per cent of the total tribal population of the State.
- *Sex Ratio:* The overall sex ratio of the ST population is 934 females per 1000 males which is lower than the national average (978) for all STs. Individually, all the

five tribes have recorded an overall sex ratio lower than the national average. While Tharu, Bhotia and Buksa have sex ratio above 900, Raji and Jaunsari have the sex ratio below 900 and 800 respectively. The sex ratio among STs, in the age group 0-6 years (973) is equal to that of all STs at the national level. Tharu have recorded the child sex ratio marginally lower than the national average whereas remaining four tribes have registered child sex ratio above 1000, showing a preponderance of girl children, Table 4.1.

Table 4.1: Sex ratio

Age Group	All STs (India)	All STs (UP)	Tharu	Bhotia	Buksa	Raji	Jaunsari
All ages	978	934	946	939	907	897	732
0-6 yrs	973	973	970	1027	1082	1019	1026

Source: Office of the Registrar General, India.

Literacy and Educational Status

The overall literacy rate of the STs has increased from 20 per cent at 1991 census to 35.1 per cent at 2001 census. Despite improvement, the literacy rate of STs is considerably lower than the national average of 47.1 per cent aggregated for all STs. Male and female literacy rates (48.4% and 20.7%) are also considerably lower in comparison to those recorded for all STs (59.2% and 34.8%) at the national level.

Table 4.2: Literacy rate

Literacy Rate	All STs	Jaunsari	Bhotia	Tharu	Raji	Buksa
Males	35.1	51.1	42.0	34.9	31.3	31.2
Females	20.7	26.1	31.3	20.0	19.1	20.7

Table 4.2 shows, among the five major STs, only Jaunsari have shown the overall literacy rate (51.1%), higher than that of the national average. All the five STs have shown female literacy lower than the national average (34.8%).

Table 4.3: Level of education among the Scheduled Tribes

Names of STs	Literate without Educational Level	Below Primary	Educational Levels Attained				
			Primary	Middle	Matric/Secondary/ Higher Secondary/ Intermediate etc.	Technical and Non-Technical Diploma etc.	Graduate and Above
All STs	45.2	37.0	25.2	16.0	10.8	0.1	2.8
Tharu	8.1	38.8	25.1	16.3	9.7	0.0	2.0
Buksa	8.2	39.9	29.7	11.5	8.0	0.1	2.7
Bhotia	7.6	26.1	21.2	14.1	17.4	0.3	13.3
Jaunsari	3.0	39.4	24.4	14.7	14.2	0.0	4.2
Raji	8.2	26.6	21.3	16.0	20.0	0.0	7.8

Source: Office of the Registrar General, India.

Table 4.3 shows, among tribal literates, 45.2 are either without any educational level or have attained education below primary level. The proportions of literates who have attained education up to primary and middle levels are 25.2 per cent and 16 per cent respectively. Persons educated up to matric/higher secondary/Intermediate constitute 10.8 per cent. Graduates and above are 2.8 per cent. Among all the STs, Raji have the highest proportion of secondary level literates, followed by Bhotia and Jaunsari. Bhotia have shown the highest proportion graduates followed by Raji. The percentage of the tribal literates decline sharply from the secondary level onwards.

Table 4.4: Percentage of school going children in the age group 5-14 yrs

Age Group	All STs	Tharu	Buksa	Bhotia	Jaunsari	Raji
5-14 yrs	40.3	40.8	26.8	44.0	58.1	25.1

Out of total 31,994 ST children in the age group 5-14 years, 12,889 children have been attending school, constituting 40.3 per cent only. As many as 19,105 children in the corresponding age group have not been going to school. Jaunsari have more than half of the total children in the above mentioned age group are school going; this proportion is below 50 per cent among Tharu and Buksa, (Table 4.4).

Marital Status

The data on marital status show that more than half of the ST population is 'never married' (53.6%) whereas 'married' persons constitute 43.6 per cent. 'Widowed' persons form 2.7 per cent while a negligible 0.1 per cent is 'divorced and separated'. The proportion of married girls below 18 years (2.9%) is slightly higher than that of all STs at the national (2.1%) whereas married boys below 21 years constitute 5.4 per cent which is considerably higher than the national average of 2.8 per cent. Among all tribes, Jaunsari and Bhotia have registered the proportion of married girls below the stipulated age higher than that of the State. On the other hand, Raji and

Tharu have shown the proportion of married boys below legal age higher than the State average.

Religion

Hinduism is the predominant religion of the tribes of the State (80.6%). The STs professing Hinduism account for 98.5 per cent. Muslim tribes constitute 0.9 per cent. Tribes following Christianity (0.3%), Sikhism and Buddhism (each 0.1%) together constitute half per cent only.

Work Participation Rate (WPR)

The Work Participation Rate (WPR) of the ST population is 40.3 per cent which is lower than that of all STs at the national level (49.1%). There has been a slight increase of 2.4 per cent in the overall WPR of STs during 1991-2001. Male and female WPR (49.9% and 30.1% respectively) are lower than those of the national average. Among the total workers, 66.6 per cent are main workers and this proportion is marginally lower than the national average (68.9%). At the individual level, Buksa, Jaunsari and Bhotia have overall WPR lower than the State average. Except Raji and Tharu, other three tribes have female WPR lower than that of the State.

Category of Workers

Table 4.5 shows, 'Cultivators' constitute the highest proportion (44.6%) among the total tribal workers, which is equal to that of all STs at the national level (44.7%). 'Agricultural Labourers' account for 31.4 per cent, which is lower than the national average of 36.9 per cent recorded by all STs in this category. 'Other Workers' form 21.6 per cent which is higher than the national average of 16.3 per cent. Workers engaged in 'Household Industry' (HHI) constitute 2.4 per cent which is same as that of the national level (2.1%).

Table 4.5 clearly demonstrates that at the individual level, Tharu have more than fifty per cent workers are 'Cultivators'. Buksa have the highest proportion of 'Agricultural Labourers' (42.3%) whereas more than 70 per cent of Bhotia workers are 'Other Workers'. Among all tribes, Raji have the highest proportion of 'HHI' workers followed by Bhotia and Buska.

Table 4.5: Percentage distribution of workers in four economic categories

Economic Category	All STs	Tharu	Buksa	Bhotia	Jaunsari	Raji
Cultivators	44.6	54.5	18.3	12.2	15.0	8.6
Agricultural Labourers	31.4	32.0	42.3	10.1	31.8	18.1
HHI Workers	2.4	1.3	5.0	5.8	1.8	12.1
Other Workers	21.6	12.3	34.4	72.0	51.4	61.1

Source: Office of the Registrar General, India.

Relations with the Mainstream

Although such secluded tribes have been a part of Indian society since ancient times, the mainstream does not seem to have taken a favorable view about them though they were not treated as low as untouchables. Main reason for disliking must have been the difference in religion and the unwillingness of these societies to assimilate in Hindu religion and culture. Tribal represented an antithesis to the Brahman and hence invited neglect and contempt in Brahamnic traditions, notwithstanding the fact that knowledge of Brahmanic scholars about these tribes was extremely limited. However, due to large size of sub-continent and no pressure of population, there was no cause of friction. Mostly, the tribes were left to themselves and were free to practice their own religion and culture as well as to use their habitat for their livelihood like hunting and gathering, grazing and shifting cultivation.

However, situation changed during colonial period. The British administrators had no idea about living conditions of these tribes. Whatever little knowledge they got, came through Brahmanic and Sanskrit traditions which held negative views about the tribes. This coupled with the desire of colonial administration to maximize profits, led to a specifically insensitive approach to these sections. A series of Forest Acts was enacted which rested the rights of forests in the state thereby restricting the traditional rights of the tribal people. This shattered the economic base of the tribes. In an economy which was only at self-sustainment levels, the effects were devastating. Economic problems led to increase in usury and moneylenders and contactors made profits at the expense of simple tribal people.

Issues with Tribes

Some main issues with Schedule Tribes are as follows:

- Land alienation has been the most important problem being faced by the tribal people. This had started in the colonial period itself with the enacting of the Forest Acts and opening of mines in tribal people areas. Expansion of railways came at a heavy cost to the forests. All this caused destitution and displacement among the tribal people. During the period moneylenders became active in tribal people areas and started usurping land of the tribal people resulting in land alienation at an unprecedented level.
- Land alienation has continued in the post independence period in the name of development projects, though the Government is more conscious about the humanitarian and rehabilitation aspects.
- Tribal economy is essentially intended for self sustainment. Primitive technology is used for production which does not have much profit earning capacity. As a result large numbers of tribal people live below poverty line. In 2004-05, percentage of urban and rural population below poverty line was 16 per cent and 16.1 per cent for general people while for tribal people it was 39.9 per cent and 47.2 per cent.
- Status of education differs from tribe to tribe. However, as a group, these tribes were also lagging behind in literacy rate which in 2001 was 64.84 per cent for all social groups and 47.1 per cent for ST. Dropout rates are high for a number of reason one of which is that medium of instruction is different from the tribal language and the curriculum neither suits their needs nor is comprehensible to them.

- Health is another cause of concern among these groups. Water borne diseases and malnutrition are rampant leading to deficiency diseases. In 2005-06, infant mortality rate, which was 48.9 for other population was 62.1 for STs. Child mortality rate which was 10.8 for others was 35.8 for STs.

Legal Provisions and Governmental Interventions

Recognising the special needs of STs, the Constitution of India made certain special safeguards to protect these communities from all the possible exploitation and thus ensure social justice. While Article 14 confers equal rights and opportunities to all, Article 15 prohibits discrimination against any citizen on the grounds of sex, religion, race, caste etc., Article 15(4) enjoins upon the State to make special provisions for the advancement of any socially and educationally backward classes; Article 16(4) empowers the State to make provisions for reservation in appointments or posts in favour of any backward class of citizens, which in the opinion of the State, is not adequately represented in the services under the State; Article 46 enjoins upon the State to promote with special care the educational and economic interests of the weaker sections of the people and, in particular,... the STs and promises to protect them from social injustice and all forms of exploitation. Further, while Article 275(1) promises grant-in-aid for promoting the welfare of STs and for raising the level of administration of the Scheduled Areas, Articles 330, 332 and 335 stipulate reservation of seats for STs in the Lok Sabha and in the State Legislative Assemblies and in services. Finally, the Constitution also empowers the State to appoint a Commission to investigate the conditions of the socially and educationally backward classes (Article 340) and to specify those Tribes or Tribal Communities deemed to be as STs (Article 342).

The Constitution (Scheduled Tribes) (Uttar Pradesh) Order, 1967 (C.O. 78)

In exercise of the powers conferred by clause (1) of article 342 of the Constitution of India, the President, after consultation with the Governor of the State of Utter Pradesh, is pleased to make the following Order, namely:

1. This Order may be called the Constitution (Scheduled Tribes) (Utter Pradesh) Order, 1967.
2. The tribes or tribal communities, or parts of, or groups within, tribes or tribal communities, specified in the Schedule to this Order, shall, for the purposes of the Constitution of India, be deemed to be Scheduled Tribes in relation to the State of Uttar Pradesh so far as regards members thereof resident in that State.

Constitutional safeguards have been provided for stopping exploitation of these people and to ensure equality is listed below:

- Seats are to be reserved for them in legislature. Further, 7.5 per cent of the government jobs have been reserved for Scheduled Tribes.
- Certain areas have been notified as Scheduled Areas. This allows the Government to frame certain regulations like restriction on transfer on land and regulation of money lending business in such areas.
- Forest Rights Act was enacted in 2006 as per which 'forest dwelling scheduled tribes' and 'other traditional forest dwellers' were granted certain rights in forests. The said act has recently been amended in 2012 for its effective implementation and removal of impediments.
- Many schemes under Ministry of Tribal Affairs have been started which included establishment of schools, girls and boys hostels and vocational training institutions in tribal people areas. Schemes have also been initiated for providing scholarship for ST students at various levels.
- A comprehensive scheme has been launched for welfare for Particularly Vulnerable Tribal people Groups.
- National Scheduled Tribe Finance and Development Corporation has been formed at the Centre with the similar structure in the states/U.Ts. For providing support for employment generating schemes/projects

and for providing training to the tribal people. The corporation sanctioned more than Rs. 192 crores during the year 2011-12.

- National Commission for Scheduled Tribes was established in 2004 for enquiring into the specific complaints as well as monitors the rights and safeguards of the tribal people.
- Tribal Co-operative Marketing Development Federation of India Limited (TRIFED) was set in 1987 for the purpose of creating market for tribal people products. TRIFED established exclusive showrooms for tribal people products under the name 'Tribes India' and has also taken up other promotional activities.

Conclusion and Suggestions

In spite of the government taking initiative steps in improving the living condition of the tribals, but in reality the tribals are still lacking in many facilities such as drinking water, proper sanitation, primary health centre, nutritional food security and quality education. Hence there is a need to make a review of the tribal situation. His review would indicate that the strategy for development would require an intensive approach to the tribal problems in terms of their geographic and demographic concentration, if the faster development of the community is to take place. While these achievements are a matter of some satisfaction as various development plans, policies and programmes have brought forth a perceptible improvement in the socio economic status of the Scheduled Tribes, a lot more needs to be done with concerted focus on the issues crucial to improve their status on par with the rest of the population. These are; prevention of land alienation from tribal to non tribal; review of National Forest Policy and Forest (Conservation) Act 1980; consideration of symbiotic relationship that the tribals are having with forest; provision of clean drinking water and medical facilities; effective rehabilitation of the tribals who are displaced on account of setting up of development projects; and legal measures to curb the activities of money lenders and traders by effective implementation of laws and regulations. The government is working hard towards a new social order based on social equality and social harmony, but still it is not adequate enough for the development of tribal people in India as well as in Uttar Pradesh.

REFERENCES

Bose, Nirmal K., (1972), Some Indian Tribes, National Book Trust, India, New Delhi.

Debbarma, Khaken, Status of Tribal in Tripura State of North-East India- An Overview, 2011.

Ghurye, G. S. (1959), The Scheduled Tribes, 2nd Edition, Popular Book Depot, Lamington Road, Bombay.

Panda, N. K., Policies, Programmes and Strategies for Tribal Development (2006), Kalpaz Publication, Delhi.

Pradesh, Himachal Pradesh University Journal, July 2011.

Sharma, Davendra, Schedule Tribes in India.

Uttar Pradesh, Data Highlights: The Scheduled Tribes, Census of India 2001.

Vaid, P. K., Kumar, Ajay and Kumar, Ravinder, Policies and Programmes for Tribal Development in Himachal.

5

Problem and Prospect of Tribal Habitant Due to Industrialization

A Theoretical Perspective

Pallavi Kumari*

INTRODUCTION

In an industrialized India the destruction of the tribal life is inevitable. According to The International Fund for Agricultural Development IFAD, Indigenous peoples suffer higher rates of poverty, landlessness, malnutrition, human rights violation, unemployment even after industrialization due to lower level of literacy and less access to health services. The tribal were dislodged from their traditional sources of livelihood and places of habitation due to industrialization. Not conversant with the details of acquisition proceedings they accepted whatever cash compensation was given to them and became emigrants. With cash in hand and many attractions in the nearby industrial towns, their funds were rapidly depleted and in course of time they were without money as well as without land. They joined the ranks of landless

* C/o B.M Tripathy (Senior Advocate), Swami Vishnupuri Marg, Burdawan Compound, Ranchi - 834 001. Jharkhand. Mobile: 09304187807, E-mail: pallavi_timesjob@yahoo.co.in

labourers but without any training, equipment or aptitude for any skilled or semi-skilled job. Thus, state governments are still free to reverse their policies and to take up a system of forest exploitation compatible with tribal interest.

Tribals in India

Tribal in India are economically and socially very backward. More than 3/4th of Scheduled Tribes women are illiterate. They have high drop-out rates in formal education, resulting in disproportionately low representation in higher education. They have very low levels of nutrition. The proportion of Scheduled Tribes below the poverty line is substantially higher than the national average. Most of the Tribal are engaged mostly in low-skilled, low-paying jobs, especially in primary sector. As per the 1991 Census, the Scheduled Tribes account for 67.76 million representing 8.08 per cent of the country's population. Scheduled Tribes are spread across the country mainly in forest and hilly regions. The essential characteristics of these communities are primitive traits, geographical isolation, distinct culture, shy of contact with community at large, economically backward.

Pre-Independence Features

The Subjugation and exploitation of tribal is something not new, only the scale and rate at which it has taken place in 18th century onwards is unprecedented. Tribal have always lived in a bad condition marked by common ownership of land and forest resources. So, historically, they have either adopted or were subjugated and mainstream cultural, social, political, religious, economic structures and practices imposed upon them. Earlier tribal societies had a hierarchy of clans, lineages or even villages. The alien rulers claimed sovereignty over tribal territory and collected revenue from tribal cultivators through tributaries/zamindars who were often outsiders and sometimes included tribal chiefs whose power increased. Tribal village councils were superseded by the council of the chiefs/rajas that often comprised of the king's followers and friends. Grants of customary rights over villages were made to such followers. Thus the jagirdaari system or the system of service grants was introduced in tribal areas. Privatization of land during British era led to a flow of capital and penetration by market opened the gates for influx of non-Tribal especially money-lenders and traders into tribal areas. This opened up the way for large scale alienation of land from tribes to non tribes, especially after tribal areas came to be linked by roads and railways.

Post-Independence Features

After Independence, it was thought that Tribes are backward due to their isolation from the mainstream and assimilation with mainstream is the only way for their development. The different measures taken up for their upliftment are usually divided into three categories:

1. *Protective:* Include constitutional and legislative rights that safeguard their interests.
2. *Mobilization:* Reservations extended to Tribal in various fields.
3. *Developmental:* Programmes and activities initiated for promoting their welfare.

Much of the forested land was declared as government land after survey and settlement. Earlier, Tribal only had to part with a portion of their produce and land belonged to them, but once the land was declared as belonging to Government in British era, the Tribal were declared encroachers upon the very land that they had lived on for centuries. In most cases, as tribal land was commonly owned it never had a owner which government can recognise. Claims of tribes over vast tracts of land were dismissed. Trees and Forests became government property who was now free to exploit them. They were compelled to find employment as labourers in nearby quarries, coalfields and emerging towns. One of the most important sectors that Tribal was the plantation sector that opened up in Bengal and Assam. They have also been affected by two more sectors of modern economy-industry and mines. Work in these sectors is divided into various types and grades depending upon skill and knowledge required for work. Not used to work other than cultivation and not being in possession of modern skills and knowledge a very large majority could secure only lowest paid jobs. The entry into white collar occupation has been very difficult.

Pre-Industrialization and Tribals

The primitive societies have passed through several stages of economic development everywhere in the world. The tribes living in the forests and hills usually earn their livelihood by means of food gathering, hunting and fishing. The tribes living in dense forests, full of wild beasts, live on hunting. The hunters leave the females to carry out household activities in the morning and return in the evening after hunting. In some tribes there is a usual custom of hunting collectively. Some tribal use spears and arrows and bows. The tribes living near rivers and seas usually earn their livelihood by catching fish. The hilly tribes rear the cattle and some tribes also carry out cultivation, but they are generally shifting from one place to another. Cottage industries, such as weaving cloths, preparing ropes and skins and utensils of different metals are prevalent in many tribes.

Post-Industrialization and Tribals

One of the main problems which the Indian tribes face is industrialization of backward areas and consequent urbanisation. The government policy of industrializing remote areas has led to the emergence of high-tech industries in tribal belts. The impact of such industrialization is manifold: Development in terms of economic prosperity might mean doom to the tribal identity. The first and major impact which tribal population faces is in the shape of loss of tribal identity through the establishment of industries. With major tribal tracts being depopulated to give space for establishment of factories, tribals are ill-ease in the new environments. Their customs and traditions come under pressure. Due to contact with the town – culture that industrialization brings and consequent urbanisation a revolutionary change in the attitude of tribal can be seen.

Social problems devastate tribals through industrialization. Urban conditions which the industry ushers into the tribal areas will mean introduction of completely alien way of social contact to the population. Economically the urban culture is highly materialistic. Tribal economic systems will disintegrate in the industrialized environment. Tribal modes of cultivation and crafts are steadily declining.

Benefits Due to Industrialization among Tribals

The benefits of industrialization should also be taken into account. Tribal's who were used to depend upon shifting cultivation and lived liked nomads are now settling down. Their children are exposed to better living conditions including education and health care services. Better sanitation means better health to the community. Yet the drive for modernization and industrialization pursued by all Indian governments committed to the improvement of the country's standard of living does not augur well for the future of tribal populations affected by projects promising to raise industrial output. There can be no doubt that the establishment of vast industrial enterprises in tribal zones lends urgency to the extension of protective measures to all tribals whose rights and way of life have been placed in jeopardy. Further, the state government has agreed to acquire land from the local residents as well as to look into all matters relating to displacement, rehabilitation, and resettlement.

Response of Governments and Non-government Organizations

In this respect there are certain discrepancies between the policies advocated by the central government and those pursued by individual states. India is one of tolerance towards the beliefs, customs, and way of life of the tribal people, whereas some of the state governments have shown themselves sensitive to the right of tribal communities to follow their traditional pattern of life.

The Indian Government: Laws Relating to Indigenous People

Ministry of Tribal Affairs

The Ministry of Tribal Affairs was constituted in October 1999 with the objective of providing more focused attention on the integrated socio-economic development of the most under-privileged sections of the Indian society namely, the Scheduled Tribes (STs), in a co-ordinated and planned manner. The Ministry of Tribal Affairs is the nodal Ministry for the overall policy, planning and co-ordination of programmes for development of STs. To this end, the Ministry of Tribal Affairs undertakes activities that flow from the subjects allocated under the Government of India (Allocation of Business) Rules, 1961.

National Scheduled Tribes Finance and Development Corporation

NSTFDC is the apex organization for providing financial assistance for scheme(s)/project(s) for the economic development of Scheduled Tribes.

Trifed

The ultimate objective of Trifed is socio-economic development of tribal people in the country by way of marketing development of the tribal products on which the lives of tribals depends heavily as they spend most of their time and derive major portion of their income from collection/ cultivation of Non-timber Forest Produce (NTFP). They develop market intelligence related to supply, demand, price trends, supply/market chain, value addition and processing facilities, product quality specifications, product applications, market trends, buyers for the tribal products and disseminate the information to the members as well as planners, researchers and associate organizations and business circles etc. They also act as an agency for canalization of export and import and facilitate, wherever necessary inter-State trade of tribal products under any Scheme formulated by Government of India or any other State agencies.

Industrialization and Forest

Many tribal places are in hilly and forest areas and the tribal activities mainly depended on the resources from forests. Forests and tribal have a symbiotic relationship. In spite of being threatened by modernization of the country, some of the tribal continue to live in forest areas. Some of them survive only on the collection of minor forest produce. The tribal have been using forest from generation to generation as their source of livelihood. However, with the enactment of the Forest Conservation Act 1980, their rights to collect minor forest produce and other forest produce has been restricted considerably. In the view of this, the National Forest Policy 1988 stipulates that all agencies responsible for forest management should ensure that the tribal peoples are closely associated with the regeneration, plantation, development and harvest of forests so as to provide them with favorable employment. Although the government has passed many Laws and constitutional provisions to respect the constitutional rights of Adivasis, Although there are constitutional rights provided, the excessive political influence and pressure on the Panchayats and the Department Officials, should not deny basic rights to the Adivasis. The political parties are concerned only about the mainstream communities, while Adivasis are not a vote bank in most of the states in India. Most Non-Government Agencies should also take up a Rights-Based Approach to tackle the issues faced by Adivasis as they fear of losing Government funds. The Government must take Adivasis into priority and implement all the schemes with their active participation of tribal peoples.

Non-Government Organizations: Programmes with Different Approaches

The Non-Government Organizations (NGOs) have been spending a great amount of time and money to uplift the Adivasi communities in the past 25 years. The NGOs conducted various training programmes and awareness sessions on human rights to Adivasis. However, these programmes have focused more on increasing welfare provision than raising the human rights consciousness and developing people's movement. The Adivasi communities become over-dependent on NGOs for providing their necessities. Recently, initiatives have been taken by some networks with rights-based approach to instill right consciousness in Adivasis and to form a national movement to fight for their rights. Only this approach will enable efforts of Adivasis to demand their rights in both public and private sectors.

In India we have enough laws and regulations, policies and welfare schemes to uplift the life situation of Adivasis. But the root problem is lack of commitment and determination to implement the laws properly. It is important that the international community pressurize the welfare-related Departments to protect the rights of Adivasis.

Major Concern Issues Related to Industrialization

This new trend in public opinion represents as great a threat to the future prospects of tribals as the greed of land-grabbers does to their present well-being. The manner of the integration of the tribals into the wider Indian society will ultimately be determined by political decisions, and these will be made on the basis of moral evaluations.

Land Issue

Land has been a major issue of Adivasis since 1950s. Few tribal families were allotted a portion of land by their erstwhile landlords. Government provided small holdings, but most of these holding are not viable and without proper title deeds. For the traditionally agricultural communities, land alienation has brought serious impacts on their livelihood, as a major portion of their land was alienated to settler farmers.

Economic Issue

The lifestyle and livelihood of most Adivasis are dependent on forest and agriculture which is the major source of their income. Adivasis became landless due to the large scale migration of people from the other districts. This leads to low family income and reduced employment opportunities in the agricultural sector. The poor marketing infrastructure, changes in cropping pattern, supply of poor quality of seeds, pesticides, low-levels of agricultural yields due to non-adoption of improved agricultural methods, entry of large number of non-tribal in labour market and the decline of price for cash crops resulted in low-income levels of tribal groups. In addition, diminishing traditional skills, non availability of alternative skills, regulations on non-timber forest produce have also caused low income of Adivasi families.

Health Issue

Most Adivasis live in poor hygienic condition in industries resulting in various problems such as low life expectancy, low nutritional intake, high morbidity and high infant mortality rate. The inadequacy of public health care delivery system, poor preventive measures, insufficient income and high consumption of tobacco and alcohol have led to an unhealthy life. Comparing to the earnings of Adivasis, the expenditure on health is a heavy burden which keeps tribal living in a poor health conditions.

Education Issue

The lack of motivation of parents and teachers to educate the young generations, high level of drop outs from schools and unsatisfactory performance of staff in schools cause low results in higher secondary levels and, thus, low educational attainment. Lack of infrastructure in schools, lack of transport facilities and low income of parents are some reasons for failure of retaining young people's interests.

Human Rights Issue

In terms of human development index, tribal are at the bottom of the rank in every state, every district and every village. No one can question the basic fact and truth that the tribal are the poorest of the poor in India. The ST population in India (except north east region) is living below the poverty line. Low literacy rate, high drop-out rate in school, nutritional deficiencies, endemic diseases and poor living conditions, low bargaining power, indebtedness, forcible eviction, migration, mortgage, atrocities, violence, exploitation of traditional knowledge, and degradation of forest resources, negligence are the long-term problems faced by tribal people.

Suggestions

In spite of disturbing the habitants if tribal and avoiding their problem the country can learn much from the beauty of tribal social practices, their culture of sharing and respect for all – their deep humility and love of nature – and most of all – their deep devotion to social equality and civic harmony. However, in the increasingly industrialized and modernized world, the indigenous peoples always become marginalized with their distinct relationship with the nature. The government and civil society movements should ensure that means of livelihood for indigenous peoples are available to them. The culture and traditions of indigenous people should be protected at all cost. The society at large should be ready to learn from the value system of indigenous people to keep the world with greater sense of equality and fraternity. In a recent study, the All India Coordinated Research Project (AICRP) credited tribal communities with the knowledge about 9,000 species of plants, including 7,500 used for human healing and veterinary health care. Dental care products like datun, roots and condiments like turmeric used in cooking and ointments are also the discoveries of tribal, as are many fruit trees and vines. Ayurvedic cures for arthritis and night blindness owe their origins to tribal knowledge. Tribal also played an important role in the development of agricultural practices – such as rotational cropping, fertility maintenance through alternating the cultivation of grains with leaving land fallow or using it for pasture. The country can learn much from the beauty of tribal social practices, their culture of sharing and respect for all – their deep humility and love of nature – and most of all – their deep devotion to social equality and civic harmony. In order to protect their interest , the government should try to focus on meeting the following needs of the tribal:

- Eradication of extreme poverty and hunger.
- Promotion of alternative livelihoods and employment opportunities.

- Education to increase school attendance and reduction of school drop-outs.
- Protection and promotion of forest rights of the indigenous communities.
- Revival of indigenous knowledge and traditional identity and wisdom.
- Regeneration of forest resources and conservation practices.
- Preservation of gender equality and promotion of women's empowerment.
- Creation of political education and awareness on reservation policy.
- Development of civil society action for the sustainable development.

Conclusion

The government policy of industrializing remote areas has led to the emergence of high-tech industries in tribal belts. The first and major impact which tribal population faces is in the shape of loss of tribal identity through the establishment of industries. With major tribal tracts being depopulated their customs and traditions come under pressure. Due to contact with the town – culture that industrialization brings and consequent urbanisation tribal economic systems is disintegrating in the industrialised environment. To what extent structural adjustment has been made following liberalization and globalization since 1991 to suit the present condition is a big question. It is the people who are called upon to make the sacrifice. The situation needs a thorough analysis and great understanding by the policy-makers. Whether we live in an age of nationalism or globalization it is the people who matter. The most important issues which have surface the movements are livelihood issues and rights of the certain sections people which include the tribals for whom the compensation package and rehabilitation measures hold out no promise. Industrialization through foreign investors inducing displacement of local people may be an issue with which people may not reconcile easily. The rehabilitation and resettlement policy needs to be formulated in such a way that the people feel that they are not the losers. The offer needs to be made attractive and make the people willing to accept it.

REFERENCES

Fried, Morton H. The Notion of Tribe. Cummings Publishing Company, 1975. ISBN 0-8465-1548-2.

Helm, June, ed, 1968. Essays on the Problem of Tribe, Proceedings, American Ethnological Society, 1967.

http://en.wikipedia.org/wiki/Forest_Rights_Act

http://socyberty.com/history/the-impact-of-industrialization-and-urbanisation-on-indian-tribals-2/#ixzz1ttaSEtC2

http://tribal.nic.in/forestright/pdf/E-Act-2006.pdf

http://tribal.nic.in/tribes/introduction.html

http://www.aitpn.org/Issues/II-09-06-Forest.pdf

http://www.vanashakti.in

Indo-European Language and Society, Translated by Elizabeth Palmer. London: Faber and Faber 1973. ISBN 0-87024-250-4.

Nagy, Gregory, Greek Mythology and Poetics, Cornell University Press, 1990. In Chapter 12, Beginning on p. 276, Professor Nagy Explores the Meaning of the Word Origin and Social Context of a Tribe in Ancient Greece and Beyond.

Sutton, Imre, Indian Land Tenure: Bibliographical Essays and a Guide to the Literature (NY: Clearwater, 1975): Tribe – pp. 101-02,180-82, 186-87, 191-93.

6

Endangered Life of Tribes Due to Development, Displacement and Resettlement

Durgesh Narpat Valvi*
Vilas Shriram Soyam**

INTRODUCTION

India is a country with the largest tribal population in the World. These tribes are considered original settlers, they are still living in rural, forest and mountain areas and prove that they have been living here from very ancient times. The Scheduled tribes population of the country, according to 2001 Census, was 8,43,26,000 and constitutes 8.20 per cent to the total Indian population. But about 40 per cent of them are displaced persons due to modern development projects. Truly, they are victims of and refugees of development.

The land of tribes is taken away for developmental projects. From food gathers, Craftsman and Farmer, today they have become agriculture labors, landless labors, bonded

* Assistant Professor, Department of Social Work, SIBER, Kolhapur - 416 004. Maharashtra. Mobile: 09423943462. Email: ukantvalvi@gmail.com

** Deputy Registar, Shivaji University, Kolhapur - 416 004. Maharashtra. Mobile: 08421549229, Email: vmaitryee@indiatimes.com

labors, seasonal laborers (sugar cane cutters), wage earners and unskilled labors. In rehabilitation sites the problems of backwardness, exploitations, underdevelopment, illiteracy, malnutrition, alcoholism, indebtedness, conversion and poor human development has been challenge for Government and NGOs till today.

Development and Displacement

According to Government of India estimate, between 1981-85 the coal mine alone had displaced 1,80,000 persons and had provided one job per family to only 36 per cent. In Jharkhand the tribal land alienation and displacement have been going on from 1907 with the establishment of Tata Iron Steel Company. The magnitude of land and number of displaced persons has been increasing since then (Singh, A. K. 1996). It has been estimated that about at least 185 lakh persons have been displaced by the development projects during 1951 to 1990 (Fernandes, 1995).

Dam and Displacement

India now boasts of being the World's third largest dam builder. According to Central water commission, the country has 3600 dams that qualify as big dams, 3300 of them build after Independence. 1,000 more are under construction. Yet one fifth of our population, 200 million people does not have safe drinking water and two third, 600 million lack basic sanitation.

During the inauguration of Panchet hill dam across Damodhar River in 1959, Nehru said, 'Dams are the temples of Modern India'. Dam building is equated with Nation building. While speaking to villagers displaced by Hirakund dam, Nehru expressed, 'If you are to suffer, you should suffer in the interest of country'.

Moraji Desai speaking at a public meeting in the submergence zone of the Pong dam in 1961 said, "We will request you to move from your houses after the dam comes up, if you move it will be good, otherwise we shall release water down on you all". The above statements of the Great leaders reveal the intensity that have been cherished by the power centres towards the people, who are negatively affected by the project. (Roy, 1999)

According to a detailed study of 54 large dams conducted by Indian Institute of Public Administration, the average number of people displaced by large dams is 44,182. If 10,000 people are displaced per dam as compared to 3300 dams, thirty million people are displaced by the dams alone in the last fifty years only. According to secretary of planning commission N. C. Sexena, 50 million people are displaced in this region of which 40 million were displaced by the dams only. 50 million is more than a population of states like Gujurat.

Table 6.1: Dams and displacement of tribal people

No.	Name of the Project (*)	State	Population Facing Displacement	Tribal People as Percentage of Displaced
1.	Karjan	Gujarat	11,600	100%
2.	Sardar sarovar	Gujarat	2,00,000	57.6%
3.	Ukai reservoir	Gujarat	52,000	18.92%
4.	Maheshwar	Madhya Pradesh	20,000	60%
5.	Koel Karol	Bihar	66,000	88%
6.	Mahi bajaj sagar	Rajasthan	38,400	76.28%
7.	Upper Indrawati	Orrisa	18,500	89.20%
8.	Pong	Himachal Pradesh	80,000	56.25%
9.	Inchampalli	A. P. - Maharashtra	38,100	76.28%
10.	Tultuli	Maharashtra	13,600	51.61%

(*) Projects are either under construction or have been planned.

Source: Satyajit Singh, taming waters OUP, 1997 and Government figures.

Huge percentage of displaced in the above projects are the tribal people. If we consider tribal people account for only 8 per cent of the India's population, it opens up whole other dimensions of a story. India's poorest people are subsidizing the life style of her richest. Displacement affected the total livelihood of tribes.

Adivasi's believes, 'The soul of their fore fathers lives in the forest'. They cannot fulfill life and culture without forest. The socio-economic life of tribes was depended on, 'Water, forest and land'. The tribes are forcefully displaced from generation to generation for various reasons under the name of development. The self-sufficient life of tribal was always introduced by selfish and ambitious people.

Former Commissioner of Scheduled Castes and Tribes Commission, Dr. B. D. Sharma noticed in his report that, 'The 10-15 per cent of Adivasi are displaced and deserted by various causes'. To build Nation, one is ruined for one's development. And it comes to the share of poor adivasi.

Rehabilitation/Resettlement

The rehabilitation of project affected people has always been recognised as storm of conflict. The projects have created various problems like displacement, resettlement, socio-economic exploitation and environmental disasters to tribal life. The developmental project submerged the tribal houses, fields, villages, forest not only ruined present status, but given pain for many generations.

It is very true that the rehabilitation of displaced person will never be satisfied. The resettlement created disharmonious relation among local tribals, was never in the history of tribes. Due to improper rehabilitation facilities, many displaced persons have lost economic status and many other problems come out.

In view of the above, the present study was conducted to understand the problems of displaced tribals due to Sardar Sarovar project in Nandurbar district of Maharashtra with the following objectives.

Aim and Objectives

The main aim of the study was to explore the impact of the development projects on the tribals affected by Sardar Sarovar project. The specific objectives are to study the nature of acceptance of displacement and resettlement, to understand the problems of displacement and resettlement of tribals, to find out the causes of dissatisfaction, to know the problems faced by respondents after resettlement.

Methodology

This research is based on primary data collected on the problems faced by the tribal community at rehabilitated site with help of an Interview schedule. The respondents selected for study was affected by Sardar Sarovar project on Narmada River rehabilitated at Maharashtra site. According to Maharashtra State Government report on Sardar Sarovar project rehabilitation department, there are 1168 families rehabilitated at various sites. For the study 100 families were selected using Simple random lottery method.

The interview schedule covers the information on nature of acceptance of displacement, satisfaction with quality of remuneration and rehabilitation, causes of dissatisfaction, personal, social and economical problems faced by the respondents.

Results and Discussion

Following are the findings based on the primary data collected for study:

Acceptance of Displacement

Regarding the nature of acceptance of displacement, majority *i.e.* 81 per cent of respondents expressed that they are pressurized by Government officials and 19 per cent did not have any choice other than accepting it showing their helplessness and vulnerability.

Satisfaction with the Quality of Remuneration and Rehabilitation against Displacement

A good majority (62%) of the respondents are not satisfied with the quality of remuneration and rehabilitation against displacement. The satisfaction is found to be as less as 38 per cent.

Causes for Dissatisfaction

Majority (88%) of the respondents did not receive community facilities like community hall, bus stand toilet etc.,

31 per cent had lack of irrigation, 25 per cent were not paid subsistence allowance, 19 per cent did not receive agricultural land and 14 per cent did not receive agricultural land legally. It was found that the tribes are dissatisfied with the resettlement made to them due to displacement. Though tribes are displaced against their wish, they did not receive ideal benefits. Administrator's red taped strategy and corruption policy seems to have exploited them.

Personal Problems Faced

As regards major personal problems faced by respondents due to displacement and resettlement, the study revealed that 78 per cent of the respondents received ill treatment by government officials, 69 per cent of them claimed that they are unaware of Constitutional measures and Protective Acts, 64 per cent experienced psychological pressure by non-tribal, 57 per cent had feeling of backwardness and inferiority and 54 per cent said that they are unaware of schemes due to illiteracy.

Social Problems Faced

Regarding the social problems faced by respondents due to displacement and resettlement, nearly 70 per cent said that they lack active leadership to enjoy rights and privileges, 59 per cent of the respondents do not get any support from non-tribals, 45 per cent had feeling of hopelessness and disadvantages, 39 per cent feel ignored by Government officials and 25 per cent are exploited by non-tribals.

Economic Problems Faced

Insufficient Income due to unproductive agriculture was the most cited economic problem for a great majority (85%) of them. When seasonal unemployment and incapability to enter into secondary and tertiary occupations accounts for nearly one third of them, only a quarter of them lack exposure to outside areas for skills and capacity development. While for 19 per cent of the respondents indebtedness seems to be another major problem.

Conclusions

Forceful displacement agitated the tribes, broke their attachment with Land, Forest and River (Goddess of their civilization) to accept wish less migration into the trap of resettlement.

Issues regarding displacement and resettlement have created tensions among tribals and administrators. Tribes have fallen into the trap of ignorance, ill treatment, psychological pressure and exploitation by non-tribal and government officials.

Though resettlement has taken place, it covered only shifting of houses and live stocks, allotment of agricultural land with or without irrigation etc; but completely ignored personal, social, economical and psychological distress due to displacement.

The status of tribals at resettled colonies is deplorably low due to insufficient income, indebtedness, unemployment, adoption of primary occupations and inactive institutional setup. This has further resulted to raise problems like illiteracy, poverty, malnutrition, poor technology and lack of leadership.

The analysis shows that though government has taken all the care for resettlement of tribal community, many are still facing problems due to faulty strategy, failures of schemes and programmes, and inappropriate efforts to bring tribal resettlement.

The results obtained in the study have important implications for the Government and suggests that more appropriate measures are needed to rehabilitate and resettle the tribes for a better quality of life.

There is abundance scope for further research in this area which can unveil many more facts and suggest for better legislative measures.

REFERENCES

Fernandes, W. (1995), Planned Development and Tribal Deprivation. In Deogaonkar S. G. (Ed): Tribal Panorama in India, Inter-India, New Delhi.

Gare Govind, (1985), Tribal Culture, Problem and Development in Maharashtra.

Ram, R.N. (NBA), Sardar Sarovar: Sachai and Dave.

Roy, Arundhati (1999), The Common Gods, Frontline, April.

Singh, A. K. and Jabbi, M. K. (1996), (Eds) Status of Tribals in India: Health, Education and Employment, Har Anand, New Delhi.

7

The Problems of Displacement among Tribal Communities in India

P. Sailaja*

Prof. K. Visweswara Rao**

INTRODUCTION

Indigenous people also known as tribal people or tribals are at the bottom of society in India and they are the poorest, most marginalized, oppressed, and deprived people in the country (Nathan 2004a; Rath 2006) displacement induced due to development is quite historical in India. Since, colonial period there has been enormous segment of displaced people. The most attractive zones for developmental projects have always been the forest resources, river systems and mineral base and have displaced many parts of the Indian society. Moreover, most of the developmental projects are located in the most backward areas and populated by tribals. India has one of the highest development-induced displacements in the world. There is however no reliable official statistics on the number of development related internally displaced in India.

* Guest Faculty, Department of Social Work, Andhra University, Visakhapatnam - 530 003. Mobile: 8801308999. E-mail: sailupilla @yahoo.co.in

** Professor, Department of Social Work, Andhra University, Visakhapatnam - 530 003.

The Indian tribes are believed to be the primitive settlers in India. They are usually called as adivasis implying original inhabitants. The constitution of India has documented these tribal groups as Scheduled Tribes (STs). The Scheduled tribes population of India, as per the 2001 census, is 8.43 crore, constituting 8.2 per cent of the total population. The population of Scheduled tribes had grown at the growth rate of 24.45 per cent during the period 1991-2001. More than half the Scheduled Tribes population is concentrated in the States of Madhya Pradesh, Chhattisgarh, Maharashtra, Orissa, Jharkhand and Gujarat (Government of India, 11) they are scattered throughout India, but most live in two contiguous areas. The first is the forested hills and mountains of the northeast, and the second is the broad belt of hilly, forested country across north-central India from Gujarat and Rajasthan in the west, through Madhya Pradesh and Chattisgarh, to Jharkhand and Orissa in the east. (http://www2.adb.org)

Post-Independent Displacement

Post-independence India sought to achieve rapid economic growth through planned development under the successive five-year plans. Large-scale investment was made in projects like: dams, roads, mines, power plants, industrial establishments, defence bases, new cities and others. Emphasis was on industrial and modern agricultural development and the main needs were power and irrigation. Accordingly, emphasis was on major dams. According to one estimate, 15 per cent of the world's large dams built from 1947 to 1979 were in India (Nag, 2002). A pre-requisite of these projects was land acquisition. This brought irreversible changes in land use and in the lives of millions of people who has earlier depended on that land (Pandey, 1998).

The development projects require a huge land area, most of it in the resource rich 'backward regions'. Many of these are inhabited by tribal and other rural poor classes whom the project forces to sacrifice their sustenance in the name of 'national development'. But its benefits do not reach them. While displacement thus alienates a large number of persons from their livelihood as, rehabilitation has also been weak in most states.

In India around 50 million people have been displaced due to development projects in over 50 years. Around 21.3 million development-induced internally displaced persons IDPs include those displaced by dams (16.4 million), mines (2.55 million), industrial development (1.25 million) and wild life sanctuaries and national parks (0.6 million) (IDMC, 2007). Development-related Displacement may be divided into two subcategories – direct and indirect. Direct displacement refers to those cases, where the installation and commissioning of development projects lead to a direct displacement of people who have inhabited these sites for generation together. In India alone, between 1955-90 as a result of the installation of such projects as mines, dams and industries, wildlife and other projects, about 21 million people were internally displaced (Gaekwad and Nochur, 1995). Indirect displacement emanates from a process whereby installation and functioning of projects continuously push up the consumption of natural and environmental resources, thereby depriving the indigenous people of the surrounding regions of their traditional means of wherewithal and sustenance (Das, Banerjee and Kumar, 2004). In the 1950s and 1960s, it may be said that the dominant view in development was informed by modernization theory, which, put crudely, saw development as transforming traditional, simple, Third World societies into modern, complex and westernized ones. Seen in this light, large-scale, capital-intensive development projects accelerated the pace toward a brighter and better future. In recent decades, however, a 'new development paradigm' has been articulated, one that promotes poverty reduction, environmental protection, social justice, and human rights. In this paradigm, development is seen as both bringing benefits and imposing costs. Among its greatest costs has been the involuntary displacement of millions of vulnerable people (Robinson, 2003).

According to a report, 'during the last fifty years, some 3,300 big dams have been constructed in India. Many of them have led to large-scale forced eviction of vulnerable groups. The situation of the tribal people is of special concern as they constitute 40 to 50 per cent of the displaced population' (Kumar, 2005). The brutality of displacement due to the building of dams was dramatically highlighted during the agitation over the Sardar Sarovar Dam. It has been called 'India's most controversial dam project'. Medha Patekar, spearhead the anti-dam movement known as the *Narmada Bachao Andolon*. This movement for the first time systematically revealed how building dams can result in total dislocation of tribal societies. The beneficiaries of the dam are meant to be large landowners; but the tribal people are paying the price. The Narmada Valley Development Project (NVDP) is supposed to be the most ambitious river valley development project in the world. It envisages building 3,200 dams that would reconstitute the Narmada and her 419 tributaries into a series of step-reservoirs. Of these, 30 would be major dams, 135 medium and the rest small. Two of the major dams would be multi-purpose mega dams. The Sardar Sarovar in Gujarat and the Narmada Sagar in Madhya Pradesh, would, between them, hold more water than any other reservoir in the Indian subcontinent. The official figure indicates that about 42,000 families would be displaced but non-governmental organizations such as the *Narmada Bachao Andolan* (NBA) the figure to about 85,000 families or 500,000 people. They argue that the official figure has not counted people who would lose their livelihood as a result of these dams as 'Project Affected Families' (PAFs). The official figure counts families who would lose their land or homes as the only PAF. The Narmada Valley Development Project would affect the lives of 25 million people who would in the valley and would alter the ecology of an entire river basin (Das, Banerjee and Kumar, 2004). The Tehri project is a multi-purpose irrigation and power project in the Ganges valley, 250 km north of Delhi, located in the Tehri Garhwal district of Uttaranchal state. Initially in 1969, the Tehri Dam Project Organization (TDPO) estimated that about 13,413 persons would be affected by the construction of the dam. But a working group for the Environment Appraisal of Tehri Dam established in 1979 put the figure of expected internal displacement to 85,600 persons. According to the 1995 report of TDPO, out of 135 villages affected, 37 would be fully submerged once the dam is completed. The total land affected by the project is 13,000 hectares (Das, Banerjee and Kumar, 2004).

According to one observer (Das, Banerjee and Kumar, 2004) Dams are built, people are uprooted, forests are submerged and then the project is simply abandoned. Canals are never completed... the benefits never accrue (except to the politicians, the bureaucrats and the contractors involved in the construction). The first dam that was built on the Narmada is a case in point – the Bargi Dam in Madhya Pradesh was completed in 1990. It cost ten times more than was budgeted and submerged three times more land than engineers said it would. To save the cost and effort of doing a survey, the government just filled the reservoir without warning anybody. 70,000 people from 101 villages were supposed to be displaced. Instead, 114,000 people from 162 villages were displaced. They were evicted from their homes by rising waters, chased out like rats, with no prior notice. There was no rehabilitation. Some got meagre cash compensation. Most got nothing. Some died of starvation. Others moved to slums in Jabalpur. Today, ten years after it was completed, the Bargi Dam produces some electricity, but irrigates only as much land as it submerged. Only 5 per cent of the land its planners claimed it would irrigate. Barring a few exceptions, most pre-1980 projects did not have a clear-cut resettlement plan. Resettlement was undertaken on a case-to-case basis. To mention a few, there were projects like the Nagarjunasagar, Hirakud, Tungabhadra and Mayurakshi dams; the Rourkela, Bhilai and Bokaro steel plants, several defense establishments, coal mines, etc., which did offer resettlement in the form of house sites to the displaced. In 1951-95 completed in six states and between 1947-2000 is probably around 60 million (Fernandes, 2004). It was clear from the start that mega-projects would require the displacement or forced uprooting of substantial populations, particularly for hydraulic projects which entail large-scale submergence for reservoirs. However, national leaders and policy-makers typically viewed these as legitimate and inevitable costs of development, acceptable in the larger national interest (Hemadri and Mander, 1999).

Globalisation has further intensified displacement. The state needs to acquire more land than in the past in order to encourage Private Indian and foreign investment (MRD, 1994). That has more implications for the tribals than the others since the focus today is on mining by private companies in Middle India and water resources in the Northeast, both of these in the tribal areas (IWGIA, 2004). Also the situation of the Displacement is bound to deteriorate because of a loss of jobs through mechanization. Thus, even the jobs lost because of land takeover will not be replaced.

The Impact of Displacement

Impact of displacement on Joblessness and increase in the proportion of workers, Homelessness, Landlessness, Food insecurity, Social Disintegration, Loss of access to common property, Decline in Joint Family System and environmental components and their family members of tribals.

Joblessness and Increase in the Proportion of Workers

When people were displaced from their habitat, they lose their means of livelihood. Creation of new jobs or alternative sources of income for them becomes very difficult since the oustees do not possess any skill to learn new methods of earning their livelihood. Hence those who were owners of the means of production before displacement have now become daily wage earners. When the company provide by the policy a job to each displaced family, the other members of the displaced families remained jobless. The policy also discriminated against the landless labourers, artisans, share croppers and petty businessmen among others.

Homelessness

Loss of house and shelter may be only temporary during the transition period for most of the displaced. But for some, homelessness remains a permanent feature. The project authorities only provided homestead plots while the displaced persons have themselves built their houses. Again when a split occurs in the family, those who leave the family become homeless.

Landlessness

India being a farm dominated society with agriculture as the main occupation, displacement from land, removes the main foundation on which people's productive systems, commercial activities and livelihood are based. Unless this foundation is reconstructed elsewhere or replaced by steady income-generating employment, landlessness sets in and the affected families are impoverished. In most of the cases/ projects, land for land, norm could not be followed. But cash compensation is inadequate to make up for the loss of land.

Food Insecurity

Forced displacement increases the risk of chronic food insecurity. In India, crops are grown to provide food to the family while vegetables are grown in the kitchen gardens that take care of the food needs of the family. Surplus is also sold in the market. But forced displacements deprive the oustees from their former resource of livelihood rendering them landless. Even when homestead land was provided, the oustees could not properly reclaim and level the hilly area. The displaced families have to buy everything including food items from the market.

Social Disintegration

Forced displacement tears apart the social fabric of the oustees. Production systems are dismantled, kinship groups and family systems are often scattered and cultural identity of the people is under threat. Social and community networks that help people to cope with poverty through exchange of food and clothing, mutual help with farming, building houses and caring children are disrupted. Social disintegration has been a major impoverishment risk in all the projects undertaken. There is also the danger of parasitic and vector born diseases in the relocated sites because of unsafe water, poor sewerage etc. In fact, lack of food, unhygienic living and environmental degradation in the new place were found in the project area to have a serious impact on the health of the oustees. By the project, pollution caused by coal dust and frequent blasting has caused skin diseases, eye irritation, gastric disorders, diarrhoea and other ailments. Though medical centres have been opened in the resettlement colony they are dysfunctional in the absence of the doctors.

Loss of Access to Common Property

For the poor people, particularly, the landless and otherwise assetless people, loss of access to common property (forest lands, water bodies, grazing land, etc.,) leads to a major deterioration in their income and livelihood levels. The economic impact gives a glimpse of aspects such as the availability and access to jobs and their quality, and ownership of land and other assets before and after the project. The tribal most dissatisfied with components like compensation. When they are paid compensation its quantum is low. It cannot replace the livelihood lost. No tribal has a government or project job. Such lost resources are rarely compensated by the Government in the relocation sites. There are also frequent conflicts between the host population and new settlers over the use of forest land and other government land. As a result, the resettler do not get fuel wood and other minor forest produce, which they used to collect from the forests in their old habitat. Decline in Joint Family System. The pre displacement level both tribal and non-tribal families showing the same trend of breaking down of joint family to nuclear families. This is a general feature noticed in most of the development projects.

Impact on the Environment and Family

The environment has deteriorated because of the projects. One of the consequences is new diseases on a rise. Studies show that water borne diseases increase substantially after a project. Some areas also experience a rise in diseases like asthma. Medical persons say that it is caused partly by air pollution and is partly psycho-somatic linked to the trauma of forced displacement. Some other diseases are linked to the quality of facilities like housing, toilets and drainage. That is the main reason why diseases are included in the environmental impact of the project. Women and children feel the negative impact more than adults do. Tribal women suffer more after losing their forests. They maintain their family with the reduced resources and also bear the mental suffering born out of poverty. An impact many mention is absence of good opportunities for children in general and girl children in particular. Most of them pulled their children out in order to work and supplement their family income which had declined after land loss (Fernandes *et al.* 2001).

Rehabilitation and Resettlement in India

An important cause of the struggles of the displaced persons or Project affected persons (DP/PAPs) is poor resettlement. Resettlement is one-time physical relocation with or without other social and economic support. Rehabilitation involves rebuilding the economic resources, cultural systems, social structures and community support mechanisms that the DP/PAPs lose as a result of alienation of their sustenance.

One knows what has preceded that land loss without livelihood alternatives results in impoverishment and marginalization. The former is expressed in landlessness, joblessness, homelessness, poor food security, malnutrition, higher exposure to diseases, morbidity and mortality. The latter entails disruption of their social, cultural and economic networks (Mahapatra, 1998).

Rehabilitation and Resettlement Policies

In 1952, after independence, a new national forest policy added further restrictions on tribal people. The traditional rights of the tribals were no longer recognised as rights. In 1894 they became 'rights and privileges' and in 1952 they became 'rights and concessions'. Now they are regarded as 'concessions' (Fernandes Waltair, 2008).

All of this shows the need to rehabilitate the DP/PAPs, but the country did not have a rehabilitation policy or law planned development. The contemporary policies that have now been promulgated are weak and also not accommodated the government's own experience of Rehabilitation and Resettlement in the past 65 years of dealing with development, disaster, and ethnicity induced displacement (Sah, 2003). India adopted its first rehabilitation policy in February 2004 and a second one with a few changes on October 31, 2007. Most persons involved in action or studies among the displaced persons or project-affected persons (DP/PAPs) have expressed dissatisfaction over these documents. One has, therefore, to work for a better policy and law. Before the promulgation of the national policy, some projects like Sardar Sarovar and Upper Krishna had rehabilitation packages and Coal India promulgated its policy in 1994 (CIL 1994). NTPC prepared its policy in 1993 and revised it in 2005 (NTPC 2005). Orissa, Rajasthan, Madhya Pradesh, Andhra Pradesh, Haryana and some other states have rehabilitation policies. A few of them are for specific categories of projects while others include all projects. Maharastra has a comprehensive rehabilitation act. Karnataka and Madhya Pradesh have laws for water resource displaced persons (DPs). Despite this, all India level documents are very few.

The draft of the government's 'National Policy for Rehabilitation' states that a figure around 75 per cent of the displaced people since 1951 are still awaiting rehabilitation (The Hindu, 2011). However, it should be noted that displacement is only being considered with regard to 'Direct Displacement'. These rehabilitation policies do not cover fisher folk, landless labourers, artisans, etc.

Conclusion

Displacement has been high and resettlement has been poor. The policies only speak of the need to minimize displacement without specifying the modes of doing it. The rehabilitation policies have but in their present form they cannot result in rehabilitation. The larger issues of the triabals their such as participation of the tribals protecting rights, to customs, traditions effect on their livelihood due to displacement are much neglected. By and large the availability of some facilities like schools and roads has improved but the access of the DP/PAPs to them is limited. An important reason for this contradiction is that the project builds facilities like schools and hospitals for their staff, not for the DP/PAPs. The resettlement area should provide infrastructural amenities including schools and playgrounds, health centres, roads and electric connections, assured sources of safe drinking water for each family, Panchayat Ghars, fair-price shops and seed-cum-fertilizer storage facilities, places of worship and burial and cremation grounds. The tribals feel the negative impact more than the others do because they find it more difficult to adjust to the new environment they are pushed into. There is need to undertake an immediate extensive project-wise survey of number of displaced as well as affected tribals across the country. Rehabilitation and Resettlement (R and R) policies at the National and State Levels, though are expected to safeguard the interests of the displaced persons, they are not practiced in the right spirit. Absence of rehabilitation Act at national level and violation of protective laws, regulations, legislations, and court orders causing deprivation of tribal and weaker sections. The National Land Acquisition and Rehabilitation and Resettlement Bill, 2011 introduced, debated without allowing dilution of its key proposals. It should preferably be passed with retrospective effect, so that major tribal displacements of recent years can be soothed away.

REFERENCES

Chittaroopa Palit, 2004, 'Short-changing the Displaced: National Rehabilitation Policy', in *Economic and Political Weekly*, Issue July 3 2004, XXXVIV, XXVII, 2961-2963.

G. Nancy and N. S. Ganesh (eds) (1995), National Conference on Development, Displacement and Rehabilitation: Policies and Strategies: A Report, Mumbai: Tata Institute of Social Science Research and NAPM.

Government of India Ministry of Tribal Affairs (2011) Annual Report. p. 28.

Fernanades Walter, Nafisa Goga D'Souza, Arundhati Roy Choudhury and Mohammed Asif. 2001. Development-Induced Displacement in Andhra Pradesh 1951-95: A Quantitative and Qualitative Study of Its Extent and Nature. New Delhi: Indian Social Institute and Guwahati: North Eastern Social Research Centre.

Fernanades. Walter (2004), 'Rehabilitation Policy for the Displaced', *Economic and Political Weekly*, XXXVIV, XII, 1191-1193.

Hari Mohan (2009), Land and Cultural Survival: The Communal Land Rights of Indigenous People in Asia, Tribal Land Issues in India: Communal Management, Rights, and Displacement, pp: 164-192.

Hemadri Mander R. Hemadri and V. Nagraj (1999), Dams, Displacement, Policy and Law India, Working paper of the World Commission on Dams.

Internal Displacement Monitoring Centre (IDMC) (2007), India: Large Numbers of IDPs are Unassisted and in Need of Protection: A Profile of the Internal Displacement Situation.

IWGIA. 2004. The Indigenous World (2004), Copenhagen: International Work Group for Indigenous Affairs.

Kumar Madhuresh (2005), Incorporating Gender Issues in National Responses, Compiled for Presentation at the Regional Workshop on NHRIs and IDPs Organized by APF, Colombo, October 26-28-2005, www.idpproject.orgIndia, date accessed on 25 October 2010.

Mahapatra, L. K. (1998), 'Good Intentions or Policies are Not Enough: Reducing Impoverishment Risks for the Tribal Custees, in Hari Mohan Mathur and David Marsden (eds.). Development Project and Impoverishment Risks: Resettling Project Affected People in India. Oxford University Press. pp. 216-236.

Ministry of Rural Development (1994), National Policy for Rehabilitation of Persons Displaced as a Consequence of Acquisition of Land, New Delhi, Ministry of Rural Development, Government of India. (Second Draft).

Nag, Sajal (2002), 'Whose Nation is it Anyway: Nation Building and Displacement in Indian Sub-Continent' in CJ Thomas (ed.)

"NAC's Seven-point Test for Land Acquisition Bill" The Hindu (Chennai, India). 10 June 2011.

Nathan, D. 2004a. The Future of Indigenous People, Seminar 537. May: 33-37.

Pandey, Balaji. (1998), Depriving the Underprivileged for Development. Bhubaneswar: Institute of Socio-Economic Development.

Rath, G.C., ed. (2006), Tribal Development in India: The Contemporary Debate. Delhi: Sage Publications.

Sah D. C. (2003), Involuntary Migrations. Jaipur: Rawat Publications.

http://www2.adb.org/Documents/Books/Land-Cultural-Survival/chap06.pdf

8

Economic Crisis among the Katkaris in Maharashtra

Prof. Dr. Anjali Kurane*
Dr. Jyoti Shetty**

INTRODUCTION

Every society has some wants and demands that are satisfied by supplying goods and services. This whole system is considered as economic organization. The meaning of word 'Economic' is 'enough to give a good return for money or effort laid'. And meaning of 'Organization' is 'act of uniting the separate elements into a smoothly working unit'.

So economic organization deals with the resource management of a particular community processes of production, distribution and consumption and in turn it connects different aspects of culture like ecology, religion, family and kinder system of that community. In this way we get to know the holistic nature of culture.

* Head, Department of Anthropology, University of Pune. Pune - 411 007.

** Documentation Consultant, Yashwantrao Chavan Academy of Development Administration (Yashada), Pune.

Economic empowerment is the foremost and basic component in the overall development of any individual or society. Economic empowerment is absolutely essential for raising the status, expected to show a positive impact on the people's control over resources and their participation in decision-making leading to their development in society.

The concept of development is multidimensional, total, qualitative and quantitative in nature that involves economic, political, social, material, legal, administrative, cultural, psychological, and cultural values on that the full development of human personality and dignity of man in the society is depended. It is value-laden concept that improves socio-cultural, economic material and non-material well-being of the society.

According to R. P. Misra (1985) for a poor landless agricultural labour development would mean a piece of land and a pair of bulls to till land for hungry man it is a piece of bread, for an unemployed urban youth it means employment, for one who has one car it would probably mean two cars.

Anjali Kurane (2009) says "Development means growth of human capabilities and freedom and meaningful participation in each and every aspect of life. For instance, meaningful participation in decision making process at family as well as society level, freedom to have choice and opportunities in socio-cultural, educational, economic and political sphere of life and freedom from domination, exploitation and economic dependence".

Therefore development is a human centered process. A prerequisite for development is participation of all people in building their society. People are the ends as well as the means in this process. Therefore in order to understand development we should see it from the several perspectives simultaneously.

The issue of development is of primary concern for a country like India. Despite all planned programmes, special provisions and strategies to improve the economic conditions of the tribes in India, they continue to remain in poverty, misery, servitude, aloof from the main stream of the modern life of the society.

Tribal development problem in India is not only limited to socio-economic development but also adaptation to new situations. Therefore Anthropologists now have greater role to contribute to the tribal development as the success or failure of development programmes depends upon the understanding of socio-cultural, economic, geo-ecological and politico-administrative perspective of the different tribes for whom development schemes are meant.

The present study emphasises on the economic crisis among the Katkaris in Maharashtra. When we are considering any primitive tribe, it is obvious that they are technologically less advanced and hence natural resources play very important role in producing goods and services which help people satisfy their needs and wants. K. S. Singh (1982) states 'economy of the tribe is a response to the eco-system in which it is placed'.

Background of Katkaris in Maharashtra

Katkaris are counted as a primitive tribal group by the government of India from 1975-76 on the basis of pre-agricultural level of technology, very low literacy and declining/stagnant population.

The Katkaris have their origin in Maharashtra, but in search of work and livelihood they migrated to Rajasthan and Gujarat, therefore today they are also found in Rajasthan and Gujarat. The term katkari is derived from the Marathi word 'Kat'. Their traditional occupation was 'Kat Kadane' or 'Kat padane' that means making of catechu, so they were 'makers of catechu' from the bark of a 'khair' tree or Acacia tree and hence the name 'Katkari'. 'Kat' is used in 'Pan' or 'betel leaf'. The Katkaris are reported to be of Bhil tribe origin. Their dialect contains some words common among Bhils and their customs to some extent indicates Bhil origin. According to them, they descended from the *Vanaras*, whom Shri Ram took with him in his expedition against Ravana. Though they speak Marathi, their language is mixed traces of Marathi, Hindi and Gujarathi.

The Katkaris are classified into two groups 'Son Katkaris' and 'Dhor Katkaris'. According to them, initially there was no division among the Katkaris but many generation ago under the stress of famine some of the Katkaris started eating carcasses and since that time the two section have been distinct namely 'Son Katkari' and 'Dhor Katkari', The Katkari including 'Son Katkari' and 'Dhor Katkari', were first notified as scheduled tribes against the name 'Kathodi' or 'Katkari' under constitution order, 1950.

Today the Katkaris are teetering on the brink of extinction. They are landless; most economically backward people living in abject poverty. They are used to live in forests; and are basically people of the jungle but as forest land is becoming less and less living in the forest is becoming difficult for them and they have started working as farm labourers. At present they are engaged in charcoal making, brick making, and mainly working as bonded labourers on their master's field. Almost all the Katkaris still wear their traditional dresses. They are known for their alcoholism and cold-heartedness for strangers. The vulnerable condition of Katkaris has come out because they are semi-nomadic and landless workers in search of livelihoods.

Location of the Study

The present study was conducted in Chikhalgoan group gram panchayat located in the Sudhagad Taluka, of Raigad District of Maharashtra state. The gram panchayat consists of six villages or padas:

1. Unehere.
2. Karanjai.
3. Ghodgaon.
4. Keshavnagar.
5. Dharanachi Wadi.
6. Chikhalgoan.

The Chikhalgaon group gram panchayat is west to the Pune and is very near to Pali that is one of the 'Ashtavinayak' places; holy place for Ganesh devotees, Pali is about 114 km away from Pune. It takes approximately three to four hours to reach Pali from Pune and from Pali it takes another twenty minutes to reach the Chikhalgoan. The distance of various padas is 2 km to 7 km from the main Chikhalgaon village.

Unhere pada is situated very near to Chikhalgaon approximately 4.5 km. This place is known for hot spring. Unhere is completely dominated by Katkaris. Karanjai pada is 4 km and Ghodgaon pada is 7 km from Chikhalgaon and are located on the hilltop so there is no proper tar road to go these places. In Ghodgaon pada there are katkaris as well as Thakars. In the Keshavnagar pada Maratha community is dominant and is 2 km., from Chikhalgaon , where as Dharanachi wadi pada is about 3.5 km., and has only eleven families of Katkaris and five families of Thakars. Thus the Chikhalgaon gram panchayat is dominated by the Katkaris. The data was collected from all the six padas.

People under Study

The Chikhalgaon group gram Panchayat is inhabited by different tribal communities such as Katkaris, Thakars, as well as upper caste Hindus such as Marathas, and Agris. The present study was conducted on the Katkari community one of the primitive tribes residing in Raigad District and Thane district of Maharashtra State. There were in all 126 families of the Katkaris in Chikhalgaon group gram Panchayat and data was collected from all.

Objectives

The present study focuses on the economic crisis among the Katkaris through understanding:

1. Their land ownership, occupational pattern, migration rate, sources of income and their expenditure pattern.
2. The structure and nature of various development schemes run by Government, Gram panchayat and NGOs for their development.
3. The rate, causes and failure of the various schemes run by Government, Gram panchayat and NGOs for their development.
4. The villager's own perception about the development schemes and their awareness and participation in it.

Sample Profile

The total population of the village was of 433 individuals out of which 232 are males and females are 201 in number. The literacy rate is found to be very low (21.01%) among the Katkaris under study. The female literacy was found to be 22.56 per cent whereas male literacy was 30.33 per cent. The migratory nature of the tribe in search of jobs hampers the unremitting flow in education of the tribes. Regarding their occupation it was seen that more than half (51.20%) of the males were agricultural labourers and even some (41.72%) of the females were agricultural labourers.

A Study by an NGO Jagruti (2005), working in four geographic locations namely Pune, Nashik, Velhe and Nagercoil, established in 1993 points that the literacy rate among the Katkari is only 22 per cent. Economically they are poor, backward, still relying on traditional occupation for day to day needs, continue to live in isolation and practice primitive or no agricultural practice. Most of them are still in food gathering and seasonal occupation stage which make them almost a stagnant population.

The Students Action Committee (SAC) of Tata Institute of Social Sciences working among the Katkari tribals in the Khalapur taluka of Raigad district point that, about 90 per cent of Katkari children do not attend schools; the Katkaris earn their living by working as landless agricultural labourers by taking fields on lease, fishing from the nearby river and working as construction labourers. Driven to supplement their meagre incomes, few of the tribals resort to measures like the domestic manufacture of local liquor.

Economic Profile of Katkaris

Land

Land is the basic source of production for each human group. The land in Chikalgoan is fertile and good for cultivation of rice and millet. The total fertile land in Chikhalgaon is 1968.85, acres and Unhere it is 664.67 acres.

Out of this available land only 0.37 per cent of land is owned by katkaris (five families) staying at Unhere pada where they practice very primitive agriculture and cultivate rice, millet, sweet potato, that they use for their own consumption which is hardly enough to satify their own needs and so these families also work as farm labour when needed. Land cultivation is done only in rainy season and hence rainy season is the season when most of the Katkaris from Chikhalgaon are indulged in farm labouring.

Maharashtra State Development report (2005), Maharashtra, states that landlessness is high among PTG's, it is 83 per cent among the Katkaris, uprooted from their traditional livelihoods they are forced to migrate for survival hence their actual numbers and living conditions are not accurately reflected in census and other records.

The present study also shows that, all the 126 katkari families of Chikhalgoan Panchayat are Below Poverty Level (BPL), stay in abject poverty and are landless people and they work as farm labourers on daily wages on land owned by Maratha upper caste people in the rainy season.

Men work on farms and women are engaged in household work, collecting and selling wood and grazing livestock, if any and they also work on farms during rainy season. Men and women get only Rs. 40/as daily wages along with the meal twice a day. This is hardly enough to meet their needs and hence they expect the contribution of their children and consider their children as economic assets. A child starts helping their parents at very early age (at around 14 yrs). By looking after the goats and their young siblings, fetch water and fuel and engaging in some kind of domestic work they help their parents economically. The parents do not give importance to education of their children and get them out of the school due to their poverty.

Migration

Majority of the katkaris migrate seasonally (seasonal migration is 70.65%) to nearby places such as Chiplun,

Nagothana to work in coal manufacturing and brick manufacturing factories and are paid approximately Rs. 1800-2000/month. The whole family migrates to the place of work thus affecting the education of the children. At Chiplun they also work as woodcutter in forest for 8 months during winter and summer. No organization of labour is seen and this might be the reason for different pay scale in Chikhalgaon and other nearby padas like Unhere. In Chikhalgaon the wages are Rs. 40 per day while in Unhere it is Rs. 45 per day.

No significant pattern like forced labour is seen. Also there is no relationship found between labour pattern and kinship system. But some kind of association is seen between the economic system and religious beliefs. They worship 'Tahal Deo' before new rice cultivation. Most of the Katkaris have sickle, axe and spade which are considered as traditional equipments.

Other Sources of Income

1. *Domestic Work:* When there is no agriculture work, the Katkaris do domestic work such fetching water from the well, house repair works in the Marathas houses and are paid according to the nature of work but at the most it is Rs. 40/- per day. At times children are engaged in the household work such as cleaning utensils, sweeping and fetching water.
2. *Collection and Selling of the Forest Products for Livelihood:* The study area, Chikhalgaon is surrounded by forests that provide much valuable products that Katkaris use for their livelihood. The total forest land available is 1697.5 acres. Forest provides many valuable products like Garuli and Bharjamun, which they sell for Rs. 5-6 per Kg., to a private contractor, whose truck comes every alternate day to collect it and are used for preparation of medicines. Since contractor cannot cut trees himself available in the forest he gets it cut by katkaris and then buys it from them. The katkaris eat Kadu Karande and also collect *Nivadi* wood, which is used for cooking purpose while

Karavi wood is used for building their huts. Forests also provide plants having medicinal importance like Bharangmul, Moh, Umber, Adulsa etc., which they use for treatment of some pathological conditions. Mostly it is the women and children who are engaged in the collection of the forest products but while selling it to the contractor the men are present. They were also engaged in making country liquor once but now it is being done by the Agri community.

3. *Livestock:* Livestock is an important source of income. There is no secondary occupation like goat domestication, poultry etc., however few katkaris have livestock such as goat (36.07%) and poultry (17.9%). When in need of extra money for celebration of festivals and in case of some lifecycle events such as marriage, child birth, death and sometimes even for their alcohol needs the livestock is sold.

Market Place

As they are primitive tribes who do not produce any goods on their own and also surplus is not there, there is no local set up of the market place. Whenever required, the Katkaris visit the market in Pali.

Expenditure Pattern

1. Food: As we know food is the primary need of human beings. Very rough estimate of need and amount spent on food is given in the following table. However this need of food is not always satisfied because nobody can guarantee them that they can get work each and every day and hence whenever possible they spent maximum earnings on food.

2. *Festivals:* Festivals play an important role in the lives of primitive people. These are the only occasions for them to celebrate and have fun. Also festivals help them to turn back to their traditional beliefs and values and also help to increase solidarity among them.

Name of Item	Rs. Per Kg.	Maximum amount Available in Kgs.	Weekly Need per Person in Kgs.	Amount Spent per Week
Wheat*	5	10	5	25
Rice*	6	25	10	60
Nachni	5		3	15
Sweet potato, potato, onion etc.	—	—	When available	125

*Available on Ration Basis.

Festival	Reason	Money Spent in Rs.
Mahasatyanarayan Pooja	Post monsoon and pre-migration pooja	Up to 500
Sarvapitri Amavasya	Honoring Ancestors	Up to 300
Holi	10 days festival	300
Ganpati Utsav	5 days festival	200

3. *Other Expenditure:* The last but not the least, they are known for their consumption of alcohol. Daily Rs. 10 is spent on alcohol. This is the average estimate but during festivals there is no estimate of how much they spent on alcohol. Whenever such extra money is needed for festivals, for different rituals such as marriage, death etc., and sometimes even for alcohol livestock (if any) is sold otherwise they take some loan from landowners which is to be repaid by doing farm work without any pay.

Social Profile of the Katkaris

The Katkaris life is just to work the whole day on daily wages, earn little and flirt that earnings in the evening in liquor, with no remains for the next day. Various studies and number of NGO's working among the Katkaris have pointed out that the katkaris are an alcoholic tribe and are known for their alcoholism and cold-heartedness for strangers.

Marriage	About Rs. 5000-6000 at a Time (may vary)
Death rituals (10th/13th day food feast)	Average Rs. 1000 at a time.
Others (house repair, equipment maintenance etc.)	Up to Rs. 500 per year.
Health	Average Rs. 30 to 40 at a time (depends on nature of sickness)
Alcohol	Daily Rs. 10, during festivals more is spent

Animal	Selling Price
Goat (depending on physical condition)	Rs. 1000 -1200
Poultry	
Hen	Rs. 50
Cock	Rs. 100

Men as well as women consume alcohol regularly almost daily after the day's work. Certain recreational activities and on occasion like wedding, births, deaths, and on festivals such as Holi, Sarvapitri Amavasya involve massive and extravagant consumption of alcohol. They also consume tobacco by chewing and rarely smoke. Most of the time, the katkaris borrow money from their landowners to buy liquor or sell livestock if any. The above expenditure pattern table among the Katkaris of the present study also substantiates the findings of others.

Schemes for Development of Katkaris

Knowing their economic condition the Government and NGOs have come up with different schemes. There are many schemes on paper but very few are successfully implemented. Some of them are:

(I) Government Schemes

1. *Sanjay Gandhi Yojana:* This is a pension scheme for elderly people, above 65 years for males and above 60 years for

females. All the people registered get 250 rupees per 2 months from the government subsidy. In Chikhalgoan only eight beneficiaries were found under this scheme. Due to some administrative problems they did not get the money orders on time, as people are illiterate there were problems with money receiving process and due to postal insufficiency they were not able to get the deliveries on time. Now one bank account has been opened in either State Bank of India or Co-operative Bank of Mahad.

If the beneficiary is illiterate an NGO Nirmiti comes to their help. The Nirmiti people help them in the process by directly taking them to the bank or by withdrawing the money for them. This NGO controls money transactions by checking frequent withdrawal of money by the villagers.

2. *Swarajayanti Swayamrojgar Yojana:* The aim of the scheme is to make them earn at least Rs. 2000/- per month and to bring them above poverty line. To achieve this government provides them with loans for buying goats, poultry, for sheep rearing, etc. Very few *i.e.,* six families have taken loan under this scheme and are having goats and poultry. The mental set up of the Katkaris being poor did not make them fetch benefits from this scheme. They either did not take the loan or if taken they used it for other purposes.
3. *Mahila Bachat Gat Yojana:* A scheme meant exclusively for the empowerment of tribal women established and initiated by the government and then carried forward by the NGO Nirmiti working for the Katkaris.

Nirmiti has formed three groups of 8-9 women in Chikhalgaon, Unhere and Keshavnagar. Groups have account in State Bank of Mahad. Under the guidance of Nirmiti each group try to save Rs. 25/- per month in bank from their own earnings and day-to-day expenses. Two members, president and secretary from the group both literate collect this amount and deposit in the bank.

They get group loans and individual loans. Individual loans are upto Rs. 500 and for group loan there is no such boundary. The interest rate is 25 per cent per annum.

The group has taken a loan of Rs. 25, 000 with interest rate of 25 per cent per year. The money was divided into two parts 20,000/- and 5000/-.

Rs. 20,000 was used to buy goats which are tagged on the earlobes by the government. As the number went on increasing, females were retained back for rearing and males were sold at their maximum growth age which is determined physically and not by years or weight. Each goat is sold around for Rs. 1000/- to 1200/-. The money is used to return the loan, the loan is now cleared and the group owns the sheep. Rs. 5000/- is used for their rearing purpose. It is the responsibility of all the group members to rear them. If any of the tagged animals dies or is lost they have to pay the fine.

They have also invested Rs. 10, 000 to take ownership of lake and fish seeds and fish nets. Now fishing is done to repay the loan taken.

The Katkari women were satisfied with the Mahila Bachat Gat Yojana. They said "It is good to run such schemes. It gives confidence to us. It makes us economically independent".

4. *Indira Awaas Yojana/Gharkul Yojana:* The objective is primarily to help construction of dwelling units for the scheduled castes/Scheduled tribes, freed bonded labourers and also non SC/ST rural poor below the poverty line by providing them with grant-in-aid. The Government implements this scheme in the field through the Gram Panchayat.

   Criteria for getting the benefits are:

1 The person must be BPL.

2. The person must not have own permanent house. Even if he owns then it has to be thatched house made of Karvi sticks.

3. If the person is widow or handicap, he gets the preference.

There are some government norms devised for construction:

1. Government grant-in-aid is of Rs. 28,500 for a new construction.
2. The total construction area should be not be more than or equal to 250 sq. ft.
3. The support of government is mostly economical. The actual construction work is expected by Shramadan (willing efforts of people).

After few years, due to money crisis the contractor as a third intermediate institution was introduced. Due to mis-co-ordination between government officials, contractors and the Gram Panchayat the scheme faced several problems but was partially successful.

Data of Gharkul Yojana in Chikhalgaon is as follows:

Total No. of Houses	71
Cement House	17
Cement Houses with Karvi Extension	15
Karvi Houses	30
Unconstructed Houses	5
Unused Houses	4

It is seen that though all the 126 katkari families of Chikhalgoan are below poverty line, only 20.7 per cent (17) had taken advantage of Gharkul yojana.

There are two sub-schemes under this scheme:

4a. *Gruha Durusti Yojana:* Under this scheme loan is provided by the government for renovation of their own houses or for repairing work of the allotted house. Any member can avail of this Yojana by applying to the Gram panchayat;

1. Total loan given is Rs. 10,000/-
2. While renewing old house, toilets have to be constructed beside the house with two septic tanks.

The scheme was not successful as money circulation was not scrupulous. The toilets were either not constructed or if constructed were never used. Due to their illiteracy they didn't knew the formalities, the procedure of the government, filling up of forms and so on. This scheme was not at all successful; no one has taken advantage of this scheme.

4b. *Pradhanmantri Awaas Yojana:* The person should be BPL without his own house to avail the benefit of this scheme. The government norms are:

   1. The loan given is Rs. 22,000.
   2. The minimum area of construction of the house is limited to 200 sq. ft.

Here also the scheme was not successful, only two houses were constructed under this scheme but even these two houses were incomplete and half constructed.

According to the katkaris perspective, the house scheme of the Government has not made any considerable changes in their life style. They say that just changing the house, never changes the status of living.

5. *World Bank Funded Drinking Water Scheme:* The scheme was such that the World Bank was to arrange 90 per cent funds and the remaining 10 per cent was to be contributed by the villagers. The pipe line system was to be made underground and big cement water storage tanks were to be placed on particular intervals. The system was partially installed but the 10 per cent to be given by the villagers was never paid, they being poor and daily labourers. So the scheme failed.

6. *Navasanjeevani Yojana:* This project was undertaken by the government for common food storage and distribution. It was proposed to give Khavti of 100 Kg grains per family per year. It was distributed in off seasons *i.e.,* rainy seasons and the villagers were expected to return it back in equal amount or by adding 25 per cent or 10 per cent to it (*i.e.* 125 Kgs. or 110 Kgs.) after the rainy season. It was also proposed that the government will construct

big storage godowns called *'Dhanya Kothar'*. The returned grains would be accumulated in *'Kothars'* for use the next time. This scheme failed as the *'Kothars* 'were never constructed, the grains distributed were never returned back as they do not have their own land to cultivate and also due to some administrative difficulties.

(ii) Rashtriya Chemical Fertilizers (RCF) Schemes

Rashtriya Chemical Fertilizers, a chemical factory from Mumbai took up some developmental programmes in Chikalgoan group gram panchayat. Unhere village was selected and adopted by RCF for 5 years. Some of the programmes taken up were:

1. *House Scheme* RCF built cement houses for some of the families in Unhere village. More than half of the amount is paid by RCF and remaining amount is given by Gram Panchayat. The land on which Unhere pada is established was not their land. Here it was seen that in front of the newly constructed cement houses there were sheds made of karvi sticks. The families were staying in these sheds and were using the cement houses as dumping rooms. When asked why they were staying in the Karvi sheds they said that the houses didn't have cement roofs so there is leakage of water, walls get wet, base is not strong, construction of roof using tiles is not done well. Also at times due to excessive wind, the roof sheds were flown off.

They said that house is not their need, to built a house for them is very easy, they go to the forest, cut some Karvi sticks and construct a shed with a thatched roof. Their immediate need is money for food. While doing the field work we came across a tribal who sold his house for Rs. 24 to the truckwala with whom he was going with his family to a brick-kiln for working as a labourer. He said *"Mala ghar kasala pahije. Mi parath aalya var junglathtun lakdi aaun ghar banavnar"* (Why do I need a house, after returning back I will go to the forest, get some wood and will build a house.)

According to the villagers, RCF house scheme was completely implemented but was never maintained. They said "RCF has given us houses but the after care and monitoring was never done. The construction of the houses was not proper so we had to leave the houses and come back to the Karvi houses".

2. *Nal Yojana:* Another project by RCF carried forward by the Gram Panchayat is the Nal Yojana, in which a well is dug at the base of the hill outside the village. One distributing pipe line was circulated through the village underground, but the water is not available at the top were the Katkaris stay, hence this scheme was of no use to the Katkaris.
3. *Tree Plantation scheme:* The RCF Company distributed some plants to each house like Cashew, papaya, custard apple. The instructions about how to plant and grow these plants are given through camps. But it was seen that many plants were dead due to lack of water and no monitoring, no guidance, Katkaris were not taken into confidence.
4. *Kitchen Garden Scheme:* The seeds of lady finger, lentils, Chilies, cucumber, tomato etc., and also the brochures explaining the technical aspect of plantation, cultivation, harvest were distributed among the villagers by the RCF. Katkaris being illiterate were unable to read the brochures and there was no proper guidance and monitoring. Hardly four kitchen gardens were located during the fieldwork but katkaris said that RCF had no connection with that, they had made the gardens on their own.

(iii) Welfare Schemes undertaken by Grampanchayat

1. *Well Repairing:* There were total 11 wells in the Chikhalgoan Gram Panchayat. The Chikhalgoan Gram Panchayat had spent about Rs. 30, 000/- on the well repairing. Repairing includes side wall construction ensuring stone construction with cement, constructing staircase and constructing the surrounding passage. To

prevent the pollution of water of the well purification chemical called as TCL is sprinkled on the surface of the water after every 15 days. A sample of water is taken from each well and is sent to the lab at Pali and according to the pollution levels of the water the amount of TCL is regulated. Hence the Katkaris were getting pure water.

2. *KT Bandhara:* The Dam is constructed for blocking and channeling the river water near Unhere on the river Amba. The percolated water is stored, gathered and circulated by the system of – KT Bhandharas, which is cement square with a depth of about 10 ft. This water is further tunneled through stone channels with open tops. As the katkaris are landless the scheme is not useful for them. The water from the KT Bandharas is used for agricultural purpose on the fields owned by high caste Maratha Kunbis who stay in areas as Pali, Nagotna, Kumbharsheth, Keshavnagar, Pen etc., and the Katkaris work as labourers on these fields.
3. *Chikhalgoan Shed:* A common shed is proposed to be constructed for public ceremonies, common rituals etc. Till now about Rs. 25, 000/- has been spent on it by the Gram Panchayat and the construction is still going on. But this shed is being used by Maratha people and not by Katkaris.

(iv) Non-Governmental Organization - Nirmiti

An NGO called Nirmiti is exclusively working in the field for empowerment of the Katkaris. Their aim is to empower them by creating awareness about their basic rights and benefits such as rights on land, electricity, ration and so on. The NGO works for entire material as well psycho temporal development of them. Nirmiti may not have actually implemented any scheme or development programme in the field but through various camps, lectures, seminars, the institute is very much successful in developing an insight in them about their own benefits.

In case of Sanjay Gandhi Yojana by the government meant for the elderly people, if the beneficiary is illiterate Nirmiti comes to their help. The Nirmiti people help them by withdrawing the money for them or by directly taking them to the bank. This NGO controls money transactions by checking frequent withdrawal of money by the villagers.

Few years back there were some problems about monthly rationing of tribals. They didn't get ration and if they got it they received insufficient quantity. Nirmiti frequently visited the ration shops as well as the concerned government officials for their rights of rationing. Their efforts were partially successful.

Katkaris are landless people working on the fields of some high caste people. Under the banner 'Kasel Tyachi zameen' (Who works on the fields holds the ownership) also called as Dali, Nirmiti is creating awareness among them for their land rights.

The villagers seemed very neutral about their concept of Development. Their entire economy revolves around 'Earn for the Day' and never consider future assurance of money. They are not at all concerned about various developmental schemes planned by the government as well as non-governmental organizations. As their concern is only 'for the day' they never entertain future prospective schemes of the government.

Conclusion

- The literacy rate is very low *i.e.* 21.01 per cent among the Katkaris.
- They stay in abject poverty, are below poverty level and are landless people; mainly working on daily wages as agricultural bonded labours. The seasonal migration rate is very high (70.65%) to work in coal and brick manufacturing factories.
- They do domestic work in the landowner's house. They collect and sell the forest products for their livelihood. They borrow money from the landowners and repay that by doing farm work without pay or by selling livestock if any for celebration of festivals and other expenses.

- They are known for their alcoholism and cold-heartedness for strangers.
- Most of schemes implemented were not successful; very few beneficiaries were there. Due to their illiteracy they didn't knew the formalities, the procedure of the government, filling up of forms, some administrative problems, postal insufficiency and their mental make-up.
- 100 per cent katkaris of Chikhalgoan are below poverty line, but only 20.7 per cent have taken advantage of Gharkul yojana.
- Only the Mahila Bachat Gat Yojana is somewhat satisfactory.
- High caste Marathas are taking advantage of some schemes as katkaris do not have their own land.
- Almost all the Schemes run by the RCF failed as there was no proper guidance and monitoring.
- An NGO called Nirmiti is exclusively working for empowerment of the katkaris.

Suggestions

- As they live with high food insecurity there is a need for strengthening of PDS system.
- Ensuring sustainable livelihoods by granting land to the landless.
- Compilation of correct census on the PTG's.
- Special programmes to render their traditional agricultural practices sustainable, upgrade skills and ensure food security.
- Compulsory registration, proper wages and social security benefits to the migrant labourers.
- Need of creating awareness about their condition and various issues by organizing workshops, training camps etc.
- Organizing, sensitizing the community about their rights and responsibilities. Efforts should be undertaken to change their mindset.

- Lastly a great deal of Anthropological study of the Katkaris is necessary for designing an effective pedagogy for them.

REFERENCES

Kurane Anjali, 2005, Socio-economic development among the Warlis of Maharashtra" in Dimensions of Research in Anthropology, Vol. 2, Serial Publication, Delhi.

Maharashtra State Development Report, 2005.

Singh, 1982, "Economics of the Tribes and their Transformation", Concept Publishing House.

Websites Visited

awakeningjagriti.org/tribal_development.asp Accessed on 7th January 2013.

www.ashanet.org/pune/old/katkari2.html Accessed on 7th January 2013

cultural.maharashtra.gov.in/english/.../people_communities.html Accessed on 9th January 2013.

9

Educational Achievement and Empowerment in Tribal Area through Public Private Collaboration

A Case Study of Odisha

Janmejay Sahu*

INTRODUCTION

Education is most effective tool for human beings to understand the society in the right perspective and live accordingly. Further, Right to Education has arguably empowered the people and enabled their children to pursue compulsory basic elementary education as part of their fundamental right. Lack of education renders people ignorant about the society and its many dimension thus making it difficult for them to set priorities and make appropriate life choices. Tribes or indigenous people live in and around the forests or hilly tracts where development process reaches very late. The inaccessibility to the tribal habitations makes it very difficult for the administration to provide basic education to the tribal children as teachers either refuse to go there or adopt dubious means to avoid duties and take salary.

* Ph.D Scholar, Department of Political Science, Central University of Hyderabad. E-mail: janmejaysahu23@gmail.com

In view of this institutional discrepancy and denial of basic entitlement several NGOs, agencies and sensitized groups decided to lend a helping hand to the local Primary Schools in the tribal areas of Keonjhar and Sundargarh districts that have substantial tribal population. The collaboration of the Government Schools with the private organizations has resulted in maximum enrolment of children in the schools in those areas and it has created a hope among the tribal people about the future of their children. Thus the public private partnership or an alliance has led to greater school participation of the children of tribal communities. This paper presents a detailed and analytical account of the collaboration and seeks to assess the outcome in the form of empowerment of the tribes.

Educational Achievement and Tribal Empowerment

It was uncritically assumed that education could cure all kinds of social problems and particularly that it could bring about more equality among men. As the sociology of education developed, this was progressively reversed and a new philosophy, a pessimistic one, emerged more and more convincingly. It may be summarised in the statement that schooling is unable to reduce to any considerable extent the inequalities among individuals which result from social background (Raymond Boudon, 1974).

Tribal people are empowered when they acknowledge that they have or can create choices in life, are aware of the implications of those choices, make an informed decision freely, take action based on that decision and accept responsibility for the consequences of those actions. Empowering tribal people means creating and supporting the enabling conditions under which tribal people can act on their own behalf than at the directions of others. Education is the basis to empower the tribal people who are out of the school in various tribal communities. However, lack of facilities to include the tribal children in the school education in tribal area of the country is a main concern to the process of tribal empowerment through education.

Public Private Collaboration/Partnership and Education

Public-private partnerships (PPP) is the new face of development where the state and private actors, who have had a long history of conflict now work in collaboration, and co-operate with each other to further common goals of a market driven, growth-oriented agenda. State actors "enter into partnerships with organizations in civil society, the market, and with transnational organizations, to affect the governance of globalisation. The fanning out of the state, the spanning out of the state, the privatisation of state and para-state institutions, and the subcontracting of state functions, is what governance is about" (Chandhoke 2003).

The approach to PPPs must remain firmly grounded in principles which ensure that PPPs are formulated and executed in public interest with a view to achieving additional capacity and delivery of public services at reasonable cost. These partnerships must ensure the supplementing of scarce public resources for investment in infrastructure sectors, while improving efficiencies and reducing costs... Public private partnerships must aim at bringing private resources into public projects, not public resources into private projects (GoI 2007: 256). According to Shaol, partnerships are "policies that enrich the few at the expense of the majority and for which no democratic mandate can be secured" (Shaol in Hodge and Greve 2005: 550).

According to Kingdon (2007), the system of government grant-in-aid to privately managed schools at the secondary and higher levels accounts for a very substantial proportion of the education budget. Public-Private Partnership in school education is projected as a strategy to distribute thc ownership of institutions, rather than tasks within institutions, between private entrepreneurs and NGOS on the one hand, and the government or state on the other. While the rationale for PPP is inefficiency of the government, the means offered to overcome it actually promise no relief or improvement. PPP is not an idea, but rather an ideology which promotes privatisation as a means of reducing the government's responsibility to increase the number of schools. (Kumar Krishna, 2008)

It shows that community participation in improving education is negligible and that members of the SEMCs have limited awareness of the SSA (Rao, V. S., 2009). According to Aggarwal (2000), the elementary education system shows the signs of a dual system where public schools are meant for the poor, who are unable to pay for quality education, characterised widely by teacher absenteeism and private schools cater to the requirements for quality education involving high user costs.

PPP may be interpreted as an apolitical model, indicating the blurring of the private and the public, but PPP, as a marriage of the best of the private and the best of the public, seems shaky (Datta, 2009). There is widespread recognition of government failure in the delivery of education and PPPs are broadly seen as a solution to the problem. At the World Economic Forum, 2004, 54 participants, involved in PPPs in basic education from various parts of the world reported the key obstacles of partnerships between public and private sectors as 'capacity to negotiate with non-traditional partners', 'political will and public support', 'agreeing key performance targets' and 'transparency and accountability between PPP partners'. (World Bank 2004)

Methodology and Limitations

The methodology for this study is descriptive in nature. It is based on a qualitative research that includes observation method, document analysis; and in-depth personal interviews. The data are collected from both the sources *i.e.,* primary as well as the secondary sources to generate a comprehensive idea to the problem of this study.

The limitations of this study are limited availability of time and cost. As it was individual research work, it did not include more respondents which were. During data collection particularly in personal interview, it was a challenge to meet the respondents in their available time and also they were asking frequently various questions about the intention of the study.

Education Scenario of Odisha and RTE, 2009

According to census 2001, Orissa has a population of 3,67,06,920. The population in the age group of 0 to 6 is 51,80,551. The number of literates is 2,05,53,786. The literacy rate of persons of seven years age and above is 63.61 per cent. The age of seven and above is taken for this purpose because children below seven years of age are not expected to learn alphabets. Male literacy is 75.95 per cent and female literacy is 50.97 per cent. Among the districts, Malkangiri has the lowest literacy rate of 31.26 per cent. Among the women, lowest literacy level is in Nabarangpur district, at 21.02 per cent, and Malkangiri district at 21.28 per cent. Khurda district which includes Bhubaneswar city has the highest literacy of 80.19 per cent. This district also has the highest female literacy of 71.06 per cent. The high literacy figures of Khurda district is certainly influenced by the inclusion of the state capital in the statistics. Next to Khurda comes Jagatsinghpur district with 79.61 per cent literates. The literacy level in Orissa at 63.61 per cent is comparable with all-India average of 65.38 per cent.

However, there are considerable regional disparities between areas, and communities. Non-formal and adult literacy programmes are run in various districts and are at different stages of implementation. Out of 30 districts, 9 are continuing total literacy campaign (TLC). 10 districts are either continuing or awaiting approval of post literacy programme (PLP). 11 districts have completed PLP, and some of them have received sanction for Continuing Education Programme.

According to the data available by Ministry of school and Mass Education, Government of Odisha, 66 lakh children of 6 to 14 years age group are in-school, out of which 12 lakh are SC and 17 lakh are ST. 1.87 lakh children of 6 to 14 years age group are out-of-school from which 0.3 lakh are from SC and 0.9 lakh are from ST community. Out of them 56,995 Children were admitted to regular existing and New Schools under Enrolment Drive in districts. Though the Government of Orissa has been making significant progress in school education in terms of enrolment of children in schools, concern on the poor quality of education and high drop out of ST and SC students, girls and children belonging to other marginalized group still remains to be addressed. There are substantial social, regional and gender disparities in literacy.

Over 86 per cent of the budget for School and Mass Education in Odisha is spent on salaries to primary and secondary school teachers and as grant-in-aid to aided institutions, leaving very little for development of infrastructure in government schools. There are an estimated 2.7 lakhs children who are out of school (not enrolled or dropped out from schools) and, even as efforts are being made to bring them to school, the need for additional resources has been growing rapidly. The system faces shortage of resources, schools, classrooms and teachers. There are also concerns relating to teachers training, the quality of the curriculum, assessment of learning achievements and the efficacy of school management. Given the scarcity of quality schools, many children drop out before completing five years of primary education; many of those who stay on learn little.

Right of Children to Free and Compulsory Education Act, 2009 is a Central Government Act which came into force from 1st April 2010. Government of Orissa has already promulgated the Orissa Right of Children to Free and Compulsory Education Rules, 2010 on the basis of the model rule prepared by Government of India. Right To Education (RTE) Cell has been setup with support from UNICEF. The objective of the Cell is to act as facilitation cell to co-ordinate and bring in national/state experts, academicians, planners, implementing agencies/departments, institutions to facilitate the Department of School and Mass Education to develop strategies and Plan of Actions to implement Right of Children to Free and Compulsory Education Act, 2009. State Commission for Protection of Child Rights (SCPCR) Rules has already been notified. State Commission for Protection of Child Rights has been setup. The policy of eight years of Elementary Education (Class-I-VIII) has been adopted by the State of Orissa. 8276 nos. of Upper Primary Schools have been upgraded to Class-VIII.

To maintain the desirable Pupil Teacher Ratio (PTR) instruction has been issued to rationalise teachers in Primary and Upper Primary Schools through Collector Headed Committee in each district. The Right to Education (RTE) Act stipulates engagement of Trained Teachers. In order to train the untrained candidates, steps have been taken to strengthen the existing teacher training institutions. 216 Lecturers and Teacher Educators vacancies are going to be filled up. 324 new Teacher Educators posts have been created. In-service training is being provided to the untrained 11 teachers through Distance Mode by Director, Teacher Education and State Council of Educational Research and Training (TE and SCERT). To meet the challenges relating to teachers for implementation of Right To Education (RTE) Act 2009 the State Government had taken steps to fill up 17820 nos. of teacher posts. But the advertisement made in this respect has been quashed by Honble High Court in their order dated on 29.06.2010 in WP(C). Expeditious steps are being taken to fill up these posts very shortly. (Activity Report, 2010-11)

Education of Tribal Children in Odisha

The Scheduled Tribes communities have very low levels of literacy. The ST female literacy has increased from a very low level of 4.76 per cent in 1981 to 23.23 per cent in 2001, which is significantly lower than SC and general female literacy. Though the ST male literacy has increased from 23.27 per cent in 1981 to 51.48 per cent in 2001, there is still a big gap between that and the general male literacy. (Economic Survey, 2011-12)

The system of Multi Lingual Education (MLE) covers 8 districts with 10 tribal languages including 02 primitive languages (Juanga and Bonda). It is planned to add 10 more tribal languages during 2010-11 covering another five districts. Textbooks are distributed to 19,786 enrolled children. Multi Language Education is now operationalised in 544 schools. Ministry of Human Resource Development has initiated a study through National Council of Educational Research and Training and Multi Language Education, Orissa for its innovativeness.

Srujan, a community based child centered retention drive was taken up in 180 blocks covering 2064 CRCs of 30 districts. Around 16 lakh children have been covered through this Programme. Its aim is to create linkage between community and school and strengthen their bond. More than one lakh stories have been collected by the children from the community through story telling festivals. Efforts have been made to create innovation like Rupantar as a teacher training module is used in tribal areas to train both tribal and non tribal teachers on tribal pedagogy (in 141 blocks). Also, to strengthen the community relation with the schools in tribal area initiatives have been taken that has achieved to make Village Education Committee (VECs) in place in all Primary and Upper Primary schools; to encourage the Village Education Committees to participate in Civil Works, Micro Planning and School Mapping and developing School Environment and Supply of uniforms and also formation of School Management Committee (SMC) at elementary level is in progress.

Public Private Collaboration and Odisha

As per the School Support System, it aims to convert backward rural and urban Government and Government aided schools into quality schools (sundar vidyalayas) in 2-3 years of time so that they are on par with the best run schools in terms of infrastructure and performance. The key objectives of this scheme are:

1. To mobilize community support and other resources to address issues of provisioning access to quality education.
2. To make an appeal to the 'partners in progress' to support schools to contribute in kind towards infrastructure, school provisions and facilities for children and teachers.
3. To seek the help of local community to improve the academic performance of the schools.

Also, it provides abundant scope to the 'Partners in Progress' to contribute in kind in the interest of education in the state which includes Corporate houses, Elected representatives, Academicians/academic institutions, Individual donors, Voluntary/socially-committed organizations,

Industrial Establishments, Public Sector Undertakings, Banks and Financial Institutions, Associations of Trade and Industry, Media Groups and other interested groups/organizations/ individuals who can contribute time and attention for improvement of enrolment, retention and achievement in the school, home-makers etc. As per the scheme, the partner can choose to take up any one or any number of activities such as:

(i) Provision of water and toilet facilities to the schools separately for boys and girls.

(ii) Construction and renovation of existing building.

(iii) Provision for developing school garden, fencing or compound wall.

(iv) Provision of equipment and furniture.

(v) Provision of utensils for mid-day meals.

(vi) Providing computers for the students.

(vi) Building or strengthening of laboratory and library.

(vii) Developing of play ground/provision of play materials.

(viii) Sponsoring literary and scientific activities in the schools.

(ix) Providing aid and appliances for children with special need.

(x) Helping raise kitchen garden with specific focus on papaya and drumsticks.

(xi) Improvement in hostel infrastructure.

According to RTE Act, it is mandatory on the part of government to ensure 8 years of elementary education to all children in the age group of 6-14 years. The RTE calls for a paradigm shift in the educational provisioning and processes which till now worked like service providers. The Act interprets it as the responsibility of duty bearers and stakeholders to remain accountable for provisioning the schools for all children and completion of 8 years of elementary level schooling by all children across the State. This means addressing the core issues such as, poor infrastructure, inadequate teaching and learning materials, poor water and toilet facilities, etc., to ensure continuation of elementary education by the children.

Case Studies in Keonjhar and Sundargarh Districts

A rigorous field visit was made to understand the functioning of the schools in the tribal area and the role of the private organization for school education for tribal children in three various levels of the schools in two gram panchayats such as Kadalkala and Patmunda of Keonjhar and Sundargarh districts in Odisha respectively. The area for this study was choosen purposefully as this area covers maximum iron ore and most of the private mining companies are working in that area.

The selected area of this study covers Schools of Uppar Kadakala Village, Kriakudar and Kadalia villages of two gram Panchayats those are situated in and around 5 km distance of each other in the mountain and vast forest area. People living in that area have been facing various problems in term of road transport, tele-communication, availability of electricity and adequate facilities for drinking water and at the same time, this area has a vast stock of natural resources such as iron ore, manganese ore and other minerals which has been adding huge tax to the state government treasures. However, most of the schools running in that area have been facing various problems such as inadequate number of teachers, government facilities as well as most of the government teachers are not interested to come these schools due to lack of communication facilities and as it is in the hilly forest area.

Case - 1: Uppar Kadakala UGUP School of Kadakala Gram Panchayat, Bansapal Block of Keonjhar District

Uppar Kadakala UDUP School is situated in the village Uppar Kadakala of the Kadakala Gram Panchayat of Bansapal block in Keonjhar district. Uppar Kadakala is a village with two hamlets such as Uppar Kadakala Mundasahi and Uppar Kadakala Naiksahi where most of its population are tribals. This village location is on the top of the hilly area of Bansapal Gram Panchayat. This village is at a very separate location from the Kadakala panchayat in which periperial area are mining areas controlled by various mining owners or companies.

This school covers from 1st standard to 8th standard with about 300 students that require minimum eight government teachers. However, there are only two government teacher available to run the school. Out of two government teachers, one is tribal government teacher there as the category of the students is both tribal and non-tribal students. As the number of students is increasing and there are student's upto 8th standard, it is a problem to run the school smoothly.

Keeping the above problem as well as the Odisha Government's scope for Public Private Partnership in School education as per School Support System, private organization have given their supporting hands to this school's improvement namely Odisha Sponge Iron Ltd (OSL) and Mesco. Orissa Sponge Iron Ltd have been helping financially i.e the salary of 3 contract teachers @ Rs. 2500.00 per month through the government proper channel whereas Mesco has been helping financially *i.e.,* the salary of 2 contract teachers.

By personal interview with Mr. Prakash Ghana one of the five contract teacher of the school, it is understood that now the functioning of school is good and regular classes are being taken to cover all the classes for both tribal and non-tribal children of that village. He also said that out of five contract teachers, there are two more tribal teachers engaged to handle the tribal children. He said, there are seven teacher including two government teachers where three teachers from the tribal community are engaged to understand the problems of the tribal children and lead them in the process of schooling education. He shared that their initiatives are being taken to include more tribal children in the school as most of the tribal children still are not coming school engaged with various activities such as collecting wood from the jungle, helping their parents in agricultural works.

Case - 2: Kriakudar Primary Project School, Patmunda Gram Panchayat of Koira Block of Sundargarh District

Kriakudar is a village with a tribal hamlet of the Patmunda gram Panchayat of Koira Block of the Sundragarh district. It is located in the hilly jungle area. The population of that village including the tribal hamlet covers around 350. This village is having a school called government Kriakudar Project School that includes upto 5th standard for both tribal and non-tribal students with having around 74 students including 74 male and 50 female students of all five classes. However, only one lady government teacher was in the school to run whole five classes students which is supposed to have five teachers to function the school effectively. The language problem is another concern to teach the tribal children however, most of the tribal children do not come to the school as there is lack of awareness among the tribal children and the tribal community.

To bring the school in order, a good initiative is taken to utilise the help of the local private organization. Therefore, through the School Support System of Odisha government, Nilanchal one of the local mining company has extended its hand to support this school and the community. This company has been providing the salary @ Rs. 2000.00 to one lady contract teacher through the government process.

During field visit and personal interview with the lone lady contract teacher of the School Smt. Jyosnarani Barik, she informed that there were only 50 students for all five classes before her joining in the school. However, the enrolment is increased after her joining from 50 to 74 as a result that she is very young and from the community itself who visits each house of the village and hamlet to convince the people about the education and it is important for the children as well as the community. She also told that even though the strength of the students *i.e.* 74 for 5 classes is very low, it is difficult to teach all of them and care them as the nature of the students is most of them are from the tribal community who needs special attention for their education.

Interestingly, she said that she has been engaging all the students to create interest of the tribal students in school education to come regular to the school. However, he opined that it is need of hour for government to engage more teachers to the school for its smooth functioning.

Case - 3: Kadalia Uppar Primary School, Patmunda Gram Panchayat of Koira Block of Sundargarh District

Kadalia is a village with a tribal hamlet having the population around 400. The location of the village in the hilly area of Patmunda Gram Panchayat of Koira block of Sundargarh district in Odisha. The tribal hamlet of this village is situated in the down side of the village and the mountain surrounded it. This village has a Uppar Primary School, called Kadalia Uppar Primary School. This School has capacity upto 7th standard. Both the tribal and non-tribal students come to the School to have education from both the tribal hamlet and Kadalia villages including the 6th and 7th standard students from its peripheral areas such as Kriakudar too study in this school. Around 160 students are studying in all classes in this School. As per the capacity of this School, it should have 8 teachers to run all 7 classes. However, only two government teachers were managing the school to handle all the students of 7 classes that was not adequate to run the school. Seeing this concern, government functionaries tried to solve it by engaging the private organization, as a result Neelanchal Mining Company who is active in the work in this peripheral area of this village. This company has been providing financial help to this school by engaging one contract teacher from this village @ Rs. 2000.00 per month through proper government process.

Mr. Bipin Munda, a tribal youth of the village who is engaged as contract teacher in Kadalia Uppar Primary School said during a personal interview that now, they are three teacher working in this school including two government school and one contract teacher. All the classes are being functioning even though there is lack of teachers' availability. He further, opened that less tribal children are coming to the school regular as most of the tribal children are being engaged with various works. He said that as he is a tribal boy from the community, more tribal children are coming to school and at the same time, he also use tribal local language to make understood the tribal students. At the end, he told that as this village in very hilly area and no adequate teachers, it is very difficult to manage students all the seven classes and hoped that government should solve this problem by providing more teachers to the school with adequate facilities to empower the tribal students.

Results and Discussions

The literature has shown that there is a need of the public private partnership in education to improve the educational facilities and strengthen the educational institutions with community participation towards betterment of the children's education. Further, School Support System of the Ministry School and Mass Education, Government of Odisha to engage Private organizations in the improvement of School education. However, lack of the developmental activities and facilities in the tribal areas of Odisha particularly in the mining tribal belt of Keonjhar and Sundargarh districts has again initiated the necessary of PPP in education.

From the field study in three schools of the Keonjhar and Sundargarh district in Odisha, it is revealed that most of the tribal children are deprived of school education in the area of the study due to inadequate government teacher's availability in those schools. This also shows that even though this tribal area is full of natural resources, they are yet to be connected in the mainstream of the development process. This study establishes that available private organization in the tribal area and their association with educational institutions has resulted in increasing the tribal children's enrolment and their regular attendance in the Schools. This study demonstrates that due to PPP in education, most of the community people are engaged in the school to educate the tribal children who are from the same communities.

Moreover, this study again explains that most of the contract teachers have been taking initiative to aware the tribal community to send their children to the schools. During field visit, it is observed that the tribal people in the community are happy with PPP in Education that is enhancing their children's education. Therefore, all these findings of the study are the basis that directs towards the real empowerment of the tribal through education.

Few Suggestions

From this study in both tribal areas Keonjhar and Sundragarh districts of Odisha, it is arrived with various specific suggestions for betterment of education in the tribal areas such as:

- Arrangement should be made at government level to provide basic facilities in the schools.
- Government should appoint more teachers to meet the lack of government teachers in those schools.
- Government should encourage more participation of private organization in terms of strengthening government school's infrastructure as well its quality of education.
- Government should increase the salary of the contract teachers sponsored/supported by the private organiztion that will help them to meet their livelihood.
- Innovative approaches should be initiated to include more tribal children in having school education.
- Adequate tribal teachers should be given appointment to teach the tribal people in tribal language as well as government should initiate steps to prepare texts in tribal language which will be easily accessible by the tribal children.
- More private organizations should show their helping hands to the development of the educational institutions that will facilitate the local community.

Conclusion

Educating the tribal children and empower them is a challenge which can be achieved by the collective effort of all the stakeholder of the society such as village community, private organization, teachers, government functionaries, elected representatives and the people in general. This study reveals that it is essential to involve the community and private, corporate organizations in the educational achievement in the tribal areas where most of the educational institutions are facing various challenges.

Further, it is seen from the observation during field visits that local community are supportive to send their children to the schools. However, inadequate facilities and lack of initiatives towards making tribal community is a great concern. This study again says that due to public private public partnership, both the teachers from the community and the children from the community are getting benefited which is a good signal to decentralisation of education and also a sign of empowering the community as well as the children of the community. Consequently, government should prepare innovative approach to involve the entire stakeholder at various levels to enhance the educational system and make easy for community accessibility that will increase more literacy level of the children the community.

REFERENCES

Aggarwal, Y (2000), 'Public and Private Partnership in Primary Education in India: A Study of Unrecognised Schools in Haryana', www.dpepmis.org/downloads/pub_pri.pdf

Chandhoke, N (2003), "Governance and the Pluralisation of the State: Implications for Democratic Citizenship", Economic and Political Weekly, 12 July.

Datta, Amrita, 'Public-Private Partnerships in India: A Case for Reform', EPW, August 15, 2009 Vol XlIV No 33.

GOI, (2007), "Public-Private Partnerships in India", Ministry of Finance, Government of India, (http://www.pppinindia.com/index.asp)

Hodge, G and C Greve (2005), The Challenge of Public-Private Partnerships: Learning from International Experience (Cheltenham, UK: Edward Elgar Publishing).

Kingdon, G G (2007), "The Progress of School Education in India", Oxford Review of Economic Policy, 23 (2): 168-195.

Kumar Krishna, Partners in Education, EPW, January 19, 2008.

Rao, V.S, 'Lack of Community Participation in the Sarva Shiksha Abhiyan: A Case Study', EPW, February 21, 2009.

Raymond Boudon. Education, Opportunity, and Social Inequality: Changing Prospects in Western Society. John Wiley and Sons, New York, 1974. P xu.

World Bank (2004), "Reforming Infrastructure: Privatisation, Regulation, and Competition", World Bank, June.

Internet Sources

http://www.orissa.gov.in/schooleducation/pdf/Resolution_of_School_Support_Scheme.pdf

http://www.orissa.gov.in/schooleducation/pdf/Note_on_School_Support_Scheme.pdf.

http://www.odisha.gov.in/schooleducation/pdf/Activity_report_2010-11_final_.pdf

10

Relocation and Rejuvenation

A Case of Yanadis in Vedullapalli Village of Guntur District in Andhra Pradesh

Dr. Noorbasha Babavali*

India is home for 635 tribes with a population of 8, 43, 26, 240 (8.20%) as per the census 2001. The state of Andhra Pradesh consists of 35 tribes with a population of 50.24 lakh distributed among all the 23 districts. Out of 35 groups in Scheduled Tribes, three groups Yanadi, Yerukula and Lambada mostly live in out side the scheduled area. According to 2001 census, there are 4, 62,167 populations of Yanadis are living in the state of Andhra Pradesh which is second largest tribe in the state. Nearly 86 per cent of the Yanadis were live in rural areas and the remaining 14 per cent lives in urban area. The Yanadis habitats are mostly found at the banks of rivers, lakes, tanks and canals. Their main livelihood is fish hunting. Besides fish hunting they also engaged in catching the field rats especially for their consumption and also for their earning.

* Research Assistant, Centre for Study of Social Exclusion and Inclusive Policy, Andhra University, Visakhapatnam - 530 003. Mobile: 09440316883. E-mail: babavali67@rediffmail.com

The Yanadis are mostly concentrated in Nellore district and distributed costal Andhra region. Most of the Yanadis engaged in agricultural activity (76.2%) as agricultural labourer. According to 2001 census the literacy rate of Yanadis is 35.35 per cent only.

Inclusive Policy for Yanadis Provided by Government of Andhra Pradesh

The State Government has also introduced land assignment schemes to provide land for cultivation to the landless Yanadis. The Yanadi Development plan has been prepared for the development of Yanadis inhabitating in 3722 villages in 166 mandals on Nellore, Chittor and Prakasham districts. The Government vide G. O. Ms. No. 136, issued orders for establishing a separate ITDA for Yanadis. Headquarter of ITDA is located at Nellore town in Nellore district.

In the Guntur district there are 51,088 Yanadis are living. Coming to the Vedullapalli village where the researcher observes the Yanadis are just 241 in number (127 and 114 male and female) with 76 households, living in small huts which were located at the bank of a canal. Almost all the Yanadis are practicing both the religions of Hinduism and Christianity.

Location, Occupation, Migration and Relations

Earlier settling in the present habitation they lived besides the south side of the rail track in Vedullapalli village which is almost all centrally located to the other habitations of the village. It is very convenient to Yanadis to purchase their regular commodities and also to sell their hunting catches like, fish, bird and mushrooms. Because the market is very near to their habitation. The Yanadis are forced to migrate to the other place by the local dominated forward communities and the Yerucala tribe who are advanced and numerically strong. The present habitation is two km., away to their original habitation and to their market place. It is also half a km., distance to the other habitation. So they feel loneliness and facing some adjustment problems. The migration is also cuts their access to their earlier relations with the other communities and also lost their confidence levels. Before their migration they maintained good relations and access with the other communities. They get hand loans from others and they get grocery on barrow from the traders with their intimacy and access with the traders. At present it is difficult to them to get the same co-operation on the same persons. Because of their migration the others and the traders are not allowed them to get the hand loan and to barrow the grocery. Earlier they have frequent interactions with each other at their habitation or at market or on the roads. The effect of their migration it is not happening in every day. So the villagers are hesitating to give loans, and the traders also not co-operating to the Yanadis. It is clear to say that the migration looses the confidence of the others on the Yanadis and at the same time the Yanadis are also loose their confidence when they loose their access to the public. It is fact that the displacement has results the creation of problems to the marginalized communities like yanadis.

Occupation based Caste Name

The Yanadis of this village is also called as Engili Yanadi (Engili means left over food). The people of Yanadis are collecting food from the other communities who left over their cooked food after their consumption and also collecting food whenever ceremonies occurred in the other communities of their village and nearby villages. Hence they are also locally called as Engili Yanadis. Usually the villagers engaged these people to clean the vessels of their house holds in regular basis and also at the time ceremonies. After completion of vessel cleaning activity usually the owners of the households will allow them to collect the remaining food items. Basically these people belong to Challa Yanadi and Paki Yanadi tribe. But for their food collection habit from the other communities they acquired another name as Engili Yanadi.

Discrimination

Regarding discrimination, inequality and exclusion the Yanadis are facing many troubles. They are not treated equally at the functions. They have to wait to take their food at the end of the function. At the time of their travelling in the short distances they are sitting at the back side of the Auto rickshaws because they are not allowed in to side of the Auto Rickshaws both by co passengers and the vehicle driver. When they traveled on long journeys they sit at the back seat of the busses because of their earlier experience and their inferiority complex. It show their marginalization in the public and private sectors.

Government of Andhra Pradesh (2008): The challa Yanadis and Paki Yanadis are considered to be unclean and low among Yanadis. Each division of Yanadi is further divided in to a number of patrilineal exogamous groups representing their lineage names (intiperulu).

Village Profile

The village *Vedullapalli* is situated 6 km., away from Mandal head quarter of Bapatla in Guntur district. The village has 1347 households with 4572 population. There are 19 castes in the village. The entire population is engaged in agriculture. The major religious groups found in the village are Hindu, Islam and Christian. The village is also influenced by urban culture, as it is situated in between two towns Bapatla in Guntur district and Chirala in Prakasam district. Both the towns are located in sea cost of Bay of Bengal, and are in the proximity of the Bapatla Mandal head quarter.

Infrastructural Facilities

The village Vedullapalli has proper infrastructural facilities like: road, rail, electricity, drinking water, post office, market, schools, Primary health centre, Veterinary hospital vocational junior college for deaf and dumb, library, community hall check post to check the transport permits of agricultural produces, post office, nationalised Bank. Railway station, 'Anganwadi' centres vegetable, fish and flower markets. Milk collection centres (private), fly ash brick industries, nursery, medical stores, fertilizer shop hotels, tea stalls cable connections, provisions shops, tailoring shops, charitable trust hospital, R. M. P. doctors, coin box telephones, barber shops, fire wood shops, rice mills, cloth shops, Flour mills and one wine shop. The village is a market centre for about 15 villages. With regard to the places of worship, one Siva temple, one Ramalayam, One Masque and 4 Churches are located in the village. In addition to these, 5 village deities and one 'Durgha' are also there.

Numerically Reddy's are dominating with their major share of 487 house holds, the second place is occupied by Vaddera cast with 188 households. Yadava caste stands in the third place with 84 households; by 81 households Yerukula and Suvva Yerukula in the fourth place, Gouda community stand in the fifth place with 78 households, Yanadi is placed in sixth with 76, the seventh place is occupied by Uppara with 75 households, eighth and ninth places are occupied by Turaka and Dudekula Muslim households with 66 and 50 respectively. However, Mala with 42 households and Madiga with 35 households stand in 10th and 11th positions, Vysya and Brahmin with 33 and 26 households occupy 12th and 13th places respectively. The remaining communities are Telaga (11), Kummari and Mangali each 5 households, Rajaka (3), Viswa Brahmin and Kamma each one household respectively.

Occupation

The *Yanadi* earlier attended manual scavenging work, fish hunting in irrigated canals, catching the rats at agricultural fields of the farmers and worked as servant maids (women). For manual scavenging and fish hunting both male and female were attended. When the Government of India bans the manual scavenging the 'Yanadi' tribe of this village confined to the fish hunting only. The villagers also not gave the employment chances like servant maids because of their outer appearance. Both men and women had taken local liquor with their limited earnings.

According to Aiyappan "The process of Chenchu evolving into an Enadi here seen: the Chenchu of sadasivakonda changes into Kappala Enadi when he first moves down into Kalahasthi and Puttur plains, gradually he merges with the Enadi and becomes one with them".

The main objectives of tribal sub plan are:

1. Socio-economic Development of Scheduled Tribes.
2. Protection of Tribals against Exploitation.

The traditional health knowledge of the Yanadis is closely interlinked with the bio-resource and medicinal plants for the health care are derived by continuous access to and observation of the natural resource. The Yanadis have rich traditional health knowledge, including knowledge for everyday health care and specialized knowledge.

Yanadis are broadly divided into four endogamous groups on the basis of occupations and dietary habits. The sub-divisions are:

1. Manchi Yanadi or Reddi Yanadi (Cultivators and servants).
2. Adavi Yanadi (those living in forests).
3. Paki Yanadi (Scavengers).
4. Challa Yanadi (those who collect left out food from leaf plates in the dust bin).

Marriages by negotiation, by mutual love and elopement are usual modes of acquiring mates. The re-marriage of divorcees, widows and widowers is permitted. The nuclear type of family is more predominant. Yanadis are non-vegetarians and eat the meat of rabbits, fowl, goat; sheep fish etc., but abstain from eating beef. Yanadis mainly subsist on agricultural labour. They are traditionally inland fishermen and are also engaged as watchmen in the fields and orchards of farmers. Collection of firewood, rickshaw pulling, rodents catching etc., constitutes secondary occupation of the Yanadis.

'The Yanadis are not an ordinary people but extraordinary in nature'. During the last two centuries the Christian church tried its best to convert the Yanadis but with least successes. Even today the two sub-tribe hierarchy is functioning. The Manchi Yanadi, consider themselves superior in status and look down upon the Chall Yanadis as untouchables. The Challa Yanadis are treated as inferior. The Manchi Yanadis refrain from inter-dining, keep separate wells, live in separate locations and almost have no relationship with the Challa

Yanadis. The Manchi Yanadi would not even touch the earthen pots, cooking vessels or eating plates of the Challa Yanadi. The Manchi Yanadis women who marry Challa Yanadis men are lost for ever to the Challas.

Literacy

The Yanadis literacy levels are very low. Particularly in Vedullapalli village of Guntur district of Andhra Pradesh, nearly 80 families dwelling at south side of the canal bund. No one is literate. Recently one girl is taking classes weekly twice or thrice basing on her leisure time to educate the children of the displaced Yanadis. The Pastor of the church with his all efforts providing slates and books to the children. They are living in small thatched huts which are not in a position to face the simple calamities.

Reasons for Displacement

According to the local church father, the village was encroached towards rail track hence the price of the land cost was hiked abnormally. Hence, some of the persons from 'Yerukula' tribe which is numerically dominated of nearby village named Stuartpuram which was established by the British India Government in the late 19th century as settlement gangs. At the same time the dominant caste people called 'Reddy' are also ill treating the Yanadi tribe who are the residing at north side of the same rail track for the cause of occupying the places. The way of ill treating is walking through their houses in every time, using the places for taking liquor, using abused language in front of Yanadi ladies and walking side of them when the habitants are taking their lunch and dinner. But these ill treats are not found in formal but it is informal way only. Because of the victim's innocence, lack of awareness, support voice they have facing these problems. They have no guts to fight against the cause. The local governing bodies are also not act on this problem.

When it was noticed by the one of the Pastor resident of Chiral, Prakasam district which is 10 km., to Vedullapalli village he ran to the victims and enquired all the issues and searched for the safe place to accommodate victims. In his search he found a Government land at Canal bund which is located at 2 km., from their original habitation towards East side of the rail track. All the displaced people arranged their small thatched huts and living here. It is surprising to note that the same tribe people who are living in the same village and also nearby village but never attending this cause to protect or to support this people, why because their practices and style of functioning is different to the affected persons and also they have no blood relations. Another surprise is to note that some people belong to forward category occupied the places and constructed thatched houses for their livestock besides the Yanadis huts.

The Pastor, with his full efforts, by consulting with District Collector, RDO, MRO and MLA got Government site opposite their present settlement. The Government of Andhra Pradesh sanctioned and constructing houses to allot the displaced people, it is under process. The Pastor constructed one thatched church for the displaced people and trying to change their life style and giving training how to move in the society. Still they are engaged in fish hunting only. Occasionally, they attend vessels cleaning work whenever ceremonies held in their village and nearby villages. Rarely they also attending for cleaning of septic tanks. Some of the NGO's came to this place and try to get the hold on the displaced people to show it as one of their activity. Basing on this cause it is very hard to get interaction with them. Without permission of the Pastor who is their godfather they won't allow the others to know the situation.

Problems Identified

Because of their illiteracy, ignorance and lack of social and health awareness their personal hygiene is very low standard. Drinking alcohol is very common to both male and female and most of their earnings are utilising to the alcoholic habit. When the world is going to advanced stage still they are preferring child marriages and number of marriages and continuous divorces. The state level Yanadis literacy rate is rising to 35.35 per cent still these people are fully illiterates. It is pity to say no one in their habitation even semi literate. Social backwardness is still prevailing and awareness levels are very low on education, health, economic and other aspects. Still they never come out from their inferiority complex they are unable to express their thoughts and needs with authorities and local leaders still they are facing too many problems. Lack of bargaining capacity and courage they sell their catches like fish, bird and Mushrooms with low price. They are malnutrition and stunning. They are not access with the poverty alleviation programmes of both State and Central government schemes like Mahatma Gandhi National Rural Employment Guaranty Scheme (MGNREGS) and other programmes. Their children are not enrolled in the ICDS programmes like Anganwadi centres. Landlessness, Unemployment, lack of food security, psychological trauma and other issues are problems not giving chance to them to develop their personalities and to change their lifestyles.

Recommendation

Residential education system is to be implemented for their children and also need to arrange adult education progrmme for the elders. Awareness campaigns are required for them on the issues of health, personal hygiene and sanitation conditions should be done in the regular intervals. Awareness on income generation programmes may be given to the members of the female Yanadis. It is also required to form a special Self-Helf Group for these targeting group, and also required to enroll them in DWCRA programmes. NGOs involvement is essential, The Yandis of in this village are deserved to get Anthyodaya ration cards Annapoorna ration cards. Facilities of old age; widow and Handy Capped pension's to be extended to them.

Frequent medical camps will help their health improvement. It is well suggested that if the nearby college adopts this habitation to perform their both regular NSS activities and Special Camping activities to sensitize this community by organizing awareness campaigns on sanitation, immunization, health, HIV/AIDS, and STD diseases, literacy, plantation, malnutrition etc. Encourage them to participate in agricultural activities in addition to their routine activities of fish and bird hunting and collection of Mushrooms for their economical development. By arranging sensitization and orientation programmes by the involvement of different sectors like Government agencies, NGOs and Social Workers on the issues of capacity building and to develop their confidence levels. Most of the Yanadis are anemic. Hence, it is recommended that a special Anganwadi centre has to be allotted to them. It is essential to supply the nutritious food to increase their health standards. It is essential to identify the Government lands and distribute among these group for their economical empowerment. Regular counseling by Social Workers, NGOs and Government Officials will help their all round development.

11

Cultural Life of Pardhi Community

Karuna Vinayak Kamble*
Damayanti Rajpal Raut**

INTRODUCTION

The dictionary meaning of the word culture is the arts and other manifestations of human intellectual achievement regarded collectively or the ideas, customs, and social behaviour of a particular people or society. To fulfill his own needs man has created many resources, all these resources are included in culture. Social life of full society is molded by culture. The culture of India refers to the religious beliefs, customs, traditions, languages, ceremonies, arts, values and the way of life in India and its people. India's languages, religions, dance, music, architecture, food, and customs differ from place to place within the country. Culture is human beings important characteristic. Each society is recognised by its culture. When we think of Indian culture we can't forget about

* ICSSR Research Fellow, Indian Institute of Education, Kothrud - Pune 411 038.

** ICSSR Research Fellow, Indian Institute of Education, Kothrud - Pune 411 038.

the tribal's who are recognised today by their distinct culture. Tribals are found in almost all the states of country. Currently there are between 258 and 540 scheduled tribe communities exists India is home to a large number of tribes with population of about 70 million.

The ST population of the Maharashtra state constitutes 5.1 per cent of the country's ST population. The Scheduled Castes and Scheduled Tribes Order (Amendment) Act, 1976, have notified 47 STs in Maharashtra. It is found that there is no similarity found regarding social life, customs, culture, occupation, rituals, arts and music among these tribes. Each tribe is formed of its own mental set up and follows the same, one of the tribe in Maharashtra is Pardihi their main occupation earlier was hunting and as they kept moving from one place to other they were kept away by other communities. They call themselves as Kshatriyas and family of Maharana Pratap. They use cows for travelling and can make sounds of different birds and animals. They respect their culture, but still follow blind faith's, black magic etc. Hence an attempt is made in the following article to study the culture of scheduled tribes especially of Pardhi community.

The dictionary meaning of the word culture is the arts and other manifestations of human intellectual achievement regarded collectively or the ideas, customs, and social behaviour of a particular people or society. To fulfill his own needs man has created many resources, all these resources are included in culture. Social life of full society is molded by culture. *Culture* is a framework of behavioural patterns, values, assumptions and experiences shared by a social group, *Culture* is a mostly automatically or unconsciously applied orientation system of collective values, which makes its group members' behaviour comprehensible and to a certain degree predictable for each other.

The culture of India refers to the religions, beliefs, customs, traditions, languages, ceremonies, arts, values and the way of life in India and its people. India's languages, religions, dance, music, architecture, food, and customs differ from place to place within the country. Its culture often labeled as an amalgamation of these diverse sub-cultures is spread all over the Indian subcontinent and traditions that are several millennia old.

The culture of India is one of the oldest and unique. In India, there is amazing cultural diversity throughout the country. The South, North, and Northeast have their own distinct cultures and almost every state has carved out its own cultural niche. There is hardly any culture in the world that is as varied and unique as India. India is a vast country, having variety of geographical features and climatic conditions. India is home to some of the most ancient civilizations, including four major world religions: *(i)* Hinduism, *(ii)* Buddhism, *(iii)* Jainism and *(iv)* Sikhism The term culture refers to a state of intellectual development or manners. The social and political forces that influence the growth of a human being is defined as culture.

Indian culture is rich and diverse and as a result unique in its very own way. Our manners, way of communicating with one another, etc., are one of the important components of our culture. Even though we have accepted modern means of living, improved our lifestyle, our values and beliefs still remain unchanged. A person can change his way of clothing, way of eating and living but the rich values in a person always remains unchanged because they are deeply rooted within our hearts, mind, body and soul which we receive from our culture.

Few countries in the world have such an ancient and diverse culture as India's. Stretching back in an unbroken sweep over 5000 years, India's culture has been enriched by successive waves of migration which were absorbed into the Indian way of life. It is this variety which is a special hallmark of India. Its physical, religious and racial variety is as immense as its linguistic diversity. Underneath this diversity lies the continuity of Indian civilization and social structure from the very earliest times until the present day. Modern India presents a picture of unity in diversity to which history provides no parallel. Indian culture is rich and diverse and as a result unique in its very own way. Our manners, way of communicating with one another, etc., are one of the important components of our culture. Even though we have accepted modern means of living, improved our lifestyle, our values and beliefs still remain unchanged. A person can change his way of clothing, way of eating and living but the rich values in a person always remains unchanged because they are deeply rooted within our hearts, mind, body and soul which we receive from our culture.

Culture is human beings important characteristic. Each society is recognised by its culture. When we think of Indian culture we can't forget about the tribal's who are recognised today by their distinct culture. Tribals are found in almost all the states of country. Currently there are between 258 and 540 scheduled tribe communities exists in India. India is home to a large number of tribes with population of about 70 million.

Generally speaking by the term 'tribe' we mean a group of people living at a particular place from time immemorial. Anthropologically the tribe is a system of social organization which includes several local groups – villages, districts on lineage and normally includes a common territory, a common language and a common culture, a common name, political system, simple economy, religion and belief, primitive law and own education system. Constitutionally a tribe is he who has been mentioned in the scheduled list of Indian constitution under Article 342(1) and 342(2). Indian Tribal Culture speaks volumes about the diversity of the country. 'Unity in diversity' is one of the most spectacular features amongst the population of India. Among the diversified population, a significant portion comprises the tribal people, the aboriginal inhabitants of the primeval land. Tribal culture of India, their traditions and practices interpenetrate almost all the aspects of Indian culture and civilization.

The different tribes in India if ever counted can move up to a mind boggling number, with all their ethnicities and impressions. In India almost a new dialect can be witnessed each new day; culture and diversification amongst the tribal can also be admired from any land direction. The tribal population is also pretty much varied and diversified. Quite manifestly, Indian tribal culture should assimilate and mirror a definitive section of the society. The current tribal population of India is approximately 20 million altogether. Each of the tribes is a distinctive community, either migrated from a different place or the original denizens of the land. These various tribes still inhabit the different parts, especially the seven states of the North-eastern region and almost each and every nook of the country. The specialty of the Indian tribes lies in their customs, cultures, and beliefs and, in particular, the harmony in which they survive in unanimity with nature. Tribal living perfectly portrays a well-balanced environment, a procedure that in no way upset the ecological balance.

In order to comprehend tribal culture in India, to understand the uniqueness of their culture, a detailed study is very much required by travelling within the society. Affectionate hospitality, undemanding ways of living and earnest judgement of the opinions is some of the characteristic traits that earmark tribal cultures of India. Their customs mirror their confidence in simplicity. Most of the tribes in India possess their own gods and goddesses, reflecting the dependence of tribal people on nature and animals. Except for the few, most of the tribes in India are affable, hospitable and fun-loving, coupled with potent community bonding. Some of the tribes share patriarchal cultural ties and some of the tribal societies are inclined towards women-oriented issues. Thus, they have their own festivals and celebrations.

Tribal people generally cling firmly to their identity, despite external influences that had threatened tribal culture, especially after the post-independence chaotic period.

In terms of geographical distribution about 55 per cent of tribal lived in central India, 28 per cent in west, 12 per cent in North-East India, 4 per cent in South India and 1 per cent elsewhere. Tribal communities are rich in their culture, folk tales, folk songs and folk stories. Dance and songs are not only the source of entertainment in tribal people, but associated with their religion, custom and above all with their culture. The systematic and scientific study of culture of tribes whether it is folk dances, movement pattern, folk song, dress design shows that all western dances and songs have been derived or taken from the tribal folk dances, folk songs. The ancient culture and tradition are yet not researched to a great extent. In order to preserve the Indian culture we must have a systematic, scientific, anthropological study of tribal culture. The preservation of such things preserves the ancient and primitive culture of India too. The government should promote such tribal institutions for development and preservation of tribal culture. The government should make plans and programme to connect these isolated societies with the national mainstream the current tribal population of India is approximately 20 million altogether.

Each of the tribes is a distinctive community, either migrated from a different place or the original denizens of the land. In order to comprehend tribal culture in India, to understand the uniqueness of their culture, a detailed study is very much required by travelling within the society. Their customs mirror their confidence in simplicity. Most of the tribes in India possess their own gods and goddesses, reflecting the dependence of tribal people on nature and animals. Except for the few, most of the tribes in India are affable, hospitable and fun-loving, coupled with potent community bonding. Some of the tribes share patriarchal cultural ties and some of the tribal societies are inclined towards women-oriented issues. Thus, they have their own festivals and celebrations.

Tribes of Maharashtra are the primitive people of this region and are scattered in different parts of the state. Mostly they are the inhabitants of the hilly areas. Some of the tribes are of primitive and nomadic character. Tribes like Warli Tribe, Bhil Tribe, Koli Tribe and Halba Tribe are some of the tribes that inhabit in the land of Maharashtra. Constitution of India recognises some these tribal groups as Scheduled Tribes. There are certain cultural aspects, which have made the culture and tradition of these tribes of Maharashtra enriched and ennobled. In other words their dialect, clothes, folklores, rites and practices show that these tribes of Maharashtra possess a heritage that is quite unique Culture of Tribes of Maharashtra. Many of these tribes of Maharashtra have adapted to the lifestyle and culture of nomads and till today, these tribes of Maharashtra state have retained their originality intact. As per some scholars and anthropologists, Maharashtra has 313 nomadic tribal communities and 198 unnoticed tribal groups.

Following the tradition of many of the tribal communities of the Indian subcontinent, these tribes of Maharashtra have got inclination towards religion and also spiritual beliefs. Ancient customs like worship of nature in several forms, animal offerings during religious rituals, decorating their heads with tusk, etc., is still in vogue.

Pardhi are a tribe in India. The tribe is found mostly in Maharashtra and parts of Madhya Pradesh. The Phasse are a sub tribe of the Pardhi caste, which includes sub-castes like Gav-Parad, Berad-Paradhi, Gay-Paradhi, Chita-Paradhi. Pardhi is the term for 'hunter'. There are only three surnames among them, Chauhan, Pawar and Solanke.

Festivals and fairs are an integral part in the society of most of these tribes of Maharashtra. Hinduism is widely practiced by most of the tribes of Maharashtra and thus, all the festivals of the Hindus are celebrated by them in great vivacity. A lot of alcohol is consumed during the occasions. Their society is governed by the Jat Panchayat. Marriage plays an important part in the lives of the both female and male members of the tribes of Maharashtra state.

Pardhi Tribe mainly resides in the state of Maharashtra. They follow Hinduism while some follow Christianity. Pardhi Tribe claims that their first ancestor was a Gond. Pardhi tribe occupies a distinct position in the list of tribal communities and they are mainly found in the western provinces of India. The term Pardhi is derived from the word 'paradh' which means 'hunting' in Marathi language. 'Shikari' is the other term that is commonly used as their alternative name. Though the major occupation of the Pardhi tribes are hunting and gathering, some have taken up diverse occupations like cultivation and some other occupations following the traditions of most of the tribes of the country. Following the tradition of most of the tribal communities of Indian subcontinent, the Pardhi tribal community adapted to occupations like hunting, working as labourers, etc.

Pardhi tribes mainly belong to the Maratha country. The Pardhi tribal community follows numerous practices and norms, mostly related to religion. Interestingly, their customs differ largely with their different localities. Although this Pardhi tribal community has their own indigenous beliefs, nowadays Pardhi tribes also taken up religions like Hinduism and Christianity. It has been estimated that about one per cent of the Pardhi tribal community are Christians.

The main language of the Pardhi tribes is their local dialect which is of the same name. Many of them also talk a dialect of Gujrati language. In the northern parts of the country, they speak a combination of Hindi language and Marwari language. The alternative names are Bahelia, Chita Pardhi, Lango Pardhi, Paidia, Paradi, Paria, Phans Pardhi, Takankar, Takia. It belongs to the famous Indo – Aryan language family. Also these are several dialects like Neelishikari, Pittala Bhasha, Takari which are also popular amongst the Pardhi tribes. The origin of the Pardhi tribal community has got a rich history behind it. Seeing the treasures and prosperity of the Gujarat region, when the Mongol kings invaded it at the end of the 13th century, the Maratha kings counterattacked them and also established an empire in Gujarat. At that time the Pardhi came under Maratha influence and grew in exuberance. There is a reason why the anthropologists of the country have shown so much of interests on the Pardhi tribal community.

The Pardhi tribal community has several endogamous groups. Their principal sub-castes are the Bhil Pardhis and Shikari. Other groups have also been recorded. Caste system is also not prevalent and also leads a life of isolation. Records of the British era, this Pardhi tribal community is regarded as one of the 'criminal tribes'. In the contemporary period, quite a handful of these Pardhi tribes take oil from crocodiles, carry out monkey shows, or kill only birds that are black. People belonging to Pardhi tribal community never kills or sells a dog. They do not hunt wild dogs. The societal structure and formation of these Pardhi tribes have some identifiable attributes. Like for instance, Phans Pardhis are not permitted to travel in a train and some of them are also prohibited from travelling in a cart. Marriage has been held in high esteem by these Pardhi tribes. For example, these Pardhi tribes can marry only within the same tribal family. Their principal deity is Goddess Devi, also known by different names. Pardhi tribes still maintain the primitive method of trial or ordeals.

The Paradhi community is labeled as ex-criminal tribes on one side and is struggling to stand on its own feet on the other. The Paradhis have many sub-castes like Fase-Paradhi, Gav-Paradhi, Berad-Paradhi, Gay-Paradhi, Chita-Paradhi etc.

All of them were declared criminal Tribes except the Gav-Paradhis, who had taken to farming and settled well during British rule having a good population in Amravati District. They have given up hunting and very few have now guns. Fairly well educated, they are in Government employment in good numbers.

Their culture and civilization is changing fast with the changing times. Their traditional apparel used to be a 'pheta' (head dress) and 'langoti' (loincloth) only. But things are now changing. They worship nature and the goddesses more than the gods. They worship 'dhani' and 'jarane' by sacrificing goats. Mostly there are only five surnames found in Pardhi community in Maharashtra Bhonsale, Chavan, Kale, Shinde and Pawar which are also called as 'kul' of their family Marriage system resembles that of other castes. Their language is akin to Hindi that is spoken in rural Gujrath and Rajasthan. They claim descent from Rana Pratap and Prithwiraj Chauhan and original home in Gujrath and Rajasthan. Their colonies are on the outskirts of towns.

The term 'adivasi' denotes the Pardhi communities 'political and social' identity. The terms indigenous and aboriginal are used by the Imperial States to enslave whole of Africa. In India, what the British could not do, was done by Independence. In the name of 'development', Adivasis are uprooted exploited and again 'rehabilitated' and this is called story of success in modern India. The strong edifice of modern India has lives of millions of Adivasis trenched under its foundation.

In the definition of modern India, an Adivasi means backward, having queer traditions, illiterate and devoid of history. Some of those who made this definition take refuge by calling then 'girijan' (dwellers of hills) or 'vanvasi' (dwellers of forests). They are already removed from the fields of arts and literature. Because of these misunderstandings, Adivasis are faced with the problem of Identity Crisis. The reply to this question will be given by the now awakening Adivasi through the medium language in the modern terms, but still all traditions and customs would be its inseparable part.

In spite of affirmative action policies the literacy levels of the Pardhi tribes are very low. Same is the case with their health status and other areas of development. Only a few tribal groups have been able to enjoy the benefits of positive discrimination. A majority still reels under poverty and is wedded to an out dated way of life. In addition to these disadvantages the single most threat that looms large over them is corrosion of their resource base-to be more specific, loss of land.

The quality of life of tribal people during pre-independence period was more deplorable and their main occupation was hunting, gathering of wood and forest products and primitive shifiting cultivation. Due to destruction of forest and non availability of proper facilities, tribal were forced to lead a miserable life. After independence with the adoption of Indian constitution in 1950 special attention was given for the upliftment of the tribal people under the 'article 48', it was mandatory on the part of the state government to make all the efforts to improve economic, social, and educational standard of the tribal people.

Due to the welfare programmes tribal communities also made themselves conscious about their own clans upliftment. Now tribles are engaged in struggle for survival. They seek identity, autonomy equality and empowerment. They became more vibrant with new expectation, they are moving out of their isolation to participate in all struggles in all institution as equals. In context of trible study, we know that they are very rich in their art and culture and the study of tribes and their culture has always been a fascinating one for all researchers. The fascinating things are their folk dances, folk songs, their own typical kind of language. The form of their entertainment today also comes from the culture like singing songs during marriages, during their festivals. They are also keen on celebrating their festivals by visiting the temples in groups, sacrificing animals especially buffaloes to god. The existence of such things must be studied to understand the ancient culture of human being.

Despite being exonerated by the Indian government, the community is still perceived to be indulging in criminal activities. The criminal stigma is attached from birth, and by the age of sixteen, his name is usually featured in criminal records as a potential suspect. Public pressure in villages often prevents the nomadic community from settling in villages.

Thus from the discussion above it can be seen that the Pardhi community is still far away from the development as they move from place to place, they are also not accepted by the society easily. Thus they carry with them their culture forwarded to them by their ancestors, it is need of the time that they should be given preference in educational institutions, special policies should be made for their development, their culture should be protected but the blind faith's in it should be removed by counseling this community, society should change its attitude towards these people and accept them as humans.

REFERENCES

Bose, N. (1971), Tribal Life in India. New Delhi. National Book Trust India.

Dixit, R. and Ramsingh, M. (2006), Tribal Development Programmes A Critical Appraisal Ritu Publications, Jaipur.

maanaoêla.1997.ivamau@tayana: maharaYT/tIla ivamau@t jamaatI ek icaik%sak AByaasa.mauMba[-.yaSavaMtrava cavhaNa p'itYzaNa.

maaMDoÊ p'.³1983´.gaavagaaDyaa baahor AaOrMgaabaad.pirmala p'kaSana.

12

Culture At A Glance

Style of the Ho Tribe in Odisha

Snehasish Sethi*

INTRODUCTION

Culture is a term that defines the growth and development of a human being by the influence of the social and political situation. Indian culture is a blend of various cultures across the world, at different points in history and also its own rich traditions. Though development and modernity has set in the people of India remain rooted in their strong and rich heritage.

The Ho is one of the tribe in Odisha, and they are popularly called *Kola* by which the Ho are generally known to outside world. They speak *Ho* language.

The tribes exhibit varied socio-cultural identities and live in different types of ecological settings such as plains and mountains. Tribes have past, they have mostly culture bounded and giving important to their culture, religion, festival and

* Department of Politics and Int. Studies, Silver Jubilee Campus, Pondicherry University, Kalapet, Puducherry Pin - 605 014. Mobile: +919360085180. E-mail: snehasishsethi101@gmail.com

tradition. The Ho is mainly depending on the agriculture, collection of forest product, hunting and rope making. Development and social change are inter-connected phenomena, but in tribal communities only the developmental activities have impacted on the social life of the *Ho*.

The present paper is focusing on the traditional cultural value of the *Ho* tribe who inhabits in the Mayurbhanj district in Odisha state. The major findings of the study are relying on the changes of their lifestyle through the empowerment.

The Ho People and their Life Style

Odisha occupies a significant position in tribal map of India. Out of 437 tribes in India, Odisha has sixty two of them, accounting for 22.2 per cent of the state population, as per 2001 Census. It accounts for 9.7 per cent of total ST population in India. The tribal population in the state experienced a growth rate of 15.8 per cent between 1991 and 2001 (Census of India, 2001). According to 1991 census the Ho population is 50,892 and 2001 census is 43,113.

The Ho is one of the major tribes of Jharkhand and Orissa. The singhbhum district of Jharkhand is the original place of their inhabitant. In due course of time they spread towards its neighbouring areas of Jharkhand, Orissa and West Bengal and even a few to Assam. These *Ho*s belong to the Proto-Astrologic group. They are of short stature, dark complex with broad and flat nose. In the Ho language the word *'Ho'* means a man and accordingly any human being can be designated as a Ho. From the field situation it is clear that the term *'Ho'* is only used by this community to identify them, whereas the other neighbuoring communities address them by the term 'Kola'. The *Ho* belongs to the Munda branch of Austro-Asiatic languages and allied to Sandal and Mandarin dialects in certain respect. In Jharkhand (as it belonged to erstwhile Hindi state of Bihar till recently) the Hindi language based on Denair script is used for inter-community communication where as among themselves they speak *Ho* dialect. The Ho of Orissa use both Hindi and Oriya languages and Oriya script. They have a strong belief in religion, spirit and super natural powers but they practice parochial religion and Hinduism. They worship different Gods and Goddesses residing in nearby jungles and hills. The Singhbunga or the Sun God is the supreme deity worshipped by them, who is mainly responsible for the rain, crop, life, and other necessities related to life. Besides Singhbunga, the Ho also worship a number of other deities like Marangburu, Naga Bubga, Dessauli, Goodie era, Japer era etc.

The worship of both benevolent and malevolent spirits is also practiced among the Ho. They celebrate both traditional and adopted festivals. Their traditional festivals are mostly associated to their agricultural activities. The Ho traditionally being a part of an elaborate political system, have a strong traditional base with corresponding political offices to maintain social control. Thus, the Hos of Jharkhand at the lowest level were places under Piers, which were under a Mankind (a divisional headman). Each Ho village has their own headman called Munda. Birth is considered as an important landmark in Ho life cycle. Though a father plays the main role in procreation of a child, it is believed that a child is a gift of Singhbunga. The *Ho*s practice tribe endogamy and clan exogamy. Marriage within the clan is strictly prohibited and the offenders are treated outcaste from their society. Bride price is the norm and marriage is facilitated by dutam karji (marriage broker). Sororate and Levirate is practiced. Cross-cousin marriage is not allowed. Widow marriage and divorce are permitted. Traditionally, the *Ho* believes that person dies not because of its old age or disease but because of the evil spirit and black magic. They bury their dead, normally, followed by purification ceremony 'Kamani' on 21st day. Each clan has their separate burial place, located close to their houses. They are agriculturists and many landless also engage in agricultural labour. They are also known to be as hardy earth diggers. They celebrate, Maghe Parab, Baa Parab, Makar Sankranti, Salai Parab, Goma Parab, Jamnama Parab etc.

The Ho house is built very neatly as a hut with a rectangular ground plan. The Ho considers pairing as essential to fecundity. Adult marriage is the rule. A man usually marries outside his clan (khilli) and village. There are various ways to acquiring the mate among the Ho, such as andi, diku, rajakhusi, and anadar. But today andi is becoming less popular, as it invariably involves a heavy bride price (gonong). The interesting thing of gonong is, the bride side takes the dowry from groom as the bullocks or few land and sometimes money also. This system is one of the best among the *Ho* tribes.

The Ho believes natural objects exercise a beneficent influence on their life and happiness. As such they are periodically prayer and offering as part of their thanks giving service. Thus the sun, moon, river, and mountain, are the *Ho*'s principal bungas. The chief of these is *singhbungas* or the sun, who is the creator of this universe. In each village there is also a sacred grove *(jaharia)* in which resides *Dasalu*, the protecting sprit of the village. Ancestral sprits are worshipped in the home. The *Ho* is afraid to malignant sprits. They believe in black magic, and witchcraft. *Basam, thakurani, kalimuhin,* and *dwarasuni* are considered to be territorial sprits who bring calamities if they are not properly appeased. All these spirits required continuous propitiation by means sacrifices.

The Ho observed seven important festivals like *Maghe, Baha, Damuria, Hero, Jomnama, Kolon, Batauli.* These are associated with their agricultural operations, and the time and season are therefore determined by the needs of agriculture. Most of the village have a Dehuri family. The post of Dehuri is hereditary. The Ho has no caste organization at present.

The Tribals of Orissa observe a string of festivals. Some are closed affairs, relating to a birth or death within the family. Mostly a festival is an occasion for a good of Mahua liquor, a game roasted on the sprit and a night of song and dance is revelry. But that is not the end, there is an animal sacrifice too, for the deities and sprits must be appeased first, particularly the malevolent ones, so they don't unleash drought or sickness on the land. Tribals are superstitious people and the 'Ojha' occupies a position of honour since he not only prescribes medicines for the sick but is also believed to exorcise evil spirits.

Handia is famous among Ho that is popularly known as Diyeng and ABCD (Adibasi Cold Drinks). This Handia is one type of a Liquor, but not harmful, it made by Rice. They believe it makes people healthy. In each and every Weekly market Handia is available in a huge amount. It has great importance in religious festivals, and is also used as a good medicine for the stomach. Raci is also a type of liquor which they consume, that is also made by Rice. Except this For Food, Basically they prefer Rice and Water Rice, Because of most of the *Hos* are BPL, they takes green leaf, Green chilli and Salt as their curry, other than this they keep cock, hen, goat, pig, hen as their domestic animal. Every year during their festival time a large number of people together go for Hunting to the nearby Forests.

History and Cultural Relations

The view that the Munda/Ho originally entered India from Southeast Asia is based mainly on their linguistic affiliations; their own oral traditions give them instead a western origin (from Uttar Pradesh). There is some evidence of tribal Kingdoms in pre-British times (*e.g.*, the Ho/Munda kingdom of Chota Nagpur, and the Bhumij states, especially Barabhum). Mainly, however, the Munda have lived, often fairly autonomously, under the rule of outside powers. Most Munda are conventionally regarded as tribes rather than castes, despite the definitional problems this gives scholarship. It is an identity most of them promote themselves, partly because of the legal advantages they gain through being on the list of Scheduled Tribes, but mainly because of opposition to 'Hindu' (*i.e.*, upper-caste) officials and landowners, who, from early British times, have displaced many tribals from their land. This strongly tribal and anti-Hindu identity has led to rebellion in the past (the Ho rebellion of the 1830s, the Santal rebellion of 1855-58, the Birsa Munda movement of 1895-1900), but today it has become translated into political action through the Santal-dominated Jharkhand Party, which agitates, among other things, for a specifically Adivasi (Tribal) province.

Despite this, there are a number of Munda/Ho groups who have sought to gain caste status by reforming customs (banning alcohol, public dancing, cross-cousin Marriage) and acquiring a specialist occupation such as basket making. These attempts to improve their lot earn them the contempt of the 'tribal' Munda/Ho and, since they are mainly artisan castes, ironically lower their status below that of the Tribals in the eyes of the upper castes, since the tribals at least are not involved in a polluting occupation. Only the Bhumij, having been rulers, can convincingly claim a moderately high (Kshatriya) status.

Settlements

Most *Ho*s live in villages, though some live and work in towns. From the study area Many *Ho*s are gone to different cities for work, the cities are like: Gujarat, Hyderabad, Bangalore, Punjab and Chennai. Being semi-nomadic, they have temporary forest camps. Traditionally, there was a tendency for villages to be fixed only temporarily because of the requirements of shifting cultivation, but with the government trying to discourage this form of agriculture, villages now tend to be more permanent. Villages may consist of detached dwellings or sometimes (as among some Sora) of dwellings connected into a longhouse. Houses are not generally oriented toward particular compass points, but they are usually symbolically divided internally according to principles of gender and age (the eldest members sleep nearest the hearth, male members on the right of the house, female members on the left, etc.). The hearth is especially important ritually and is the spiritual centre of the homestead.

Economy

Subsistence and Commercial Activities among Ho

Most *Ho*s are agriculturalists; increasingly, permanent irrigated sites are replacing the traditional swiddens. The other main traditional occupation is hunting and gathering, with which the Birhor and some Korwa are particularly associated, though all groups participate in these activities to some extent to supplement their agriculture. Today, however, government policy is to preserve the remaining forests, which are now much depleted, and this policy militates against both of the traditional forms of economic activity. The result is an increase in irrigated land and the development of other sources of income.

Industrial Arts

*Ho*s have a traditional artisan or other specialist occupation (*e.g.*, the Asur are ironworkers, the Turi are basket makers, the Kora are ditch diggers, etc.). Some Birhor make and sell ropes. Generally, though, Hindu artisans supply most of the tribes' needs.

Trade

Few *Ho*s live by trade, though they may occasionally sell forest products or some rice to wholesalers. The Birhor obtain their rice by selling ropes and forest products, and some Korwa, Turi, and Mahali sell their basketwork in local markets.

Division of Labour

Both men and women work in the fields, but the domestic burdens fall more on the women; many occupations (*e.g.*, ploughing, roof repair) are barred to them for ritual reasons. Men hunt, women gather. Specialist occupations are mainly men's work.

Land Tenure

Swiddens are normally owned by the dominant descent group in the village, though co resident non-members are usually granted access; the individual normally has use rights only while he cultivates. Irrigated land tends to be individually or family owned, primarily because of the extra labour involved in building terraces and irrigation ditches.

Kinship

- *Kin Groups and Descent*: Descent is uniformly patrilineal, and all the *Ho*s have patrilineal descent groups. Totemic, exogamous clans, mainly significant as regulators of marriage, and lineages, normally named after localities or Village offices and mainly of ritual and economic significance, are identifiable in most tribes; sub clans are also present in the larger Chota Nagpur tribes. Clans are not especially localised, though they are often identified with particular cemeteries or memorial stones, and each village will be dominated by the members of a particular clan. No Sora descent groups are Totemic. On the whole, a common totem, shared ritual food, or village co residence are more important indicators of agnation than genealogy as such. Villages are often identified with a particular agnatic group, despite the frequent co presence of members of other clans. Clan members are not necessarily descended from their totem, but the totem usually plays some key role in the clan origin myth, and clan members must show respect to and avoid harming their own (though not others') totem species (most commonly an animal).

- *Kinship Terminology:* Basically it is symmetric-prescriptive or bifurcate-collateral terminology, but Ego's Genealogical level is normally generational, and the levels adjacent to it usually have a final term separate from those for cross kin.
- *Domestic Unit:* Both nuclear and extended or joint Families are found, though a single family often oscillates between the different forms, as new members are born and old ones die, or as quarrels split them up. For the hunting-and-gathering Birhor, the *tanda* (band) is the unit.
- *Inheritance:* Irrigated land, use rights regarding swiddens, the family home, fruit trees, and most movables are inherited in the direct patrilineal line. The eldest son receives the most, though not normally everything, as the new head of the Family (he may be responsible for the welfare, marriage expenses, etc., of his younger siblings, for example). In some cases, the sons who have remained at home are favoured (the youngest sons among

the Sora and some Santal, for instance). In default of sons, the closest collateral agnate or an uxorilocally living son-in-law (the *ghar-jawae*) inherits. There is some matrilineal inheritance of female clothes and ornaments, but women cannot inherit land, because they marry out of the clan.

- *Socialization:* Infants are brought up by their parents with the help of elder siblings, but it is the former who are mainly responsible for socialization. Other opportunities are provided by children watching and eventually helping with the daily work, and the elders play their part by telling myths and other folktales on ritual and other occasions.

Socio-Political Organization

- *Social Organization:* Many tribes are internally divided because of some ritual fault or disagreement over custom. The Birhor, Korwa, and some Asur distinguish settled groups from nomads. Most tribes distinguish landowning clans from tenant clans with use rights only, though since the clans involved vary with the village; this does not entail a tribe wide class system. Santal clans are unusual in being ritually ranked, and there is some hypergamy between them. In all tribes, village officers command a marked degree of respect, though this rarely leads to a class system or to hypergamy between them and the ordinary Villagers. Kinship remains the basis of social organization, and there are a number of ritualized friendships for both men and women, between villages and even tribes, that are assimilated to it. Although all tribes distinguish affines from agnates (*i.e.*, marriageable from no marriageable persons), these are relative designations only: despite the system of affinal alliance, there are no sociocentric categories of the sort associated with dual Organization or four-section systems of some Australian Aboriginal peoples. The Juang and possibly other tribes have a system of generation moieties in which Ego's generation is linked with those of his grandparents and grandchildren in opposition to the set formed by those of his parents and children. This impinges on both stereotyped behaviour and marriage choices: joking is only allowed with members of one's own moiety, which is also that from which one's spouse must come (and even then there are numerous exceptions in both regards), while avoidance or respect in behaviour and avoidance of Marriage and sexual relations is enjoined toward members of the opposite moiety.

- *Political Organization:* The elected government *gram panchayat* was introduced in this region soon after Independence in 1947, but it often has to compete with the traditional village assembly or *panchayat*. This consists of the headman, other officials, and typically household heads at least, if not all males in the village. It is unusual but not unknown for women to participate in decision-making, though they are often called to give Evidence in disputes. The headman ship and other offices (assistant headman, messenger, etc.) are mostly hereditary in the male line, though there may be an elective element in the choice, and the eldest son can always be replaced if believed to be unsuitable. Village headmen are no more than first among equals, for they have to consult the panchayat on all important matters and are removable for misconduct or incompetence.
- *Social Control and Conflict:* The old sanction of expulsion from the community has fallen into disuse, and fines, along with provision of a feast for the panchayat or even the whole village, are now the common penalties. Most conflicts concern land rights or marriage. Resort to violent direct action by an aggrieved party is by no means uncommon. Sometimes in major cases they goes to nearest police station.

Religion and Expressive Culture

- *Religious Beliefs:* Hinduism is an influence, though the *Hos* are not among the main guardians of Hindu traditions as followed by the Brahmans. The great deity, as protector and judge – sometimes identified with the sun (*e.g.,*

Kharia Dharam, Remo Singi-Arke, the Singbunga of the Ho, Santal, etc.), sometimes depicted as a 'diluted version' of Hindu gods (*e.g.*, Mahadeo, Bhagwan) – should normally be distinguished from the creator (Munda Haram, Santal Marang Buru), especially since the former typically destroyed men through fire or flood in order to recreate them whole and pure; sometimes, however, the two deities are linked rather like the different incarnations of Hindu gods. There are in all tribes numerous spirits, both benevolent and malevolent. They include agricultural gods and goddesses, spirits of trees, hills, forests, the village, village boundaries, ancestral spirits (especially malevolent if uncared for or allowed to wander rather than being 'brought back' to the hearth after their funeral), other household and lineage deities (some secret), clan deities, deities associated with snakes, tigers, monkeys, and other wild animals, the ghosts of women dead in childbirth or Pregnancy, the ghosts of suicides or people killed by tigers, and shamans' tutelaries. Christians are in a minority in most tribes. But now a large number of *Ho*s are converting to Christian.

- *Religious Practitioners:* Most tribes have both priests, concerned with village rituals and life-crisis rites, and shamans, concerned with illness, malevolent spirits, divining the fate of the dead, divining reincarnation, etc. Usually there is one of each to every village, though only the priest, not the shaman, sits on the village panchayat. Unlike the priests, whose offices are basically hereditary in the male line, shamans 'emerge' by demonstrating their powers, becoming possessed, etc. Sometimes priests and shamans come from different tribes. Some shamans are female, but no priests. In most tribes domestic ritual is performed by male household heads.
- *Ceremonies:* The most important life-cycle rites are those concerned with birth, marriage, and death. Initiation and puberty are usually much less marked, if at all, and it is marriage, if not parenthood, which really makes one a

full adult Member of the tribe, with the right to sit on the panchayat, etc. There are also numerous agricultural rites (fertility, sowing, transplanting, harvesting), as well as rites to promote success in the hunt (usually in March), to safeguard the village against disease and other misfortune, to honor the supreme deity and clan deities, etc. Tribals often imitate, or take part in, local Hindu festivals.

- *Arts:* On the whole, the Hos are not renowned for artistic expression, though there are some exceptions, such as the wood carvings of the Kharia and Sora and the wall paintings of the Gadaba and Sora, mostly done for a ritual purpose.
- *Medicine:* Illness is attributed to the actions of malevolent spirits, who may be ancestors who have not been sufficiently appeased or to the temporary withdrawal of soul substance from the body, etc. Shamans are frequently called in to divine the cause, often with the aid of their tutelary spirits, and to effect a cure through the sacrifice of a fowl, goat, or other animal. The *Ho*s are not so health conscious, Because of lack of Education Still people believe on superstitions. Many Ho are dying for small small diseases like malaria, snake bite, fever etc. They believe that all these happening because of their unimpressed god. So instead of taking them to hospitals, they go for worship. They have also a strong believe on Ghosts, unsatisfied soul etc. But in due course of time few educated people are became conscious about their health and by the help of some voluntary organizations, they are organizing some camps, and giving suggestions to go for hospitals.
- *Death and Afterlife:* There is no particular delay in disposing of the dead. Whether cremation or burial is followed depends on the tribe; the inauspicious dead (accidents, suicides, very young infants, etc.) are usually disposed of in a different manner from "normal" deaths; they are buried where cremation is the norm or buried with the opposite orientation from a normal burial. The person

generally has at least two souls, sometimes more (*e.g.*, a Juang has five). One is linked to the personality of the deceased and has to be 'brought back' from the funeral ground to join the ancestors behind the domestic hearth. The other-commonly called *jiv*, really another term for 'soul substance'– is usually reincarnated in a same-sex agnatic descendant, preferably a grandchild related in the direct line, though sometimes it is a collateral ascendant who is reincarnated, especially if there are several siblings. A person is usually given the name of the ancestor deemed to have been reincarnated in him or her.

Strategies for Empowerment

There are several steps has been taken for the empowerment of Ho tribes by implementing various schemes.

Constitutional Provisions

- Statutory recognition of tribal communities.
- Creation of scheduled areas for the thorough development of the tribals.
- Special representations in the parliament, in the legislative assemblies and local bodies.
- Special privileges in the form of reservation of a certain percentage of posts in government services and seats in educational institutions.
- Recognition of the right to use local language for administration and other purposes and to profess one's faith.

Schemes for Tribal Development

The tribal majority areas in the country are broadly divided into three categories, *(i)* predominantly tribal state/ union territories, *(ii)* Scheduled areas, and *(iii)* Non-Scheduled areas in the states. All the tribal-majority States and Union Territories are placed in a special category for availing funds. The development and administration of tribal areas is accepted as a special responsibility of the central govemment even though they are integral parts of the concerned states. Financial provisions for their development were considered in detail by the constituent assembly itself.

The schemes have been divided into two categories:

(i) Central sector programmes which are fully financed by the central government.

(ii) The centrally sponsored programmes which are partly financed by the central government and rest of the expenditure meted out by the concerned State government.

According to Dr. B. D. Sharma, financial resources for developmental programmes in a state may comprise the following elements.

- Investment in the central and centrally sponsored schemes.
- State revenues.
- Share from certain central revenue.
- Plan assistance from the central government.
- Grants under Article 275(1) on the basis of the recommendations.

Finance Commission

The utilisation of State funds is broadly classified under two categories. Plan and non-plan. The plan technically covers all those items which are included in the State or the Central plan. The non-plan includes expenditure on general administration as also on the maintenance of development schemes.

The Special Central Assistance (SCA) for tribal sub-plans is allocated between different states on the basis of three criteria as under.

- The tribal population of Sub-Plan area.
- The geographical area of the Sub-Plan.
- The per capita gross output of the state.

The weightage for these three elements has been fixed in a certain proportion. While the first two criteria are simple, the quantum of assistance on the basis of the third criterion is determined with reference to the difference between the inverse of the State's per capita gross product and the inverse of the per capita gross national product.

The financing agencies rendering their services in the tribal areas are Central Government, State Governments, institutions, *viz.*, commercial banks, co-operative banks, NABARD and voluntary organization.

Programmes for Tribal Welfare

A number of employment oriented and developmental programmes for tribals have been introduced by the government of India. The major programmes are Integrated Rural Development Programme (IRDP), Jawahar Rosgar Yojana (JRY), Prime Ministers Rosgar Yojana(PMRY) and Training For Self-Employment For Rural youth (TRYSEM). IRDP scheme is absolutely for rural people those belong to below poverty line and others are for both rural as well as urban youth. All these schemes are implemented in the state by District Rural Development Agencies (DRDA's) in collaboration with Commercial and Cooperative Banks. PMRY was initiated in October 1993 to tackle the burning problem of educated unemployment. PMRY relates to setting up of self-employment ventures through industries and services. Any unemployed youth who is metric failed/passed or above or ITI passed, is eligible for the benefits of the scheme subject to the condition that if he is between the age group of 18 to 35 years and his family income does not exceed Rs. 24,000 per annum. The youth should also be the permanent resident of the areas for at least three years and he should not be defaulter to any bank or financial institution. The scheme envisages 22.5 per cent reservation for Scheduled Caste/Scheduled Tribe and 27 per cent for OBC. A maximum loan of Rs. 1 lakh per candidate is provided under this scheme, at an interest rate of 12.5 per cent to 15.5 per cent. The entrepreneur has to contribute 5 per cent of project cost as margin money. No collateral security guarantee is asked on such loans. Period of repayment starts after a moratorium of six to eighteen months and range over 3 to 7 years. The government provides subsidy to the extent of 15 per cent of the total loan imbursed with a ceiling of Rs. 7,500 per entrepreneur. In case of joint venture each partner may be provided a loan of Rs. 1 lakh subsidy. In such cases the interest is calculated for each partner separately at a rate of 15 per cent of his share in the project cost limited to Rs. 7,500 for each partner.

The provision of compulsory training to entrepreneurship development is a salient feature of the scheme. Duration of this training is one month and trainees are provided stipend of Rs. 500 during the training period.

With the objective of providing technical skills to rural youth to enable them to take up self-employment in the fields of agriculture and allied activities, industries, services and business activities, the scheme of TRYSEM was introduced in the year 1979 on the Independence Day. The scheme works as a part of Integrated Rural Development Programme and aims at imparting training to about 2 lakhs rural youths every year from the 5,011 development blocks of the country and to lift them above the poverty line.

Under this scheme, those rural youth who are in the age group of 18 to 35 years with annual timely income from all sources are not exceeding Rs. 8,500 are eligible for selection. Preference is given to Scheduled Caste/scheduled Tribe (50%) women (40%) and physically handicapped (3%). The selected beneficiaries are trained into the field of agriculture and allied activities, industry, service and business activities. The trainees are paid a monthly stipend or daily allowance during the training period. The training institution is provided honorarium along with Rs. 75 per trainee per month for purchase of raw materials.

After completion of training, the beneficiaries are assisted in getting finance from the banks. A maximum of Rs. 35,000 can be sanctioned to each beneficiary as a composite loan. Trained youths are granted a subsidy by the government at the rate of 1/3 to 1/2 of the cost of the project to set up self-employment venture. Beneficiaries are also provided marketing support for their finished products. The amount spent on this scheme is contributed by the Central and the State governments in *50:50* ratios. Since 1983 the scope of TRYSEM scheme has been enlarged.

The main thrust of the development strategies during the recent past has been on the removal of poverty in tribal areas. The main causes of poverty are identified as illiteracy, unemployment, under employment and law productivity in agriculture. Since farmers in TSP area have land holding mostly on hill slopes, the fertility of land is very low. Further, droughts and soil erosion are now recurring features in the tribal areas. This has reduced employment opportunities of the tribals. For improving the economic status of tribals.

Programmes were launched, during 1980's, mainly: *(a)* the Asset Programme and *(b)* the Employment Programme.

The Asset Programme aims at the overall integrated development of rural life through the removal of poverty and unemployment in rural areas. In this programme productive assets are directly given to the poor. It is believed that income generated from these productive assets would not only be sufficient to repay the bank loans but will help the assisted families to cross the 'poverty line'. This programme is popularly known as Integrated Rural Development.

Programme (IRDP)

The Employment Programme on the other hand aims at providing employment through public works during the adverse agricultural season. The employment programme asserts that poverty persists because of the lack of employment opportunities. The earlier employment schemes were adhoc in nature but the employment programme launched from Oct 1 980, popularly known as National Rural Employment Programme (NREP) is considered as a permanent plan programme.

The travails of tribal development need to be understood properly. The programmes should be related to the specific needs of the tribal community. Also, tribal development programmes should be integrated with the ongoing rural development programmes meant for poverty alleviation. A pragmatic and holistic approach to tribal development alone can produce good results.

Conclusion

The Major findings of this study reveal that, the *Hos* are mostly culture oriented, and they have their own life style and not the followers of others. They like to live inside the forest and the followers of superstitions. Still they lives a peaceful life, no quarrel no ego, nothing is there among them. Except this The Ho tribes are also facing number of problems, which are the major obstacles for their empowerment. The government is making lot of policies for them but implementation is very low. Because of that most of the Hos are still in Below Poverty Line. But now a day they have improved a lot.

REFERENCES

Dr. M. Kunharnan, (1997), "Tribal Development in India. Retrospect and Prospect", Budgeting for Whom. *Update quarterly* No. 1, April-June.

Dr. Prakash Chandra Mehta, (2000), *Tribal Development in 20th Century,* Siva Publishers, Udaipur.

Elwin, Verrier (1955), *The Religion of an Indian Tribe.* Bombay: Oxford University Press.

K. K. Mishra (1987), Social Structure and Change among the Ho of Orissa, Gyan Books Pvt. Ltd.

Orans, Martin (1965), *The Santal: A Tribe in Search of a Great Tradition.* Detroit: Wayne State University Press.

R. N Thakur, (1997), "Tribal Development Need for a Fresh Perspective"; *Kurukshethra,* March-April.

13

Socio-economic Development of Scheduled Tribes

A Case of Adilabad District in Andhra Pradesh

Dr. P. Padmanabha Rao*

INTRODUCTION

India is a vast and second most populous country of the world. A big part of its population has been leading an uncertain economic life due to non-synchronization of employment opportunities in agriculture sector because of the fast growing population and hence increased attention is desired to improve the lot this population. So, to provide a suitable and sustainable model of development and overall reconstruction of society in the changing scenario, the need of analysis of society is imperative. In pursuance of this idea an effort needs to be made to highlight the missing aspects in the process of development along with an overall evaluation of present process of rural development in India.

The economic and social conditions in the tribal areas, in spite of adequate resource endowments, are far from

* Faculty Member, Centre for Economic and Social Studies (CESS), N. O. Campus, Begumpet, Hyderabad - 500 016. Email: ppadmanabharao@cess.ac.in. Mobile: 98494 48201

satisfactory compared to other similarly endowed areas. And, therefore, up-gradation of productive capabilities in such areas along with the protection of the ecology is of paramount importance to narrow down the gap between the backward tribal areas and the developed areas to realise sustainable growth and development and the creation of adequate employment opportunities. To achieve this, State intervention through protective and preventive measures to develop dry land agriculture, become absolutely necessary.

Utilisation of natural resources for the betterment of man's living conditions is a must. But, proper assessment and utilisation of resources for overall development need special attention. The quality, spatial distribution, extent of utilisation and potential for development are influenced by various factors, namely: physical, economic and institutional. After 50 years of constitutional provisions and concentrated efforts for uplifting of Scheduled Tribes, more than half of the tribal population is still unable to meet the basic requirement of food and continues to live in abject of poverty. The deprivation among the tribal population is reflected in almost every sphere of the daily life. Wide difference is observed in the extent of poverty and living conditions among the tribes across different ITDAs of Andhra Pradesh. The inadequate provision of infrastructural facilities in remote tribal areas is a denial of opportunity for socio-economic transformation of the tribal population in the state of A. P. The future development of the tribal areas. Poverty reduction and improvement in their living conditions lies in concentrated efforts development of existing resources and accelerated investment in the basic infrastructural facilities in the remote tribal areas.

The Government of India and Andhra Pradesh is implementing various anti-poverty and developmental programmes for the welfare of the tribes for their upliftment and development. The programmes are mainly focus on the poorest of the poor such as small and marginal farmers, artisans, indigenous people, and rural women. The present paper aims at to examine whether any change has taken place due to implementation of various developmental and welfare programmes, in their quality of life, their participation in the planning and implementation, social mobility, awareness, and in their socio-economic conditions etc. The study also looks into critical appraisal and sustainability of schemes and integrated approach, and tried to assess how the empowerment among the women actually took place.

Objectives of the Study

1. Assessment of degree of involvement of peoples participation at various levels of project formulation, identification of beneficiaries/schemes, grounding of the scheme and maintenance, management of the assets created.
2. Assessment of degree of understanding of tribal families on the project activities, on the nature of entrustment, execution of the project activities to the people, the opinion of the people on the strategy adopted, the peoples perception on the assets created.
3. Degree of involvement of tribal women in various project activities especially in formulation of the thrift credit and grain banks and other community based activities.

The Study has been conducted through:

(a) Group discussions with the beneficiaries and village community.

(b) Physical verification of the schemes for quality assessment and to examine processes involved.

(c) Collection of data relating to implementation process, scheme details, visits by officials and non-officials, nature of execution of work, peoples' participation, number of works completed, formation of VTDAs, maintenance of assets, self-help groups, meetings, training received etc.

(e) Final discussions with the field staff and sectoral officers regarding implementation process and problems encountered during the course of implementation.

Multiple stratified random sampling methods were adopted in identifying the schemes and villages. Based on the geographical distribution from each mandal 3-5 villages were selected randomly. Where atleast two major schemes were implemented. In the selection of villages care was also taken to cover remote villages and villages in the interior.

A Brief Profile of the Study Area

The district of Adilabad lies between 77° 46′and 80° 0′ of East longitude and 18° 40′ and 19° 56′ of the North latitude. It is situated in the northern most part of the state of Andhra Pradesh. It is the second largest district in the Telangana region in the state after Mahbubnagar district. The district is bounded on north by Yeotmal and Chanda district of Maharastra, on the east by Chanda district, on the south by Karimnagar and Nizamabad districts and on the west by Nanded district of Maharastra State. The district is administered by five revenue divisions and has 52 mandals (Fig 13.1).

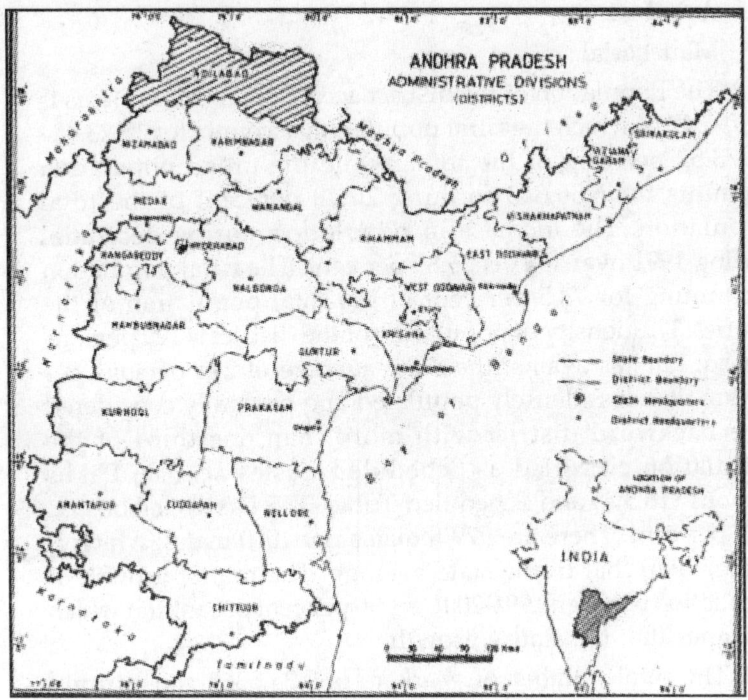

Fig 13.1:

The total geographical area of the district is 16,128 sq. kms., which accounts for 5.9 per cent of the total area of the state. The total population as per 2001 Census is 24.79 lakhs, which accounts for 3.13 per cent of the total population of the state. It is however takes the fifth rank in area with an extent of 16128 sq. kms., which account for 5.90 per cent of the total area of the State. It is however, the second largest district in the Telangana region. The District Comprises of 52 Mandals and 1743 villages of which 1557 villages are inhabited and 186 villages are un-inhabited. There are 7 Municipalities in the District. The District is conveniently formed into five divisions:

1. Adilabad.
2. Nirmal.
3. Utnoor.
4. Asifabad.
5. Mancherial.

The Population of the district according to 2001 census is 24,79,347 of which the rural population accounts for 18,23,004 or 73.52 per cent of the total, while the urban population accounts for 6,56,343 forming 26.48 per cent of the total population. The increase in population during decennial ending 1991 over 1981 is 26.85 per cent. The rural population accounting for 73.5 per cent of the total population of the district. The density of population of the district is 129 persons per sq. km., as against the State average of 241 persons per sq. km. It is less densely populated and generally considered as a backward district with more than one third of the population classified as Scheduled Castes *i.e.* 3.86 Lakhs persons (18.5%) and Scheduled Tribes 3.55 Lakhs persons *i.e.* 17.9 per cent. There are 979 females per 1000 males; which is higher than that of the state average. The rate of growth of population between 1991 2001 is 1.90 per cent per annum which is higher that the state's growth.

The total number of workers is 9,34,3365 constituting 44.93 per cent of the total population as against the state average of 45.27 per cent out of the total main workers. The classification shown that 65 per cent of the work force is engaged in agricultural activities, such as cultivation and agricultural labourers. Cultivators account for 34.09 per cent and Agricultural laboureres 34.88 per cent. The literate persons in Adilabad district are 5,78,226 forming 27.80 per cent of the total population as against the state average if 37.8. The percentage of literacy in the district increased from 18.79 per cent in 1981 to 27.80 in 1991. It is lower that the state average which increased from 30 per cent in 1981 to 37.58 per cent in 1991.

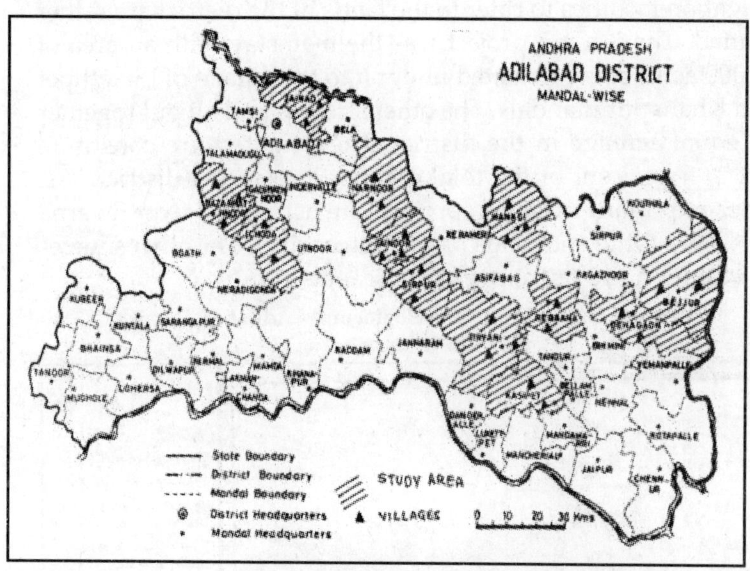

Fig 13.2:

More than 44 per cent of the geographical area is under forests, the area under permanent pastures is around 3 per cent. Net area sown constitutes 35 per cent of the area of the district, which is lower than the state's average. There is a very little double cropping (less than 10%) in the district. The mono cropping is due to the single season rainfall and lack of water storage facilities. The land use pattern in the district has remained stable over the last three decades. The district receives an annual rainfall of about 1050 mm and most of the agriculture is rainfed. The sparse irrigation facility is mostly the reason for mono crop agriculture. The gross irrigated area in the district is only 12.4 per cent of the gross cropped area, which is the lowest as against 39.9 per cent of the states and 36.1 per cent for the Telangana region.

Irrigation

Irrigation is the backbone for agriculture. Agriculture depends on the irrigation facilities available. Though the rivers all along its border surround the district of Adilabad, the irrigation facilities to cater to the lands of the district are rather limited. The Kadam project was the mainstay with an area of 55,000 acres being irrigated under it to the village of Luxettipet and Khanapur mandals. The other streams and all put together an equal acreage in the district. The irrigated are constitute just 11.5 per cent of the total cropper area in the district. The other important irrigation projects are across the river Swarna in Nirmal Taluq and Sirala project across river. The other sources of irrigation are tanks, wells and canals.

Status of Groundwater Developmenmt - Adilabad District (Sub-Basin-wise)

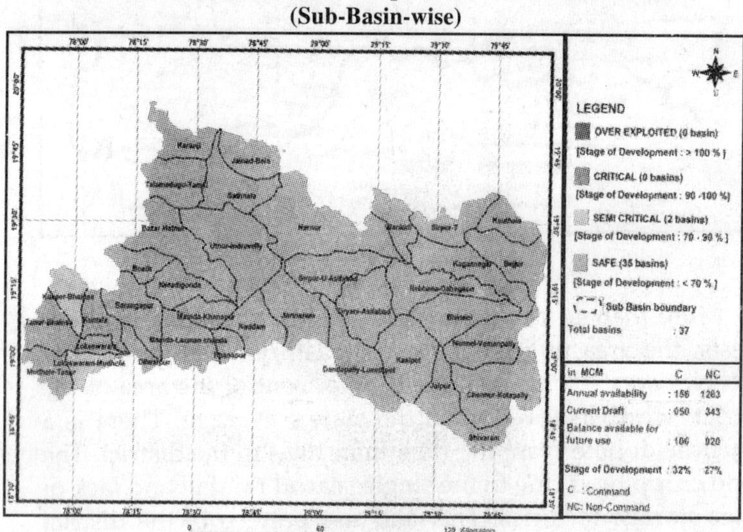

Fig 13.3:

Due to the high percentage of slopes and the forest and hilly terrains the irrigation projects are hampered in the district. Small projects of lift irrigations and bundings could be given a though to irrigate local areas in a small and medium scale for meeting the irrigation needs of the district.

There is scope for bringing large areas of cultivable lands under irrigation though several surface water schemes. The present level of 17 per cent irrigation of the cultivable area under minor, medium and major irrigation projects which is the lowest in the state needs to be improved for achieving higher yields and creating fresh employment in the agriculture sector.

The Integrated Tribal Development Agency (ITDA) extends over 45 mandals covering (412) Scheduled Villages, (234) Non-Scheduled Villages (TSP) and (12) cluster villages in the district. The tribal sub-plan area comprises (646) villages covering an area of 6353 sq. kms., which works out to be 38.13 per cent of total geographical area of the District. The tribal population is Scheduled Tribes 3.55 Lakhs person's *i.e.* 17.9 per cent. The tribal population in the Tribal Sub-Plan area is 2,35,000 covering 47,304 house holds and the remaining 1,20,000 tribal population consisting of 23,507 house holds are residing out side the Tribal Sub-Plan area in the District.

A number of different groups of the Tribals *i.e.*, Gonds, Naikpods, Kolams, Pardhans, Koyas, Manne, Andhs, Thoties, Lambadas and Yerukalas are living in the district. The Kolams and Thoties are the most backward and poorest and classified as Primitive Tribal Group (PTG) for special attention. Even the poorer Mannes (Telugu Speaking Kolams) are extended with the same benefits with a special government order.

Thus, the district is backward and subject to drought in the recent past. The land is concentrated in the hands of a few individuals and the marginal and small farmers who are in majority account for an insignificant percentage of the total land. Their illegal economic system makes the social system, hierarchical which would affect the functioning of any anti poverty programmes. Against this background, the study was conducted in 20 mandals from 960 sample households. Agriculture is predominantly rainfed, with less than 10 per cent of the area under irrigation. Most of the rainfall is not utilised due to non-availability of storage facility. Due to the absence of soil and moisture conservation measures, use of local low yielding seed varieties, time old traditional agricultural management practice, lack of capital and low yields, the tribals are forced into a debt trap. The area under cultivation, in the Project area, is less than 35 per cent. The important crops that are grown in the area are paddy, maize, jowar, pulses, oil seeds and cotton. Inter-cropping is common in these areas.

Most of the tribals, about 80-90 per cent of the work force, are engaged in settled agriculture. Very few households are engaged in household industry such as making bamboo products. Collection of MFP is one of the most important activities for Gonds and Koyas. Due to lack of education and poor levels of economic development women do not play an active role in the tribal village society. They, however, are engaged in agriculture and other labour. They participate in collection of MFP along with the men and attend to their household duties. There is no positive self-image in the community.

Though well endowed with land, due to their low productivity, the tribal households get very low incomes. Traditional agricultural management, lack of irrigation facilities and non-adoption of soil and moisture conservation measures lead to environmental degradation. Due to inadequate extension services and lack of investment for inputs, the output is not adequate. In the tribal areas, there are no opportunities for additional employment due to non-availability of wage employment. Due to degradation of forests, income from the collection of MFP is also falling. Borrowing at higher interest rates from the money lenders to meet their consumption needs leads the tribals into a debt trap.

Unless there is rise in their incomes, they will remain vulnerable. Improvement in their economic status can be achieved only through increase in agricultural production by adoption of new technology and diversification of the activities to horticulture through people participation and extension methods and increase in the income from their traditional source of MFP by regeneration of forest species. The positive factors in favour of these are abundant surface and ground water resources for irrigation development, their exposure to settled cultivation, good soils and rainfall to support dry land agriculture, coupled with soil conservation methods. By improving irrigation facilities production can be improved. Provision of infrastructure facilities such as roads, electricity, drinking water etc., will also bring development to these areas. To achieve these, the ITDA programmes would provide opportunity to reinforce and expand the innovated schemes/ intervention, so that achievements could make a major contribution to tribal development.

Community Participation and Development

In the villages Tribal Communities participation in planning and execution of the programme is a very important aspect. The general opinion is that the tribal community are lazy and they are un-co-operative with the government functionaries for taking up developmental works. When the participatory approach has been introduced the results are some what encouraging. The communities are taking up active role in the implementation of the programme. They have organising women thrift groups, grain banks. It contributes to the sustainability of the development efforts as the community has a stake in the success of the works. The VTDA are implementing the works such as small scale irrigation and soil conservation etc., by their nominal participation and managing funds through its agency under the supervision of a official in charge of that works.

Development Activities	Beneficiaries
	(708) Schemes in (490) habitations with an outlay of Rs. 45.00 Crores taken-up under Tribal Water Supply Project.
350 IFAD Villages 156 Kms Road	Under Article 275(1) programme Rs. 3.50 Crores worth of B. T. roads have been taken-up and completed (26) Kms., of distance under F. F. W. 156 kms., of road formation completed with an outlay of Rs. 213.00 lakhs.
	372 M. I. works have been taken-up with an estimated cost of Rs. 24.675 crores and created 15,749 acres of ayacut under various schemes *viz.*, IFAD, SCA, TSP, RIADP and X-Finance Commission etc.
	Systematic Land Development has been taken up in 4524 acres of Tribal Lands under SID works.
4524 Acrs for Land Development	Under IFAD Soil Conservation works taken-up with an estimated cost of Rs. 688.00 lakhs in (350) Tribal habitations and grounded 1750 works.
Rs. 82.18 Crores	(7418) Tribal BPL families have been assisted with various economic support schemes.

Some of the youth and women were trained in horticulture nursery in the HNTCs of Bhadrachalam, Eturunagaram and Utnoor. The women thrift groups are active in some of the mandals. The liason works suppose to oversee the all development works such as education, health, nutrition, small scale irrigation, horticulture and soil conservation works. But in practice, in majority of villages his role is restricted to horticulture development activities and to some extent soil conservation. He is taking his remuneration from VTDA funds and are answerable to VTDA only.

The main objective of the community development programme is that the VTDAs should be strengthened and they have to take up all the developmental works on their own, and their frequent dependence to be minimised to some extent. To achieve the objective, formation and effective functioning of the VTDAs, formation of thrift groups appointment of CDCs/ADCs/VLWs etc., and training to be given to these members for effective implementation and success for the programme.

The study finds that wherever the CDCs are appointed they are actually involved in the programme. They are mobilising the communities and pursuing them for involving in the development activities, encouraging the women to form thrift and credit groups, encouraging them to take up economic activities etc. The CDCs were succeeding in these activities to some extent. They are co-operating with the implementing agencies in the development activities of their respective areas.

The working of the functionaries like ADC is not upto the mark. On enquiry in some of the villages, the villagers informed that they are not aware about the existence of these officers. As per job chart the ADC is the main person in the implementation of the programme at ground level, and has to see the progress of the work and give advice to the farmers on agriculture and related activities, whereas, the CDCs is proposed to supervise the activities of VTDAs and women thrift groups. He has to make regular visits, and has to be activate the defunct groups. He is expected to motivate the women thrift group members and VTDAs for better performance/functioning. But practically, the performance was not satisfactory because in some places the man power is inadequate and some places their visits to the villages were not adequate. They should be made to visit the villages regularly for the proper implementation and motivation for success of the programmes.

The study finds that these personnel are working in their respective areas. But not as committed as expected. In some of the villages their visits are not regular. Where they are visiting frequently there the situation of crops and horticulture plantation is good. They are motivating the farmers to take up latest agricultural practices, hybrid seed, use of fertilizers and chemicals etc. After prolonged persuasion in some of the villages the tribal farmers are reported positively. The results are also good. There is instance of change in cropping pattern, increase in yield etc.

Still, these personnel have to work hard to motivate the community for success of the programme. They will have closed interacted and cooperative with the ADA/AO for further action and proper implementation.

Keeping in view the past experience the Andhra Pradesh Participatory Tribal Development Project was started in the year 1994-95, with the assistance of International Fund for Agricultural Development to assist tribal house holds engaged in shifting cultivation to improve household food security, for the development of rain fed agriculture and the protection of environmentally fragile areas.

The major new element introduced by the project is the stress on community-based activities and development of self-reliant communities and strong and sustainable village institutions. The strategy aims to promote the full participation of the tribal people in identifying the causes of deterioration in the physical environment, appreciating the need for change and planning and implementing new initiatives. It is an approach that requires fundamental changes, in attitudes among communities and Government staff alike.

The study reveals that in almost all the villages the VLWs were selected among the community. He is educated and enthusiastic. The required procedure was followed while selecting the VLW, by selecting him in the gramasabha meetings. He has been paid through VTDA funds. He is supervising activities/programmes undertaken by the VTDA/ITDAs or other agencies within in the village. The ITDA gave a cycle to the VLWs towards transportation. In a majority of villages the VLWs are meeting AO/HO or concerned sectoral officer once in a fortnight and informing about the crop conditions, horticulture plant conditions and progress of the work etc. If any precautionary measures, the same he is intimating to the villagers. But this type of things is not happening in all the villages. In some villages they are overseeing only horticulture crops. In some places they supervising the soil conservation works along with horticulture crops. They are not actually involving and not monitoring the irrigation, education and health aspects. The study team suggested to the VTDAs wherever the VLWs are not functioning effectively, they may be removed and take new person and same may be intimated to the PO, ITDA. This is for effective functioning of the VLW. In some villages the VLWs are assisting the women groups in maintenance of the accounts.

Women Thrift Groups

Until 1974, no attempt was made to deal separately with the problem of women. During 1974, a Committee on the status of women was formed to study the problems of poor and disadvantaged women. The Committee in its report (1979) 'Towards Equality' highlighted facts, such as declining sex ratio, lower female life expectancy, high maternal mortality, low female literacy etc.

During 2000-03 459 Women Self-Help Groups covering about 10,000 tribal families participated in execution of SMC works and turned out work worth Rs. 856.599 lakhs and saved Rs. 197.975 lakhs in their saving accounts till September-2003 which amounts to generation of 15,15,457 man days involving 10,000 tribal families in to tribal villages of Utnoor Agency in Adilabad District. The new approach has created tremendous impact on the rural Women Self Help Groups and now people from neighbouring villages where similar rural development works under DPAP, VSS, NWDAPRA are under implementation, are demanding the same approach. Recently, efforts are being initiated by ITDA, Utnoor in motivating the DPAP villages in 27 Watersheds allotted to ITDA for taking up Soil and Moisture Conservation Works. As a result, in PRA exercise conducted during micro plan preparation, 92 Women Self-Help Groups have come forward to take up work with the similar approach and saved amounts in their saving accounts which never happened earlier.

In the light of the above, the Study proposes to examine whether any change has occurred due to the implementation of development schemes in their quality of life, awareness, social mobility and improvement in their socio-economic conditions, their participation in the development activities etc., keeping in view the long-term objectives of strengthening the role of women in the development process, enabling their participation in social development and increasing their economic self-reliance. Various programmes for improving the access of women to basic services of health, child care, education, nutrition and sanitation etc., were implemented through the formation of women's' groups. The responsibility for forming such groups rests with the ITDA Officials/CDCs. There is supposed to be one CDC (Community Development Co-ordinator) for each mandal to see the functioning of the groups. During the project period, the salaries of the CDCs are met from the Project. It is seen that the formation of thrift groups in almost all the villages, has been completed. The achievement during the last four years was the formation of 413 groups with 5006 members against the target of 282 *i.e.* (146%).

The study tried to assess how the group empowerment activity was initiated and sustained, and whether the empowerment of women actually took place. It also considered the participation of non-government organizations in the ITDA's to help women thrift groups. As a result, a few alternatives are suggested for better functioning of the groups as well as the programmes.

The sample Study covered Utnoor ITDA of Adilabad district and 44 thrift groups from 40 villages. All these 44 groups were interviewed to assess the performance of the groups and impact of the programmes. These 44 groups studied include, active and non-functioning and ineffective groups.

The group leaders (President/Secretary) were interviewed on the basis of a questionnaire specially designed to capture their functioning and their role in the development process. In addition to this, information group discussions were held with CDCs/ADCs/VLWs and group members. The findings of the Study are presented in the following paragraphs.

Awareness/Motivation

The main purpose of extension education is to familiarize the target population with the aims and objectives of the Programme. In the absence of proper awareness, people do not identify the sponsored programmes and their success. In the Project area, the main sources of information to these people are VLWs and CDCs (86.4%) followed by other ITDA Officials (9%) and NGOs (4.5%). The Study found that many members (not group leaders) do not know about the ITDA programme and its aims and objectives. About 45 per cent of its members could explain one of the important programme called the IFAD Programme. The entire group members are not aware of the programmes relating to health, nutrition, and sanitation and child education. It is necessary for the field functionaries to explain the aims and objectives of the various programmes of ITDA. The CDC has to educate them in child health, sanitation and family welfare. It was observed that during the women thrift group meetings members are actively participating in the discussions.

Group Meetings

The groups meet once a month to discuss various issues relating to social, economic and other activities, besides thrift. About 14 per cent of the members are not attending the meetings regularly. The other 86 per cent attend the meetings regularly. During the group meetings, the members generally discuss about health, sanitation and savings and domestic expenditure. The group leaders said that a majority of the members (93.2%) co-operate with them. A majority of group leaders were elected by the members (97.7%). In each group, on an average, there are 15-20 members. After formation, all the groups start savings at the rate of Rs. 20 to 30 per month.

Except in few villages, in the rest of the study villages the participation and support of the NGOs, is absent. In other places, proper monitoring is lacking which resulted that some of the groups becoming non-functional (12%). They stopped their savings due to internal squabble. In such cases if the CDCs can motivate them properly by calling all the members, they can restart their activities. About 16 per cent of the group leaders participated in training programmes which is useful for better perception. About 37 per cent of groups were given matching grants to an extent of Rs. 5000 per group after completion of one year. The active groups are giving loans to the group members for the purpose of consumption (59.1%), farm inputs (34.1%) and investment (6.8%). The interest rate is 5 per cent. Those who want a loan, have to approach the group and the members will decide in the meeting whether assistance should be provided after examining the purpose and urgency, and decide the amount of loan not exceeding Rs. 5, 000.

During the group discussions, the members expressed dissatisfaction over the officials. They are supposed to visit the groups once a while and have frequent interaction, so that the women can build up confidence and mutual trust among themselves. At present, VLWs and VTDA are the most accessible persons followed by CDCs. The groups' performance is also very good. In one of the villages, they started economic activity by giving loans for purchase of sewing machines and goats. Those who have purchased sewing machines are planning to train some more members. The success stories reveal that these groups are not only saving but also lending for various purposes. In the meetings, the members exchange views and discuss other development activities which are implemented within the village. All the group meetings are taking place mostly at the group leaders' house/community centres/and Anganwadi centres.

Health and Education

Some more attention is needed to take care about health and sanitation aspects of students. During the visits of the study team, during rains the sanitary conditions were not adequate. Stagnation of water on the roads and near by ponds was observed which may cause malarial disease. During the team visit, there were incidence of fever and diahorrea in the villages. If the sanitary conditions are improved this can be averted. Regular visits of the Doctors/ANMs are to be ensured. The thrift group leaders/Anganwadi workers or educated girl children may be given training in basic health aspects and also provided with emergency safe medicines for fever, cough, diahorrea etc. The services of educated girls may be utilised in health and sanitation aspects by giving needed training.

Government and NGOs at all levels, including local authorities should ensure opportunities for women's so that they can participate in watershed development and other programmes. In every stage of watershed development women should involve, in designing, structure and site selection, execution and monitoring facilitates should be provided to improve increase women's access to environment and education about the watershed programme. Measures should be taken to integrate a gender perspective in the design and implementation of the programme and to empower women as producers and consumers, So that they can take effective environmental actions. Along with men women can also strengthen their crucial roles for better resource management and the conservation of environment.

Integrate rural women's traditional knowledge and practices of sustainable resource use and management in the watershed development which will encourage women participation. Girl and women education in science technology and economics should be promoted on a large scale so that they will get a good command in taking decisions towards watershed development programmes.

Identification and promotion of environmentally sound technologies that have been designed developed and improved in consultation with women. Technical assistance should be provided to women who are active in the watershed development programme and even in other development activities.

We should make them understand the benefits out of the watershed development and their role in the programmes. The focus should be shifted from watershed to livelihood development by making them understand that the watershed development finally improves the livelihood in addition to the environment. Addressing the issues like drinking water problem, fodder problem, fuel wood problems etc., will be as major issues and activities should be planned in implementation of various programmes. Naturally these topics will create interest in rural women and makes them to involve in the watershed programme.

Benefits out of the watershed programme especially in view of women are:

A reliable safe drinking water source within a reasonable distance and health and hygiene improvement. This helps the women's watershed needs for household purpose, livestock etc.

There will be a steady flow of income to ensure food, fuel and financial security work can be ensured in all stages of watershed development programme and after implementation, monitoring and development will create work. A secure future for their children through education will be ensured participation in household decision-making and community affairs.

The empowerments of women through watershed development activities bring them sustainable economic independence and make them involve in such development activities in future too. By paying greater attention to non-land based activities and seeking to redress inequities it is hoped that this will encourage the involvement of women in the programmes especially by taking account of their needs and interests.

The formation of VTDAs on the lines of the traditional village association, which already exists in many villages and their promotion into a community development institute, has enabled them to take up all village development activities through their participation. The agency is responsible for identifying the village priorities, identifying beneficiaries to implement the developmental activities and to protect environmental degradation. The agency may form women's groups to activate them in the developmental process, water users' association, conduct household and natural resource surveys, have discussions with elders and youth for the development of the village which gives them the necessary encouragement to increase community participation in development.

The success of any programme mainly depends upon the proper identification of beneficiaries, who really require assistance. The study revealed that in the case of 96 per cent of beneficiaries were identified on the basis of household survey, and they were selected in the gramsabha meeting.

Perception of Households Regarding the Programme/Schemes

Sl. No.	Question	Yes %	No %	No. of Respondents
1.	Are you started savings regularly?	88.6	11.4	44
2.	Group members are co-operating?	93.2	6.8	44
3.	Sanction of matching grant	38.6	61.4	44
4.	Economic activity	11.4	88.6	44
5.	All the members are attending meeting?	86.4	13.6	44
6.	Consider the ideas of group members?	86.4	13.6	44
7.	Support from NGOs/other agencies?	18.2	81.8	44
8.	Training in maintenance of accounts?	15.9	84.1	44
9.	Payments are regular?	86.4	13.6	44
10.	Advice from VLW/NGO/ Members?	63.6	36.4	44
11.	Facing any problems?	2.3	97.7	44

Under Community Participation and Development Programme, women thrift groups were formed in each village. It is observed that excepting in few mandals; all the women thrift groups are functioning well. All the members are regularly meeting at their group leaders (presidents) house and handing over their monthly savings. The groups are also lending among themselves for consumption, health, agricultural and marriage purposes at 5 per cent interest. These members are also repaying the loan amount with interest regularly. All most all the groups have got the matching grant from the ITDAs.

They are maintaining the prescribed registers properly by writing about the minutes, about member's individual contribution, loan payment and repayments, decisions taken in that meeting with the help of the VLW or educated youths. They are also discussing about health and sanitation aspects. Some of the groups are giving loans for income generating schemes such as goat rearing, sewing machines, kirana shop etc., to their members. This shows awareness among the tribal women in savings and earnings through off-farm activities.

Social mobilization enables the poor to build their organizations (Self-Help Groups) at grassroots level, in which they participate fully and directly and take decisions on all the issues concerning poverty. The government will foster mobilization and organizations of the poor and empower them to address various issues concerning poverty. The ongoing efforts in facilitating the formation and development of the Self-Help Groups of the poor, especially DWCRA groups in the rural areas, DWCUA groups in the urban areas, mothers committees, school education committees, watershed committees, and vanasamrakshan samithies would be sustained. Through these Self-Help Groups, the poor are able to harness their potential, prioritize their needs, design and implement developmental initiatives. The government would pursue policies to SHG movement and their participation in the programmes critical to poverty eradication.

With the Self-Help Groups as the building blocks, the community based organsations (CBOs) of the poor are emerging at habitation, cluster and mandal level. The government would encourage this process, so that the poor would be able to articulate their demands effectively and manage the developmental initiative professionally. The government would facilitate development of self-managed, self-reliant and vibrant organizations of the poor, at village, mandal and district level such as mutually aided co-operatives societies (MACS) of women being formed at mandal level in many districts.

Capacity building of the SHGs and their federations will be given adequate attention. The government would develop state, district and mandal level training capabilities so that the capacity building of the members of the organization is taken up depending on the need and the demand of the groups. The government would put in position an effective mechanism to regularly undertake the rating of the groups so that developmental inputs can be targeted in a more transparent way. The organizations of the poor, being participatory bodies will forge harmonious partnership with the representative bodies such as Gram panchayats and Mandal Parishads and Municipal bodies.

The growth impulses in the economy should focus on generating sustainable livelihood opportunities for the poor. This can come through natural resource regeneration such as watershed and wasteland development. These protect the poor communities from adverse climatic conditions such as droughts, erratic distribution of rainfall and excess rainfall; enhance their opportunities for employment and incomes.

An important concern in watershed development is the equitable distribution of the benefits of land and water resources development and the consequent biomass production. Public investment of a large magnitude is being made in both private lands and in common public property. Therefore the right of each individual in the village to an equitable share of the common lands, forest and water resources of the village regardless of his individual private land holding would be recognised and addressed through effective means. The support for micro-watershed development will be routed through the SHGs of the poor to ensure that the works taken up are demand driven and based on their felt needs, thereby ensuring better targeting of the interventions in favour of the poor.

Andhra Pradesh has taken bold steps to demonstrate that a convergence of conservation and development objectives can be achieved through Joint Forest Management (JFM). Pursuing one of the most proactive JFM programmes in India, the State has committed to the user groups, 100 per cent of usufruct forest produce secured from the area entrusted to the JFM committees. Widespread implementation of JFM is leading to an increased flow (both value and volume) of forest products to communities and an increase in environmental benefits resulting from improved forest condition (principally with respect to soil and water regimes). Formation of JFM Committees in Andhra Pradesh has successfully targeted remote and under-served communities, in particular tribal populations. Government is committed to ensure the success and spread of this process.

All the departments of the government will be sensitive to the issues concerning poverty and poverty eradication shall become the priority. The departments would be reoriented to look at development as an opportunity to bring changes in the lives of the poor. Each department would be mandated to articulate clearly as how the departments programmes address the poverty.

Transparency and accountability will become the hallmark of the government's interface with the people, especially the poor. The departments would revisit the procedures, processes and guidelines and make necessary changes to give space for participation of the poor through SHGs in designing, prioritizing, implementing and monitoring their developmental programmes. The government is implementing Velugu under APDPIP which aims at poverty eradication. Considering the inadequacies in the past developmental strategies in reaching the poorest of the poor, this programme mandated to focus on the poorest of the poor, who have been left out of various development initiatives.

Success stories are often cited to show that the programmes can be successful, but there may be very very few success stories. The system can be improved if there is a committed leadership and committed bureaucracy is there. The government realised that if the programmes have to be success, people should be involved in planning and implementation, bureaucratic procedures have to be simplified and funds should be directly transferred to the people. The concept of 3-tier system of administration gained importance. Government realised that the PRI should play a crucial in poverty alleviation programmes. Top-down approach gave a way to the decentralized planning. People's participation is the key word in the development.

The answer lies in social mobilization and empowerment of the community. An organized and aware community has to be involved in planning, implementation and monitoring of the programmes. Poor have to be mobilized and empowered so that they can effectively participate in the programmes meant for them. The development paradigm today puts the focus of development on the people and their participation. After joining SHG they are becoming literate, sending children to schools, going for family planning, keeping their environments clean. The encouraging response to the programme has raised a hope that an empowered community can solve their basic minimum needs themselves without middlemen provided government comes forward positively to solve their problems. They are participating in the watershed programmes and other wage employment programmes etc.

Conclusions

The study reveals that the programmes have brought some significant changes in the tribal development scene.

When participatory approach has been introduced the results are some what encouraging. The communities are taking up active role in the planning and implementation of the programmes. It contributes to the sustainability of the development efforts as the community has a stake in the success of the works. Development emphasis has changed from one of merely increasing employment opportunities for tribals by way of labour input programmes, executed and monitoring and empowering them as partners with a stake in the improvement of the natural resource base of their economy. Village development committees have become actively involved in planning and implementation, and participating in construction works. The programmes have made considerable efforts to develop participatory approach. A considerable transformation in approach to tribal development is taking place which is leading towards the establishment of sustainable village institutions.

REFERENCES

Action for Equality, Development and Peace, The United Nations Fourth World Conference on Women, Beijing, China – Sept. 1995.

Agarwal, B. 1994 A Filed of One's Own, Cambridge University Press, New Delhi.

D'Souza, M. 1999, Watershed Development: Creating Space for Women. In Farrington, J., Turton, C, and James, AJ (eds). Participatory Watershed Development. Challenges for the Twenty First Century. Oxford University Press, New Delhi.

Government of India. 1994 Guidelines for Watershed Development, Ministry of Rural Development, Government of India, New Delhi.

Government of India, 2001, District Census Hand Book, Adilabad District.

Rao, R. 1999. Gender and Participation in Watershed Management. In: Farrington J., Turton, C. and James AJ (eds). Participatory Watershed Development, Challenges for the Twenty – First Century. Oxford University Press, New Delhi.

Rama Mohan K. R. and V. Subramanyam, 2002., The Role of Forest in Tribal life: An Anthropological Study In the Eastern Ghats of Andhra Prdesh, Pondicherry University Journal of Social Sciences and Humanities Vol. 3 No. 2 pp. 67-82.

Sarkar B.. (ed) 1989; Social Perspective of Generation and Utilisation of Indigenous Science and Technology, Indian Academy of Social Sciences, Allahabad, India.

Saxena, N.C. (no date), Women in Forestry, unpublished Manuscript.

Subramanyam V, 2001, Tribes and Ecology of Andhra Pradesh: An Anthropological Study, in the Science of Man in Service of Man (ed) M. K. Bhasin and S. L. Malik, Department of Anthropology, University of Delhi, Delhi pp. 49.61.

UNDP (1998): "Human Development Report 1997 – 98" UNDP, New York.

14

Tribals and Social Justice

G. D. Kharat*

INTRODUCTION

India is the second largest country in the World after S. Africa Continent in terms of tribal population and communities. There are 370 million Indigenous People in some 90 Countries in the World. Tribal's share in the global population is about 6 per cent. Tribal population of India is 84.3 million and its share to the total population is 8.26 per cent as per the Census of 2001. There are near about 700 Scheduled Tribes in India of which most of overlapping. India started its tribal development programme through TSP from 1974-75. TSP (Tribal Sub-Plan) Strategy seeks to ensure adequate flow of funds for tribal development from the State plan allocations, schemes and programmes of Central Ministries and Departments besides financial and developmental institutions in proportions to tribal population. Madhya Pradesh,

* Associate Professor, M. G. Vidyamandir's Loknete Vyankatrao Hiray Mahavidyalaya, Panchavati, Nashik – 422 003. Maharashtra. E-mail: gdkharat@gmail.com. Mobile: 9960369291.

Maharashtra, Orissa, Gujarat and Rajasthan are the main TSP States having the largest share of tribal population in India. Tribals occupied the notable share in Indian population and they found all over the country. Tribals contribution in economy and environmental balance is noteworthy. Rich culture and social heritage is the integral part of tribal society. Social justice to these downtrodden is the challenging task before the Government in planning era. Tribals are the most neglected citizens in terms of socio-economic development and welfare.

Research Methodology

This Paper highlights the picture about social justice of tribals in India. Information and Data about the Research Paper has been collected from the various secondary sources such as Websites, Research Articles, Government Reports, Journals and Reference Books.

Objectives

1. To study the socio-economic status of tribals in India.
2. To focus on the various issues regarding social justice of tribals in India.
3. To suggest the solutions towards social justice for tribals in India.

Definition

The concept of tribal is defined through socio-economic and cultural aspects at the world level. Tribals are referred differently as Adivasis, Scheduled Tribes, Aboriginals, Natives and Indigenous People in the world. The United Nations Permanent Forum has accepted the term Indigenous People. Tribals are known as Scheduled Tribes as per the Constitution of India.

ILO Convention No. 169 Article 1d

"Tribal people in Independent Countries whose social, cultural and economic conditions distinguish them from other sections of the national community and whose status is regulated wholly or partially by their own customs or traditions or by special laws or regulations".

Constitution of India Article 342(1)

"Those Communities which have been declared as such by the President through an initial Public Notification or through a subsequent Amending Act of Parliament will be considered to be Schedule Tribes".

Need of Social Justice

Man is a social animal. There should be provision to fulfillment of social, economic, political, cultural and educational needs of the society in any social system. If the discrimination on the basis of religion, caste, gender and race exists in the society, then the goal of achieving social justice becomes very difficult. Social justice is a natural right of each and every citizen of the country. Indian social structure is discriminative and exploitive for the weaker section particularly for SC and ST. To overcome with all social evils, Indian Constitution provides safeguards to the people who are facing continuously the problem of social injustice.

Concept of Social Justice

"Social justice is the broad, inclusive and concept which deals with equal social status, political representation and economic development opportunities to the people of the society".

Parameters of Social Justice

- *Social Equality:* Equal and Class-Casteles social structure is the basic criteria of social justice. The social structure should provide equal status to all. Each and every citizen should get the development opportunities as per their will and capacity.
- *Political Representation:* Each and every section of the society should get the political representation as per the proportion of population. Share in the political system is the fundamental right of the people belonging to the society.
- *Economic Development:* All the people should get the economic development opportunities without discriminating on the basis of wealth and income.

Decentralization of economic power and eradication of economic inequality should be the targets of the Government for the overall and equal economic development.

Table 14.1: Constitutional protection to the scheduled tribes

Sl. No.	Constitution Article	Provision
1.	Article 6	Right to work
2.	Article 12	Right to live and health
3.	Article 13 and 14	Right to education
4.	Article 15	Right to cultural life
5.	Article 15(4)	Special Provision about Education
6.	Article 16(4)	Service Reservation
7.	Article 17	Right to freedom
8.	Article 21	Right to livelihood
9.	Article 23 and 24	Prohibition of human trafficking and Child Labour
10.	Article 29	Prohibition of Social injustice and exploitation
11.	Article 46	States obligation towards socio-economic development
12.	Article 243(D)	Village and ZP Reservation
13.	Article 243(T)	Corporation and Municipal Reservation
14.	Article 244	Provision about Scheduled and Tribal Area
15.	Article 275(1)	Provision of Funding for Welfare
16.	Article 330	Reservation in Parliament
17.	Article 332	Reservation in Legislative Assembly
18.	Article 335	Relaxation in marks of various Examination
19.	Article 338	Provision of National Commission
20.	Article 342(1)	Definition of Scheduled Tribe
21.	Article 350(A)	Provision about Primary Education in Mother tongue

Reference – Constitution of India.

Table 14.2: State of tribals in india

Tribal population (million)

Census Year	Total Population	Tribal Population	% of Tribal Population
1951	361.1	19.1	5.29
1961	439.2	30.1	6.85
1971	548.2	38.0	6.93
1981	685.2	51.6	7.53
1991	846.3	67.8	8.10
2001	1028.6	84.3	8.26
2011	1210.1	NA	NA

Reference – www.tribal.nic.in/html page 2 of 3 and 3 of 3.

Tribal population was 19.1 million in 1951 which has increased to 84.3 million in 2001. The share of tribal population in the total population has increased to 8.26 from 5.29 per cent in these 50 years.. Tribal population has increased after 1971 rapidly. Bogus registration as a tribal, abolition of area restriction act, first time registration and beneficiary approach are the main reasons of increasing tribal population as per the report of NCST. 92 per cent of tribals are still living in rural area while only 8 per cent are the part of urban India. The tribal population has increased in planned era but the bogus registration as a tribal is the alarming issue in India. Tribal rights regarding employment and development scheme benefits are snatched by the bogus intruders in India.

Table 14.3: Tribal literacy in india (%)

Census Year	Male	Female	Total
1961	13.83	3.16	8.53
1971	17.63	4.85	11.30
1981	24.52	8.04	16.35
1991	40.65	18.19	29.00
2001	59.17	34.76	47.10
2011	NA	NA	NA

Reference – www.tribal.nic.in.

The overall, male and female tribal literacy is 47.10 per cent, 59.17 per cent and 34.76 per cent respectively as per the census of 2001. The role of Government responsibilities of women and their changing status, functioning of Ashram schools, poverty, and migration are the reasons of unsatisfactory performance on literacy front especially for women. Tribal literacy is increasing but women and rural illiteracy is still the hurdle to overall development.

Table 14.4: Male – female ratio

Census Year	General	Tribal
1971	930	982
1981	934	984
1991	927	972
2001	933	978
2011	NA	NA

Reference – Registrar General and Census Commissioner, Government of India, New Delhi.

Decreasing ratio of women is the burning issue in India. Tribals are comparatively ahead on the front of sex ratio between women and men than main stream society. Tribal sex ratio is much better than us due to high social status of tribal women. The figures of 2001 explain that mainstream and tribal sex ratio is 933 and 982 respectively. Tribal women are respected in their society, but the contact and following of mainstream society has responsible for inside as well as outside problems. Empowerment of tribal women through education, health services, proper political representation and development opportunities is the need of hour. Tribal women are the victims of exploitation and injustice. The mainstream should follow the tribal society to maintain the proper sex ratio.

Tribal economy is still livelihood base economy in this market and commercial era. Agriculture, Agriculture labour and Cottage industries are the features of tribal economy. The dependence on agriculture is decreasing while dependence on agriculture labour is increasing. Agriculture development

Table 14.5: Tribal occupational classification (%)

Occupation	1961	1971	1981	1991	2001
Agriculture	68.18	57.56	54.43	54.50	50.90
Agri. Labour	19.71	33.04	32.67	32.67	28.40
Home Industries	2.47	1.03	1.42	1.04	1.80
Other	9.64	8.37	11.84	11.76	18.90

Reference – Annual Report 2003-04, Tribal Affairs Ministry, Government of India. Document of 11th Plan, Chapter 6.

is the main objective of TSP in India which is not fulfilled in planned era. Problems of agriculture from ownership of land to modernization are still exists and the new economic policy is also increased the complications. The share of other livelihood sources such as services and self-employment are increasing but the tempo is not as per the requirement.

Table 14.6: Political representation in india

Category	Village Panchayat (2001)	Panchayat Samiti (2001)	Jilha Parishad (2001)	Total (2001)	Vidhan Sabha (2009)	Lok Sabha (2009)
General	2580261	128581	13484	2722326	4150	545
Tribal	235445	7237	1170	243852	544	47
% of Tribals	9.1	5.6	8.7	9.0	13.10	8.62

Reference – General Election Handbook 2009, Rural Development Department, National Information Centre, Sansad Bhavan, Government of India, New Delhi.

Tribal political representation from root level Village Panchayat to Loksabha is as per the Constitutional provisions and population proportion. 9 per cent tribals are involved in the Village politics but most of them functioning as a rubber stamp. Out of 4150 Vidhan Sabha Seats, 544 seats are occupied by the tribal all over India. Tribal representatives in Loksabha are 47 out of 545 total seats. Tribal unity is not possible in politics due to various party banners. Most of the tribals are not well educated and aware about their rights. Tribal representative's attitude towards society is not much better. They lack political willpower to solve various problems of the society. Most of the representatives are engaged in self-progressive activities. They are not interested in various debates about tribal development, policy-making and its effective implementation.

Table 14.7: Poverty (%)

Year	General		SC		ST	
	Rural	Urban	Rural	Urban	Rural	Urban
1993-94	37.27	32.36	48.11	49.48	51.94	41.14
1999-00	27.11	23.65	36.25	38.47	45.86	34.75
2004-05	28.30	25.70	36.80	39.90	47.30	33.30

Reference – NSSO various Rounds including 61st Round.

Poverty is the basic problem of tribals in India. Most of the tribal families are BPL families in our country. Tribal development programmes are not much succeeded to tackle out the problem of poverty. In the reform era, General and SC poverty is declined as per the NSSO but tribal poverty is still big issue particularly in rural area. Negligence on development front, illiteracy and loopholes in the TSP implementation are the main reasons of tribal poverty. In 1993-94 General, SC and ST poverty in rural India was 37.27, 48.11 and 51.94 respectively. In 2004-05, General, SC and ST poverty has declined to 28.30, 36.80 and 47.30 respectively. These figures explain that near about 50 per cent rural tribals are still facing the problem of survival. Urban General, SC and ST poverty in 1993-94 was 32.36, 49.48 and 41.14 respectively. 2004-05 figures about Urban General, SC and ST poverty were 25.70, 39.90 and 33.30 respectively. Only 8 per cent tribals are living in urban area while the General and SC figures are much more than tribals.

As per the Government strategy, 9 per cent of budget fund is reserved for the tribals under the banner of TSP (Tribal Sub-Plan). The proper implementation of this strategy is the big problem in India. There is a huge backlog of TSP funding as per the various reports and records published by the Government.

Table 14.8: Tribal development provision (crores)

Plan	Total Provision	Tribal Development Provision	% of Tribal Development
I Plan (1951-56)	1960	19.93	0.60
II Plan (1956-61)	4672	42.92	0.50
III Plan (1961-66)	8577	50.53	0.50
IV Plan (1969-74)	15902	79.85	3.0
V Plan (1974-79)	38853	1157.67	3.7
VI Plan (1979-84)	97500	3640.25	3.8
VII Plan (1984-89)	180000	6744.85	5.2
VIII Plan (1990-95)	434100	22409.65	3.7
IX Plan (1995-2000)	859200	32087.26	–
X Plan (2002-07)	1637664	NA	NA
XI Plan (2007-12)	5507215.64	NA	NA
XII	NA	NA	NA

Reference – Occasional Paper on Tribal Development 1966, Page 1, 19, 20 Home Ministry, Government of India.

The funding provision as per the population is not achieved due to various bottlenecks and hurdles in the bureaucracy. Tribals are facing the problem of livelihood due to deforestation, acquisition of tribal land, displacement and the entrance of various selfish intruders in their habitant. As per the Article 12 of our Constitution, every citizen got the right to live with dignity. Tribals are still struggling to get the status of citizens of this country and our system and policies denied their rights.

Agriculture and labour is the main means of living for tribals in India. Tribals got the right to work and reservation in services as per the Article 6 and 16(4) of our Constitution. There is a 7 per cent reservation for tribals in India but the backlog of ST is exists in various departments and cadres. Most of the tribals are engaged in C and D Category's jobs while A and B Category posts are still vacant due to unavailability of qualified candidates.

Table 14.9: Central government service representation as on 1.1.2005

Group	Total	ST	% of ST
A	80589	3448	4.30
B	139958	6230	4.50
C	2036103	131678	6.50
D	767224	53032	6.90
Sweeper	81174	4012	4.90
Total (excluding sweeper)	3023874	194388	6.43
Total (including sweeper)	3105048	198400	6.39

Reference – Annual Report 2005-06 Ministry of Personnel, Public Grievances and Pensions, Government of India, New Delhi.

Table 14.10: Tribal enrolment (%)

Year	Primary	Higher Primary	Secondary	Higher	Professional and Technical
1995-96	8.8	6.1	4.9	3.1	3.6
1996-97	9.2	6.3	4.9	3.1	3.8
1998-99	9.6	6.7	5.1	3.1	4.0
1999-00	9.4	6.9	5.0	3.1	4.1
2001-02	9.7	7.2	5.4	3.0	4.1
2002-03	9.7	6.9	5.4	4.3	4.6

Reference – Secondary and Higher Education Section, Selected Statistics 2003-04.

Education is the base of tribal development. Tribal enrollment to the total enrollment at various levels is still not much satisfactory as per the HRD statistics. In 1995-96, the enrollment figures for primary, secondary, higher and technical education were 7.5, 1.9, 3.1 and 3.6 per cent respectively. These figures are slightly increased as 8.2, 5.4, 4.3 and 4.6 per cent respectively in 2002-03.

Tribal indebtness, poverty, lack of infrastructure and quality education, migration are the basic reasons of huge tribal drop-out rate. The drop-out rate for various States and

Table 14.11: Tribal drop-out (2005-06)

State	I to V			VI to VIII			I to X		
	Boys	Girls	Total	Boys	Girls	Total	Boys	Girls	Total
Bihar	49.71	44.17	48.00	75.8	72.66	74.15	89.35	87.49	88.27
Gujarat	40.56	40.91	40.72	61.76	68.18	64.70	73.30	72.39	72.79
Kerala	2.18	5.81	1.78	9.44	14.02	11.64	48.26	53.75	51.10
Maharashtra	28.32	27.67	28.01	47.03	46.40	46.73	59.35	61.30	60.40
Manipur	46.77	56.79	51.58	56.27	62.69	59.51	71.27	71.50	71.40
A and N	18.38	25.79	22.24	34.20	34.81	34.47	27.75	29.35	28.57
India	49.13	48.47	48.93	69.04	71.43	70.05	81.16	77.92	79.25

Reference – Secondary and Higher Education Section, Selected Statistics 2003-04.

educational level is varies in India. Girls drop-out is burning problem due to family responsibilities and lack of safety and security. Most of the tribal ashram schools are functioning as a centre's of exploitation instead of development. Maharashtra, Kerala are performing better than Bihar and other States but the drop-out problem is the national issue and it is hurdle to tribal development.

Table 14.12: Displacement 1951 to 1991 (lakhs)

Development Project	Total			Tribal		
	Dis-placed	Rehabilities	Back-log	Dis-placed	Rehabilities	Back-log
Dams	140	35.00	105.00	53.00	13.15	39.45
Mines	21	5.25	15.75	12.00	3.00	9.00
Industries	13	3.25	9.50	2.60	0.65	1.95
National Park	6	1.50	4.50	5.00	1.25	3.75
Other	5	1.25	3.75	1.50	1.40	1.10
Total	**185**	**46.25**	**138.75**	**74.10**	**19.45**	**55.25**

Reference – ISI 1994.

Tribals are the most displaced people of the country. They have sacrificed their livelihood and resources for the sake of development projects of the country. Dam and mine projects are mostly responsible for tribal displacement. Near about 20 million people were displaced in India since 1951 to 1991 of which 40 per cent displaced people were tribals. More than 70 per cent displaced tribals are still waiting for proper rehabilitation and resettlement. The chart shows that dam and mine projects, national park, industrial development and other are the main reasons of displacement. The sacrifice of displaced people should be taken seriously but instead of paying price to them the main society and Government has neglected them. The right of these displaced people should be respected and the implementation of proper R and R policy is the need of hour. Society is against the development projects because the strategy about displacement. Only 50 millions are resettled of which 20 million were tribals. Near about 150 million are still waiting for resettlement of which 60 million were tribals. The displacement has denied the right to live. Overall development is the price paid by displaced people especially tribals of the country.

Table 14.13: State of atrocities in india

Year	Total Complaints	Settled Complaints	Convicted Complaints	% of Conviction to Settled
2001	152917	16203	1965	12.13
2002	162817	33606	3748	11.15
2003	147952	20638	2727	13.21
2004	141881	20750	3259	15.71
2005	126762	24511	7110	29.01
2006	101008	24180	6782	28.04
Total	**833337**	**139888**	**23626**	**16.88**

Reference – National Crime Records Bureau.

Table 14.14: Registered cases

Year	PCR Act	Atrocities Act	Total
1997	88	643	731
1998	50	709	759
1999	45	574	619

Reference – National Human Rights Commission.

Injustice to women's especially SC, ST and their inside and outside exploitation is the unsolved issue after 65 years of independence. There is a caste base discrimination in urban and rural India in different form. Constitutional safeguards are meant to abolish such incidences in India. The data shows that we are not able to control the atrocities. The rate of settlement and conviction is not satisfactory. Loopholes in the legal system, political pressure and corrupt administration are responsible for the exploitation and injustice to the weaker section. Our social system and mentality of the so called mainstream is not supportive to banning such incidences.

Recommendations

- Mahatma Phule was the first social reformer who spoke for the social justice to tribals through his writings. M. Phule focused on the fact that tribals are the aboriginals while others are the intruders. Tribals were forcefully pushed towards forestry. Thoughts of Mahatma Phule about tribal rights should be considered to minimize the widening gap between mainstream society and tribals.
- Dr. B. R. Ambedkar's efforts through constitutional provisions for equal opportunity are the beginning steps towards social justice for SC and ST. The socio-economic and political transformation is the outcome of Constitutional provisions but there are still limitations about the social justice for tribals. Dr. Ambedkar's 'move towards urban cities' mantra should be implemented in this discriminative society.
- TSP is implemented since 1975-76 but the real change hasn't taken place about the status of tribals in India. Tribals should be involved in the decision making process instead of implementation of routine mechanism.
- Constitutional safeguards to the SC and ST is the price of traditional and social negligence. The mentality of the main society should be changed and the tribals should be aware about their rights.

- Tribal leadership should lead the society for the upliftment. Tribals should become a 'Vote Bank' for socio-economic transformation and justice.
- The globalisation has increased the problems of tribals in India. They need safeguards in this global era to get the developmental opportunities.
- There is huge developmental gap among the various tribes. This gap should be removed through providing educational, health facilities and schemes in the remote area.
- Establishment of tribal university, increased share in higher education must get the priority in the process of planning in India.
- The effective and honest implementation of reservation policy is must for social transformation.
- The criteria's about the BPL families should be changed and the modification is needed to get the proper information about the standard of living of the tribal's in India.
- Self-help groups should be promoted for empowerment of tribal women.

Conclusions

Tribals struggle to survive is still going on after the completion of 65 years of independence. Forest contractors have replaced the traditional landlords. Ashram schools should function as a centre's of development instead of exploitation. The original beneficiary of the development schemcs is disappeared in the crowd of bogus beneficiaries. Naxal movement is the outcome of hunger, exploitation and injustice. Tribals deaths due to malnutrition in Maharashtra, victims of police firing in Orissa, Struggle of Meena's in Gujrat, Marketing of PVTG'S from Andaman, Cases of bogus loans in the names of Tribals in M. P. and clash between Ranveer Sena and MCC these are the examples of their desperate position in India.

TSP is responsible for affirmative changes in the tribal life but there is a huge gap between various tribes according to opportunities, development, welfare and treatment as a human being. India needs efforts to maintain social justice through various schemes and its effective implementation for the tribal. The State Governments are responsible for socio-economic and educational development of tribal as per the Article 46 of the Constitution but the performance has to be improved. The various study reports reveals that target oriented approach is not the answer. Uniformed strategy is not suitable for the scattered and variety of ST's in India. TSP Strategy needs to be reformulation and proper implementation for the overall tribal development.

Although, the picture is changing affirmatively for the tribals which should be generalised on various fronts. India is the largest democracy and secular country of the world. Caste base society is the defective feature of India's social structure. There is a huge gap between sections of the society according to opportunities, development, welfare and treatment as a human being due to defective social system of India. India needs efforts to maintain social justice through various schemes and effective programmes for the downtrodden people. The inclusive and effective programmes of development and its sincere implementation is the need of hour. Mainstream society, political representatives, NGO's and tribals should contribute integrally for the social justice.

REFERENCES

Ph. D. Thesis entitled "Critical Evaluation of Integrated Tribal Development Programme Nashik District (Maharashtra), Submitted to University of Pune, Pune, Maharashtra.

2009, "The State of the Worlds Indigenous Peoples", Department of Economic and Social Affairs, Division for Social Policy and Development, Secretariat of The Permanent Forum on Indigenous Issues, United Nations, New York.

2009, "General Election", Reference Book, Ministry of Information and Broadcasting, Government of India, India.

2008, "A Shadow Report to the UN Committee on Economic, Social and Cultural Rights" AITDN, Janakpuri, New Delhi. May 2008.

M. Nagaraju, Director, Tribal Welfare, TSP Strategy – Concept, Practice and Relevance.

2007 – Standing Committee on Social Justice and Empowerment, Ministry of Tribal Affairs, 25th Report, LokSabha Secretariat, April 2007.

Websites

http://www.india.gov.in/

http://www.maharashtra.gov.in/

http:www.planningcommissionofindia.in/

http:www.tribal.nic.in/

http:www.trti.mah.nic.in/

15

Programmes and Policies for Tribal Development

Dr. R. B. Sathyavathi*
C. Chenchuprasad**

For the first time after the country became Independent, the Government of India is proposing the formulation of a National Policy on Scheduled Tribes.

The policy seeks to bring Scheduled Tribes into the mainstream of society through a multi-pronged approach for their all-round development without disturbing their distinct culture.

There are 67.8 million Scheduled Tribe people, constituting 8.08 per cent of India's population. There are 698 Scheduled Tribes spread all over the country barring States and Union Territories like Chandigarh, Delhi, Haryana, Pondicherry and Punjab. Orissa has the largest number – 68 – of Scheduled Tribes.

Scheduled Tribes are those, which are notified as such by the President of India under Article 342 of the Constitution.

---

* Assistant Professor.

** Research Scholar, Department of Adult and Continuing Education, S. V. University, Tirupati - 517 502. Andhra Pradesh. Mobile: 9440860859.

The first notification was issued in 1950. The President considers characteristics like the tribes' primitive traits, distinctive culture, shyness with the public at large, geographical isolation and social and economic backwardness before notifying them as a Scheduled Tribe. Seventy-five of the 698 Scheduled Tribes are identified as Primitive Tribal Groups considering they are more backward than Scheduled Tribes. They continue to live in a pre-agricultural stage of economy and have very low literacy rates. Their populations are stagnant or even declining.

The Constitution through several Articles has provided for the socio-economic development and empowerment of Scheduled Tribes. (You may list the provisions here, if necessary). But there has been no national policy, which could have helped translate the constitutional provisions into a reality. Five principles spelt out in 1952, known as Nehruvian Panchasheel, have been guiding the administration of tribal affairs. They are:

1. Tribals should be allowed to develop according to their own genius.
2. Tribals' rights in land and forest should be respected.
3. Tribal teams should be trained to undertake administration and development without too many outsiders being inducted.
4. Tribal development should be undertaken without disturbing tribal social and cultural institutions.
5. The index of tribal development should be the quality of their life and not the money spent.

Realising that the Nehruvian Panchasheel was long on generalities and short on specifics, the Government of India formed a Ministry of Tribal Affairs for the first time in October 1999 to accelerate tribal development. The Ministry of Tribal Affairs is now coming out with the draft National Policy on Tribals. Based on the feedback from tribal leaders, the concerned States, individuals, organizations in the public and the private sectors, and NGOs, the Ministry will finalise the policy.

The National Policy recognises that a majority of Scheduled Tribes continue to live below the poverty line, have poor literacy rates, suffer from malnutrition and disease and are vulnerable to displacement. It also acknowledges that Scheduled Tribes in general are repositories of indigenous knowledge and wisdom in certain aspects.

The National Policy aims at addressing each of these problems in a concrete way. It also lists out measures to be taken to preserve and promote tribals' cultural heritage.

Formal Education

Formal education is the key to all-round human development. Despite several campaigns to promote formal education ever since Independence, the literacy rate among Scheduled Tribes is only 29.60 per cent compared to 52.21 per cent for the country as a whole (1991 census). The female literacy rate is only 18.19 per cent compared to the national female literacy rate of 39.29 per cent. Alienation from the society, lack of adequate infrastructure like schools, hostels and teachers, abject poverty and apathy towards irrelevant curriculum have stood in the way of tribals getting formal education.

To achieve the objective of reaching the benefit of education to tribals, the National Policy will ensure that:

- Tribals are included in the national programme of Sarva Shiksha Abhiyan run by the Ministry of Human Resource Development.
- Schools and hostels are opened in areas where no such facilities exist.
- At least one model residential school is located in each tribal concentration area.
- Education is linked with provision of supplementary nutrition.
- Special incentives like financial assistance, pocket allowance, free distribution of text-books and school uniforms are provided.

- Teaching is imparted in tribals' mother tongue at least up to the primary level. Educated tribal youth are given employment as teachers, wherever possible. (This will obviate the need to employ teachers belonging to far-off places who find commuting is as difficult as staying in a village with no basic amenities.
- Pedagogy is made relevant so that tribals do not find it as alien.
- Curriculum and cocurriculum include aspects of meta skill up-gradation of tribal children.
- Curricula for meta skill up-gradation are to include aspects of tribal games and sports, archery, identification of plants of medicinal value, crafts art and culture, folk dance and folk songs, folk paintings etc.
- Emphasis is laid on vocational/professional education. Polytechnics are set up for studies in subjects like forestry, horticulture, dairying, veterinary sciences, polytechnics.

Traditional Wisdom

Dwelling amidst hills, forests, coastal areas, deserts, tribals over the centuries have gained precious and vast experience in combating environmental hardships and leading sustainable livelihoods. Their wisdom is reflected in their water harvesting techniques, indigenously developed irrigation channels, construction of cane bridges in hills, adaptation to desert life, utilisation of forest species like herbs, shrubs for medicinal purposes, meteorological assessment etc. Such invaluable knowledge of theirs needs to be properly documented and preserved lest it should get lost in the wake of modernisation and passage of time.

The National Policy seeks to:

- Preserve and promote such traditional knowledge and wisdom and document it.
- Establish a centre to train tribal youth in areas of traditional wisdom.
- Disseminate such through models and exhibits at appropriate places.
- Transfer such knowledge to non-tribal areas.

Health

Although tribal people live usually close to nature, a majority of them need health care on account of malnutrition, lack of safe drinking water, poor hygiene and environmental sanitation and above all poverty. Lack of awareness and apathy to utilise the available health services also affect their health status. In wake of the opening of tribal areas with highways industrialization, and communication facilities, diseases have spread to tribal areas. Endemics like malaria, deficiency diseases, venereal diseases including AIDS are not uncommon among tribal populations. However, lack of safe drinking water and malnutrition are well-recognised major health hazards. Tribals suffer from a deficiency of calcium, vitamin A, vitamin C, riboflavin and animal protein in their diets. Malnutrition and undernutrition are common among Primitive Tribal Groups who largely depend upon food they either gather or raise by using simple methods. The poor nutritional status of tribal women directly influences their reproductive performance and their infants' survival, growth and development.

Tribal people, who are self-reliant and self-sufficient, have over the centuries developed their own medicine system based on herbs and other items collected from the nature and processed locally. They have also their own system of diagnosis and cure of diseases. They believe in taboos, spiritual powers and faith healing. There are wide variations among tribals in their health status and willingness to access and utilise health services, depending on their culture, level of contact with other cultures and degree of adaptability.

Against this background, the National Policy seeks to promote the modern health care system and also a synthesis of the Indian systems of medicine like ayurveda and siddha with the tribal system.

The National Policy seeks to:

- Strengthen the allopathy system of medicine in tribal areas with the extension of the three-tier system of village health workers, auxiliary nurse mid-wife and primary health centres.

- Expand the number of hospitals in tune with tribal population.
- Validate identified tribal remedies (folk claims) used in different tribal areas.
- Encourage, document and patent tribals' traditional medicines.
- Promote cultivation of medicinal plants related value addition strategies through imparting training to youth.
- Encourage qualified doctors from tribal communities to serve tribal areas.
- Promote the formation of a strong force of tribal village health guides through regular training-cum-orientation courses.
- Formulate area-specific strategies to improve access to and utilisation of health services.
- Strengthen research into diseases affecting tribals and initiate action programmes.
- Eradicate endemic diseases on a war footing.

Displacement and Resettlement

Displacement of people from traditional habitations causes much trauma to the affected people. Compulsory acquisition of land for construction of dams and roads, quarrying and mining operations, location of industries and reservation of forests for National Parks and environmental reasons forces tribal people to leave their traditional abodes and land – their chief means of livelihood.

Nearly 85.39 lakh tribals had been displaced until 1990 on account of some mega project or the other, reservation of forests as National Parks etc. Tribals constitute at least 55.16 per cent of the total displaced people in the country. Cash payment does not really compensate the tribals for the difficulties they experience in their living style and ethos.

Displacement of tribals from their land amounts to violation of the Fifth Schedule of the Constitution as it deprives them of control and ownership of natural resources and land essential for their way of life.

The National Policy for Tribals, therefore, stipulates that displacement of tribal people is kept to the minimum and undertaken only after possibilities of non-displacement and least displacement have been exhausted. When it becomes absolutely necessary to displace Scheduled Tribe people in the larger interest, the displaced should be provided a better standard of living.

The National Policy, therefore, mandates that the following guidelines be followed when tribals are resettled:

- When displacement becomes inevitable, each scheduled tribe family having land in the earlier settlement shall be given land against land. A minimum of two hectares of cultivable land is considered necessary and viable for a family (comprising man, his wife and unmarried children).
- Tribal families having fishing rights in their original habitat shall be granted fishing rights in the new reservoir or at any other alternative place.
- Reservation benefits enjoyed at the original settlement shall be continued at the resettlement area.
- Additional financial assistance equivalent to nearly one and a half year's minimum agricultural wages for loss of customary rights and usufructory rights of forest produce shall be given.
- Tribals are to be resettled close to their natural habitat by treating all the people so displaced as one group to let them retain their ethnic, linguistic and socio-cultural identity and the network of kinship and mutual obligations.
- Free land is to be provided for social and religious congregations.
- If resettlement is possible only away from the district/ taluka, then substantively higher benefits in monetary terms shall be given.
- When tribal families are resettled en masse, all basic minimum amenities shall be provided at the new sites. They include roads and passages, electricity, drainage

and sanitation, safe drinking water, educational and health care facilities, fair price shops, a community hall and a panchayat office.

Forest Villages

Tribal's age-old symbiotic relationship with forests is well known. Recognising this fact, even the National Forest Policy committed itself to the close association of tribals with the protection, preservation and development of forests and envisaged their customary rights in forests. It is, however, a matter of serious concern that about 5000 forest villages do not have minimum basic living conditions and face a constant threat of eviction.

The National Policy suggests that any forceful displacement should be avoided. Human beings move on their own to places with better opportunities. The forest villages may be converted into revenue villages or forest villages may be developed on par with revenue villages to enable the forest villagers enjoy at least the minimum amenities and services that are available in revenue villages.

The National Policy, therefore, mandates that:

- Educational and medical facilities, electricity and communication, approach roads and such other basic amenities be provided to forest villagers.
- Public Distribution System (PDS) and Grain Banks be established to prevent food problems.
- Advanced agriculture and animal husbandry technologies be introduced so that forest villagers raise their production, incomes and economic standards.
- Bank and other institutional loans be made available for entrepreneurs with viable projects of income-generation.
- Tribals be given opportunities to partake in joint forest management and encouraged to form co-operatives and corporations for major forest related operations.
- Integrated area development programmes be taken up in and around forest areas.

- Tribals' rights in protection, regeneration and collection of minor forest produce (MFP) be recognised and institutional arrangements made for marketing such produce.
- Efforts be made to eliminate exploitation by middlemen in co-operatives like Tribal Development Co-operative Corporations (TDCCs), Large Sized Multi Purpose Societies (LAMPS) and Forest Development Co-operatives by introducing minimum support prices for non agricultural produce on the lines of minimum support prices for agricultural produce.

Shifting Cultivation

In the evolution of human civilisation, shifting cultivation preceded agriculture as we know it today. In shifting cultivation, tribals do not use any mechanized tools or undertake even ploughing. A digging stick and a sickle are the usual tools. It is widely practised in whole of North-Eastern region besides the States of Andhra Pradesh, Orissa, Tamil Nadu and to some extent in Chhattisgarh and Jharkhand. Though the practice is hazardous to environment, it forms basis of life for tribals. Traditionally, shifting cultivation has been in vogue in hilly terrains where tribals have had the right on land either individually or on community basis. Because of poor yields, crops do not meet their food requirement for more than four months or so in a year.

The tribals involved in shifting cultivation do not seem to have any emotional attachment to the land as an asset or property needing care and attention as in non-tribal areas. In shifting cultivation lands, no attention is paid to the replenishment of soil fertility. Tribals merely believe in harvesting crops without putting in efforts or investments. Land is just left to nature to recoup on its own.

To handle the problem of shifting cultivation, the National Policy will focus on the following aspects:

- Land tenure system will be rationalised giving tribals right to land ownership so that they will invest their energy and resources in checking soil erosion and fertility – which have hitherto been neglected as land belonged to no one but was subject to exploitation by every one.

- Agricultural scientists will be asked to focus on shifting cultivation and evolve suitable technologies to improve production.
- The shifting cultivators will be ensured sufficient food supply through the public distribution system and grain banks. Tribals will be encouraged to raise cash crops and horticultural plantations.
- Training and extension programmes will be organized to sensitise tribals about alternative economic strategies so that they can come out of shifting cultivation.

Land Alienation

Scheduled Tribes being simple folk are often exploited to forgo their foremost important resource – land – to non-tribals. Although States have protective laws to check the trend, dispossessed tribals are yet to get back their lands. Yet, another form of land alienation takes place when States promote development projects like hydro-electric power stations and mining and industries. These developmental activities, which do not confer any benefit on tribals directly, render them landless.

The National Policy for Tribals seeks to tackle tribal land alienation by stipulating that:

- Tribals have access to village land records.
- Land records be displayed at the panchayat.
- Oral evidence be considered in the absence of records in the disposal of tribals' land disputes.
- States prohibit transfer of lands from tribals to non-tribals.
- Tribals and their representatives be associated with land surveys.
- Forest tribal villagers be assigned pattas for the land under their tillage since ages.

- States launching development projects take adequate care to keep tribal lands intact and when not possible, allot land even before a project takes off.

Intellectual Property Rights

Scheduled Tribes are known for their knowledge and wisdom of ethnic origin. There is, however, no legal and/or institutional framework to safeguard their intellectual property rights.

The National Policy, therefore, will aim at making legal and institutional arrangements to protect their intellectual property rights and curtailing the rights of corporate and other agencies to access and exploit their resource base.

Tribal Languages

The languages spoken by tribals – tribal languages – are treated as unscheduled languages. In the wake of changing educational scenario, many of the tribal languages are facing the threat of extinction. The loss of language may adversely affect tribal culture, especially their folklore.

The National Policy aims at preserving and documenting tribal languages. Education in the mother tongue at the primary level needs be encouraged. Books and other publications in tribal languages will be promoted.

Primitive Tribal Groups (PTGs)

Primitive Tribal Groups (PTGs) are Scheduled Tribes known for their declining or stagnant population, low levels of literacy, pre-agricultural technology, primarily belonging to the hunting and gathering stage, and extreme backwardness. They were considered as a special category for support for the first time in 1979. There are 75 Primitive Tribal Groups spread over 15 States and Union Territories. The 25 lakh PTG population constitutes nearly 3.6 per cent of the tribal population and 0.3 per cent of the country's population.

PTGs have not benefited from developmental activities. They face continuous threats of eviction from their homes and lands. They live with food insecurity and a host of diseases like sickle cell anaemia and malaria.

The National Policy envisages the following steps to tackle PTGs' problems:

- To boost PTGs' social image, their being stigmatized as 'primitive' shall be halted.
- Efforts shall be made to bring them on par with other Scheduled Tribes in a definite time frame. Developmental efforts should be tribe-specific and suit the local environment.
- Effective preventive and curative health systems shall be introduced.
- PTGs' traditional methods of prevention and cure shall be examined and validated.
- To combat the low level of literacy among PTGs, area and need specific education coupled with skill upgradation shall be given priority.
- Formal schooling shall be strengthened by taking advantage of 'Sarva Shiksha Abhiyan'. Trained tribal youth shall be inducted as teachers.
- Teaching shall be in tribals' mother tongue/dialect.
- Considering PTGs' poverty, school-going children shall be provided incentives.
- Emphasis shall be on laid on vocational education and training.
- PTGs shall enjoy the 'right to land'. Any form of land alienation shall be prevented and landless PTGs given priority in land assignment.
- Public distribution system (PDS) shall be introduced to ensure regular food supply. Grain banks shall be established to ensure food availability during crises.
- PTGs' participation in managing forests shall be ensured to meet their economic needs and nourish their emotional attachment to forests.

Scheduled Tribes and Scheduled Areas

Although the Constitution is clear about the concept and strategy adopted for defining Scheduled Areas and tribal areas in terms of Fifth and Sixth Schedules under Articles as 244(1) and 244(2), there is some confusion among those concerned with implementing them.

The National Policy, therefore, envisages the following steps:

- The regulation making powers of State Governors to maintain good governance, peace and harmony in tribal areas will be further strengthened. It will be ensured that Tribal Advisory Councils meet regularly and focus on speedy developmental works and prohibition of land transfers. Money lending menace shall be curbed through implementation of money lending laws.
- Tribal Advisory Councils will be established in States which have Scheduled Areas and even in States where a substantial number of tribal people live although Scheduled Areas have not been declared.
- The Autonomous District/Regional Councils in North-Eastern States will be further strengthened. The Councils are elected bodies having powers of legislation and execution and administration of justice.

Administration

The existing administrative machinery in States and districts comprising Integrated Tribal Development Agencies (ITDA) and Integrated Tribal Development Projects (ITDP) have not been up in terms of the quality of performance and development indicators.

The National Policy seeks to revitalise the administration by proposing the following:

- Skill up-gradation-cum-orientation programmes shall be conducted for tribal administration officials.
- Infrastructure development shall be given priority to so that officials will function from their places of posting.
- Only officials who have adequate knowledge, experience and a sense of appreciation for tribal problems shall be posted for tribal administration.

- As the schemes meant for improving tribals' condition take time, a tenure that is commensurate with their implementation shall be fixed for officials.

Research

The National Policy acknowledges the importance of a good database to deal with Scheduled Tribes' affairs. Research on tribals' ethnic profiles, spectrum of problems and prospects and developmental constraints and monitoring and evaluation of schemes and projects needs priority attention.

The National Policy for Tribals proposes that the existing Tribal Research Institutes located in different States shall be further strengthened for carrying out purposeful research and evaluation studies and work towards the preservation of the rich tribal cultural heritage. It also envisages the establishment of a national-level research institution.

Participatory Approach

The National Policy recognises the importance of participatory approach to development. Non-Governmental Organizations (NGOs) and Voluntary Agencies (VAs) act as catalysts in reaching benefits of Government programmes and policies to the grass-root level and thus optimise the desired accomplishment. Such organizations have direct linkages with people and are conversant with their problems. NGOs can undertake and promote family and community based programmes and mobilise resources in tribal areas. Some well-established NGOs are eager to take part in the development of Scheduled Tribes in general and Primitive Tribal Groups in particular.

The National Policy, therefore, seeks to enlist and encourage NGOs in tribal development activities. They can play an important role in the opening of residential and non-residential schools, hostels, dispensaries, hospitals and vocational training centres, promotion of awareness programmes and capacity building.

Assimilation

To bring the tribals into country's mainstream, the National Policy envisages the following:

- Identification of tribal groups with 'primitive traits' shall be done away with on a priority basis.
- The 'distinct culture' of the tribes reflected in their folk art, folk literature, traditional crafts and ethos shall be preserved. Their oral traditions shall be documented and art promoted.
- Opportunities shall be provided for tribals to interact with outside cultures.
- Their geographical isolation shall be minimised through development of roads, transport and means of communication and provision of concessional travel facility.

16

Fusion of Warli Motifs with Kota Doria Handloom Craft

An Effort towards Promotion of Indian Tribal Art

Deepika Purohit*
Meenu Munjal**
Alka Chaudhary***

INTRODUCTION

India has a rich tradition of folk arts the custodians of which are the many tribes that live in the interiors of various states. A the age old custom are starting to disintegrate in the face of changing social patterns and new dimensions of identity but fortunately a growing appreciation of traditional art and craft in India and abroad is helping to sustain and encourage new creativity. In the present work, an attempt has been done to establish motifs of Warli Tribal Art of Maharashtra into a gossamer-fine checkered fabric woven at Kota, Rajasthan, known as Kota Doria (also known as Masuria). It is a design innovation to bring newness to traditional Kota Doria.

* Research Associate, Banasthali Institute of Design, Banasthali University, Rajasthan.

** Research Associate, Banasthali Institute of Design, Banasthali University, Rajasthan.

*** M. A. Student, Banasthali Institute of Design, Banasthali University, Rajasthan.

Warli Art

The first Indian Tribal art was developed in the western zone of India which included warli painting, it is one such highly-popular art-form. Based in the Thane District, about 150 km., north of Bombay, the Warli tribe numbers over 300,000 members.

Their extremely rudimentary wall paintings use a very basic graphic vocabulary: a circle, a triangle and a square. The circle and triangle come from their observation of nature; the circle representing the sun and the moon, the triangle derived from mountains and pointed trees. Only the square seems to obey a different logic and seems to be a human invention, indicating a sacred enclosure or a piece of land.

The paintings are simple line drawings, mere outlines with little or no detailing. The human figures in a Warli painting are simple, yet stylish – easy even for a child to master. The Warli people are famous for their beautiful and unique style of painting which reflects the close association between human communities and nature.

Kota Doria Handloom Fabric

Hand woven fabric is the product of Indian tradition, the inspiration and the cultural ethos of the weavers. The strength of handloom lies in introducing innovative designs which cannot be replicated by the power loom sector. However, market dynamics are lead by power loom fabrics due to their lower costs, handloom fabrics have been triumphant in some varieties, such as Kotadoria.

Kota district in Rajasthan, steals the show with its age old weaving and invaluable contribution to the Indian textile world through the magic of Doria. Kaithoon village is 15 kms., from Kota. It is only Muslims who are engaged in the weaving, on Kotadoria craft. In Kaithoon 2,000 weavers are engaged on the equal number of handlooms presently. Almost all weavers are working for Master weavers. Kotadoria fabric consists of cotton and silk yarn woven in different combinations in warp and weft, so that they produce square check pattern. This check pattern is popularly known as 'khat' which gives it transperant effect and fineness. So Kotadoria handloom fabric is a dynamic part of Indian handloom sector. The Kotadoria was granted a G. I. (Geographical indication) in July 2005. Under the Geographical Registration act 1999. At present kotadoria is passing through difficult days because power loom fabric ischeaper than the original doria ,and also due to less customer awareness about original kotadoria and awareness among the weavers of kaithoon for government policies is also poor.

Kotadoria Handloom Textile

Floral Motif on Kotadoria Fabric

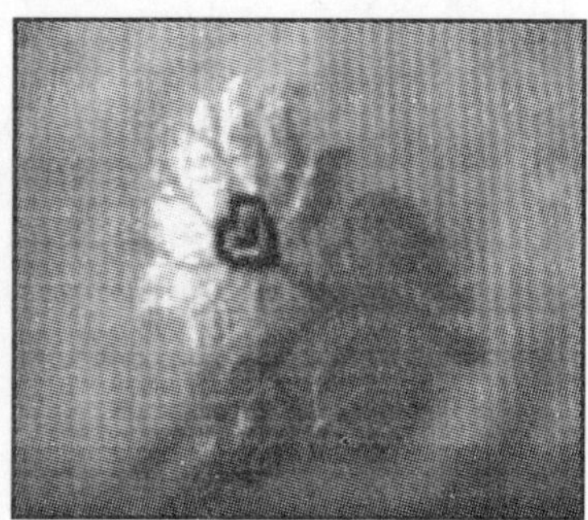

Bright Colors of Kotadoria Saris

Warli Art

Fusion of Warli Art and Kotadoria Handloom Textile

Figurative motif designing in weaving with CATD simulation inspired by Warli painting on.

Methodology

Firstly, a survey was carried out on 180 weavers of kaithoon village by interview schedule and Kota city to study the varieties of the kotadoria handloom craft and possibilities of using other art motifs and implementation on kotadoria with product diversification. After the completing first survey this study got a platform for the next consumer based survey. *Second* survey was conducted by 30 consumers, which are related to the Marketing field, mainly this type of consumer selection was done for the marketability of this fusion art product. Regarding the acceptance of merging two art forms to create design innovations, the probable market acceptance of Warli motif in Kota Doria fabric, in which product form Kotadoria fabric with Warli motif can make its mark. Warli Art has already established itself in designer products and some printed fabrics. It is probably the first attempt to take inspiration from Warli motifs for a woven fabric.

Result and Discussion

After the first data collection, it was observed that 80 per cent of the Kotadoria weavers using traditional motifs , some of them are using contemporary motifs but this type of product made only as per the special costumer demand. 72 per cent weavers wants to improve their design catalogue for offering National and international market selling, only 28 per cent weavers not respond positively because they are fully dependant on master weaver they are not aware about the costumer demand. 78 per cent of the weavers response positively for merge two types of art forms, 22 per cent weavers feel some insecurity of this type of fusion. 68 per cent weavers positively feel that Possibility of implementation of warli tribal motif on kotadoria handloom fabric.

As per the basis of first data analysis result, second survey was carried out from 30 consumer more aware from the market trend and market demand this result focused mainly these four aspects.

1. Market Demand on this Type of Fusion Work

S. No.	Response	Frequency	Percentage
1.	Yes	22	73.33%
2.	No	8	26.67%
	Total	30	100%

Most of the respondent positively believes on the marketability of warly art work on kotadoria handloom craft, like a product diversification and commercialised way to sustainable livelihood.

2. Relevant for the Long-term Production and Relationship with Both Artisans

S. No.	Response	Frequency	Percentage
1.	Yes	17	56.66%
2.	No	13	43.34%
	Total	30	100%

43.34 per cent of the Respondent said that "it is very difficult to say that about long term relationship between two art forms of different states".

3. Possibility of Government Support

S. No.	Response	Frequency	Percentage
1.	Yes	20	66.66%
2.	No	10	33.34%
	Total	30	100%

66.66 per cent respondent response positively, as per the cluster development programmes now a days Government is very actively participating to promote and support for the tribal art and artisans.

4. Idea to promotion of Tribal art and Artisans

S. No.	Response	Frequency	Percentage
1.	Yes	28	93.33%
2.	No	2	06.67%
	Total	30	100%

Most of the respondents appreciate this type of creative fusion work.

Conclusions

In order to achieve sustainable development it is imperative to promote the strategies which aim to carryout conservation and development of tribal arts and crafts. Some of the tribal paintings which were not for selling purpose, but now in the globalization scenario it is very important to make commercialised and convert according to the real fashion trend.

In any artwork, economic and cultural-artistic aspects co-exist. In creating our model, we borrowed the commonly used art market terminology 'signs' and 'signals', which we transformed into empirical criteria for analysis. It is important to emphasise that type of work.

In present study an attempt has been made to collect data for both side opinions for the practical possibilities of this fusion from weavers and consumer. After the data analysis documentation had been prepared for the design aspects. This study combined aesthetic appreciation with community development in a challenge to find another creative way to represent the Warli style of art, the growing popularity and commercialization of the Warli painting has been uplifted the many tribes and they are being integrated with the mainstream. We sincerely hope that it unfolds a possibility of new ways of seeing and interpreting our folk life. Unique museum of art objects of the rural and tribal flavor. The Warli tribe has realized that their art work is popular with tourists.

From the above analysis the following points emerge.

- Tribal artisans are unable to receive even the labour cost involved in preparing the art, let alone the profits.
- Tribal art must be promoted through product diversification, new innovative ideas and connecting their skill with other textile handloom craft, current trends through high fashion brands, fashion designers, fashion shows, patent, design rights and it must be ensured that some credit goes to the particular tribe.

- Efforts are being done by Central and State Governments for imparting training for making them commercialized and improve their marketability, providing market intelligence, establishing linkages with financial institutions, providing raw materials, providing managerial inputs in the need of the hour.

REFERENCES

Anjaneneyulu (1990), "Financial Management in the Co-operative Handloom Industries". Classical Publishing Company, New Delhi, pp. 56-59.

Annual Report 2009-10 Government of India, Ministry of Tribal Affairs.

Bhandari, K. (1996), "Participation of Rural Artisan Couple in Selected Trades and Problems Faced by them". Unpublished M.Sc. Thesis of R. A. U. Bikaner.

Dhamja, J. (1970), "Folk arts and Crafts" National Book Trusts, New Delhi.

Dhanasekar, (1993), "Handloom Sector: Impressive Export Performance" Textile Magazine Gopali and Co., 33(6):64.

Dr. M. Soundarapandian Growth and Prospects of Handloom Sector in India \\Ashok\d\Databank Ashok\Tamal Databank\Tamal Kota\Revised Diagnostic Study 2. doc

Fisher, A. (1992), "Problem and Prospects of Rural Artisan: A Case Study" Rural India ,Vol. 32, No. 10. pp. 36-38.

http://tribal.nic.in

http:/labourbureau.gov.in/ Ministry of textile textile 2008-09.

Rathore Shilpa and Purohit, Deepika (2012)" An Exploratory Study on Weavers of Kaithoon with Special Refrence to Design used, Problem fased and Interpersonal Relationship with their Family" Ph.D. Thesis , M.L.S. University, Udaipur.

www.craftsinindia.com

www.culturaindia.com

17

A Study on the Effectiveness Multilingual Education for Quality Elementary Education in Tribal Areas

K. Ramakrishna Rao*

In India the indigenous people are referred to as Adivasis, Tribal people or the Scheduled Tribes (STs). The Scheduled Tribes (STs) constitute 8.2 per cent of the population of I[illegible] The Adivasi/Tribal/Scheduled Tribe (ST) child stands [illegible] centre of an educational irony. From the mainstream perspective of education, he/she is the most deprived child in the formal system, of education. The all India drop-o[illegible] rate for STs was 52.6 per cent for Classes I – VIII. There are 623 tribal communities in India speak 218 languages out of which 159 are exclusive to them (Singh 2002). Most of the tribal languages do not have a script and are written in the script of either the dominant regional language or another major language. The *Sixth All India Educational Survey* of the National Council of Educational Research and Training (NCERT 1999) shows that, out of 41 languages used in schools (grades 1 – 10) as languages of teaching or the Medium of

* Lecturer, Government D. I. E. T, Bheemunipatnam - 531 163. Visakhapatnam (Dist.); A. P. E-mail: krkrao365@rediffmail.com

Instruction (MoI) and as school subjects, only 13 are tribal languages. Further, only three to four of these 13 tribal languages are used regularly as medium of instruction (MoI). Less than 1 per cent of the tribal children have any real opportunity for education in the medium of their mother tongues. Exclusion of tribal languages in school education is problematic since a very large number of classrooms throughout the country have a sizable proportion of tribal children. It is also quite striking that the tribal mother tongues are denied a place in formal school education in practice, despite constitutional and other policy related provisions which mandate education in mother tongues particularly for the linguistic minorities. According to the NCF-2005 children's mother tongues including tribal languages are the best medium of education at elementary level. Right to Education (RTE) Act 2009 also recommends that the medium of instruction shall as far as practicable be in the child's mother tongue When children's mother tongues are left out of classrooms, the disadvantages that accrue to them and the resultant damage to their chances of success in schools and in life are irreversible. Classroom achievement and severe learning difficulties faced by tribal children. The problems of non-comprehension, poor Academic performance in primary schools among schedule tribe Children if they were taught in a language which is different from their mother tongue The problems in tribal children's early education lead to large scale push out and cumulative failure throughout all levels of education which, in effect, push the tribal population to the lowest level of educational attainment in India. Therefore Sarva Siksha Abhiyan (SSA) has introduced an innovative tribal education programme in Andhra Pradesh and Orissa called the Multi Lingual Education (MLE) which focuses on teaching in the mother tongue for the Primary classes to improve the quality education at elementary level in tribal areas.

Multilingual Education

Multilingual Education refers to 'first-language-first' education that is, schooling which begins in the mother tongue and transitions to additional languages. Most of the MLE programmes are situated in developing countries where speakers of minority languages are tend to be disadvantaged in the mainstream education system. Research shows that children whose early education is in the language of their home tend to do better in the later years of their education. Multilingual Education is a transition programme, starting from language of child and gradually moving to languages of wider communication. Curriculum is based on local culture, using local knowledge, customs and resources through which child can develop common concepts in all areas of learning. Mother Tongue (MT) based Multilingual Education (MLE) programmes enable learners to begin their education in the language they know best. As they use their own language for learning, they are introduced to the new (official) language and begin learning to communicate in that language. At the same time, teachers help the learners develop their academic vocabulary in the new language so they can understand and talk in that language. In the MLE programmes, learners continue to develop their ability to communicate and to learn in both languages throughout Elementary Education. A widespread understanding of MLE programmes (UNESCO, 2003, 2005) suggests that instruction take place in the following stages:

- *Stage I* – learning takes place entirely in the child's home language.
- *Stage II* – building fluency in the mother tongue. Introduction of oral L2.
- *Stage III* – building oral fluency in L2. Introduction of literacy in L2.
- *Stage IV* – using both L1 and L2 for lifelong learning.

The most important features of this process are that:

- Education begins with what the learners already know, building on the language and culture, knowledge and experience that they bring with them when they start school.
- Learners gradually gain confidence in using the new (official) language, before it becomes the only language for teaching academic subjects.

- Learners achieve grade level competence in each subject because teachers use their home language, along with the official school.

Multilingual Education in Andhra Pradesh

The Rajeev Vidya Mission (RVM/SSA) Andhra Pradesh has started Mother Tongue (MT) based education *i.e.* Multilingual Education (MLE) in tribal areas to enhance the quality of elementary education provided to the schedule tribe children. There are 35 tribal groups in Andhra Pradesh. Before Multilingual Education (MLE) was implemented in the state, same textbooks, written in Telugu script were used across districts. In 2003, a pilot project was started in 8 tribal languages by the Tribal Welfare Department. Text-book primers were developed in eight tribal languages – *Adivasi Oriya, Banjara, Gondi, Kolami, Konda, Kuvi, Koya and Savara* – and the programme is being implemented in 2248 tribal Primary Schools across the State. Under this programme it is planned that the children will be taught in the mother tongue as the medium of instruction using the language primers with a gradual shift to Telugu/English medium of instruction. 20-30 schools for each language in 7 districts were identified by ITDA for the purpose. Education and Tribal Welfare departments worked out plans with Linguists and Educationists for primary schooling in Tribal languages and in 2004, the Multilingual Education (MLE) programme was finally started. All the primers have been developed in Telugu script with mother tongue language and teachers appointed preferably from local communities in these schools are imparted special training in Multilingual Education (MLE).

- *Current Status:* Currently Multilingual Education (MLE) is being implemented in the state in 7 districts and from grade I to grade V. The first grade V batch joined in 2009 Till 2008, the programme was being implemented only in 220 schools; however the numbers of schools are reported to have been up scaled to 2248 from the academic year 2010.

- *Languages:* 8 tribal languages in which Multilingual Education (MLE) is being implemented are: Adivasi Oriya, Banjara, Rajkoya (Gondi), Kolavar (Kolami), Konda, Koya, Kuvi and Sora (Savara).
- *Districts:* Srikakulam, Vizianagaram, Vishakhapatnam, Khammam, Warangal, Adilabad, Kurnool and Nellore.
- *Number of Schools*: 220 – pilot schools; 2248 – current number of MLE schools.

Curriculum Development

The curriculum is based on local culture, using local knowledge, custom and resources through which child can develop common concepts in all areas of learning. For the initial stage of curriculum development, studies were conducted on culture, habits, dialect and values of Tribal people concerned after extensive field visits by experts; Core teams along with local tribal teachers community elders knowledge keepers; NGOs Anthropologists, Educationalists took part in development of curriculum.

Curriculum planning in the MLE method:

- *Class I* – Child learns in the mother tongue and the curriculum subjects are the tribal language and math.
- *Class II* – Child learns in the mother tongue and the curriculum subjects are the tribal language and math as well as Telugu (second language) orally.
- *Class III* – Language, math, environmental studies in mother tongue and Telugu introduced as second language.
- *Class IV* – Mother tongue and second language as medium of instruction (bilingual text-books) and introducing oral third language, English.
- *Class V* – Mother tongue and second language as medium of instruction (bilingual text-books) and reading and writing of third language (English).
- *Class VI* – Transition to second language (Telugu) as medium of instruction in all the curricular subjects.

Need for the Present Study

Visakhapatnam district has the third largest ST population in the state which accounts for 11.1 per cent of the total ST population of the state and 14.55 per cent of the total population of the district. The Multilingual Education is being implemented *in Konda, Kuvi, Adivasi Oriya* Languages in 326 elementary schools in eleven mandals in the tribal area of Visakhapatnam district. Hence the investigator taken this study to know how effective the implementation of Multilingual Education (MLE) in elementary schools in the tribal area of Visakhapatnam district. This study may provide a report on MLE *i.e.* problems issues and useful suggestions for more effective implementation of Multilingual Education in tribal Areas.

Statement of the Problem

"A Study on the Effectiveness Multilingual Education for Quality Elementary Education in the Tribal Area Visakhapatnam District".

Objectives of the Study

1. To study effectiveness of Multilingual Education in the tribal area of Visakhapatnam district.
2. To study the Utilisation MLE text-books and other instructional material in Konda, Kuvi, Adivasi Oriya languages supplied to the schools in tribal area of Visakhapatnam district.
3. To study the Enrollment and Attendance of the students in schools where Multilingual Education is provided.
4. To study the achievement levels of the students in the schools where Multilingual Education is provided.
5. To study the effectiveness teaching learning activities of teachers in classroom transaction where Multilingual Education is provided.
6. To study perceptions of teachers towards the implementation of Multilingual Education in the tribal area of Visakhapatnam district.

7. To study the opinions of students towards the implementation of Multilingual Education in schools of tribal area of Visakhapatnam district.
8. To study the perceptions of parents towards implementation of Multilingual Education in schools of tribal area of Visakhapatnam district.
9. To study the problems in implementing Multilingual Education in tribal area of Visakhapatnam district.

Hypotheses of the Present Study

1. There is effective implementation of Multilingual Education in the schools of tribal area of Visakhapatnam district.
2. There is effective utilisation of Multilingual Education text-books and other instructional material in Konda, Kuvi, Adivasi the schools where MLE is provided.
3. Enrollment and Attendance are improved in the schools where Multilingual Education is provided.
4. Achievement levels are improved in the schools where Multilingual Education is provided.
5. There is effective classroom transaction and the students understand better in schools where Multilingual Education is provided.
6. There is an active involvement of teachers in effective implementation Multilingual Education in schools.
7. The students have the positive perception towards the implementation of Multilingual Education in tribal area of Visakhapatnam district.
8. The parents and community members have the positive perception towards the implementation of Multilingual Education in tribal area of Visakhapatnam district.
9. There are some problems in effective implementation Multilingual Education in the schools of tribal area of Visakhapatnam district.

Sampling and Sample Design

The researcher selected six mandals out of eleven mandals of tribal area of Visakhapatnam district. Four mandals for each language *i.e.* Konda, Kuvi, Adivasi and three schools from each mandal were selected for the study .Thus 12 schools were selected for each language and total 36 schools were selected through simple random sampling technique. The teachers from all the 36 schools were covered for the collection of data purpose. Totally 54 teachers considered as respondents for this study. Again a few Parents and two students from each school were interviewed to know their opinions towards Multilingual Education.

Tool Description

This study was designed a quantitative survey through data collection, data from schools, teachers, students, and parents through observation, questionnaire and interview schedules. For this purpose the researcher designed and developed the following tools.

- *School Observation Schedule*: An observation schedule containing part – A general information regarding particulars of the school and part – B comprises questions to collect the data to assess the implementation of Multilingual Education.
- *Questionnaire for Teachers*: It comprises the questions having three point Likert scale to find out the perceptions of teachers towards the implementation of Multilingual Education.
- *Interview Schedule for Parents:* The tool is used to assess the opinions of parents towards the implementation of Multilingual Education.
- *Interview Schedule for Students*: This tool is used to assess the opinions of students studying in schools where Multilingual Education is provided.
- *Achievement – Test:* To assess the achievement levels of the students in Multilingual Education the marks in the

school registers were taken into consideration. The marks secured by students studying class – 2 and class – 3 in Baseline test and Half yearly exams in Language; Mathematics and Environmental sciences were taken. Baseline test and half yearly marks were considered as pre-achievement test and post -achievement test marks.

Data Collection

The investigator collected the information from the selected elementary schools in tribal area of Visakhapatnam district. The school observation schedule was administered to collect the general information regarding the school and to find out the activities in implementation of Multilingual Education in the sampled schools. Through the Questionnaire the investigator collected the data from the teachers working in schools where Multilingual Education is provided. Interview schedule was used to collect the opinions of the parents and students. To assess the academic achievement of the students the Baseline test and Half-yearly marks of the students in Language Mathematics and Environmental sciences were taken into consideration for comparison. The data collected through the observation schedule questionnaire and interview schedules was used for analytical purposes.

Analysis of Data

To know the implementation of Multilingual Education in the tribal area of Visakhapatnam district the data collected through the observation schedule questionnaire and interview schedules and documentary evidence was computed and analysed in averages and percentages.

Delimitations of the Study

The study was limited to know the implementation of Multilingual Education in the selected elementary schools of tribal area of Visakhapatnam district in Andhra Pradesh. The study is also limited to collect the data from teachers, parents, students of tribal area schools where Multilingual Education is provided.

Major Findings of the Study

(i) Implementation of MLE in Schools

- It is observed that all the children in all schools have been supplied Multilingual Education text books. They are being utilised by the teachers and students for effective teaching learning process in the classrooms.
- Modules and reference books in Multilingual Education are available in 72 per cent of schools. Children Literature in Multilingual Education is available in 81 per cent of schools. It is found in schools that they are utilised for effective implementation of Multilingual Education.
- It is observed that in schools there is implementation of preparatory activities for class 1 and 2 in Multilingual Education and the children are sitting in groups and separate activities are being conducted for A, B, C Group children. Activities for remedial teaching are also being conducted for the backward students (B, C grade students) in Multilingual Education.
- It is found that all schools (100%) are evaluating the progress of the students regularly in Multilingual Education. (*i.e.* conduct of tests etc.). It is found that in 81 per cent of schools children's work, *e.g.*, notebooks, assignments etc., is corrected regularly in Multilingual Education.
- In 61 per cent of schools there is improvement in enrollment by implementing Multilingual Education It is observed that in 75 per cent of schools there is improvement in attendance and in 89 per cent of schools the School Grade is improved (when compared with previous school grading) by implementing Multilingual Education.
- It is found that schools are getting support and guidance from the school complex in Multilingual

Education. It is observed that 72 per cent of schools by the M.E.O/M.R.Ps and 47 per cent schools by the Bhasha-co-ordinator and 19 per cent of schools visited by the DIET lecturers, RVM officers, D. R. Ps on implementation of Multilingual Education.

- It is found that schools are conducting SMC meetings regularly and there are discussions on Multilingual Education and schools have community involvement in Multilingual Education.

(ii) Perceptions' of the Teachers towards MLE

- Majority of the teachers (74%) perceived that utilisation of multilingual text-books is very effective in schools. It indicates multilingual text-books are being utilised very effectively in classrooms for teaching learning process. It is perceived by the teachers that utilisation of modules and reference books in Multilingual Education are very effective.
- It is responded by 80 per cent of teachers' that pupils' participation in teaching learning process in Multilingual Education is very effective and 65 per cent of teachers' perceived that impact of Multilingual Education on students' understanding the lessons is effective. It is responded by responded 63 per cent of teachers that Multilingual Education helps the teachers maintaining discipline and classroom management.
- It is perceived by 72 per cent of teachers that the progress of the students are being evaluated regularly in Multilingual Education .It reveals that evaluating the progress of the students in Multilingual Education (conduct of tests, correction of children's work, assignments etc.,) is done regularly in all schools.
- It is responded by 67 per cent of teachers' that utilisation of children literature in Multilingual Education is very effective. It reveals that children literature Multilingual Education is utilised well in all schools by the teachers.

- It is expressed by 69 per cent of teachers that enrollment is improved by implementing Multilingual Education in schools and 76 per cent of teachers' perceived that Multilingual Education has an impact on attendance of the students and impact on improving school grade. It reveals that Multilingual Education has great impact on Enrollment Attendance and achievement levels of the students in the tribal area.
- It is perceived by 74 per cent of teachers' that academic guidance and support from Bhasha co-ordinator regarding implementation of Multilingual Education is very effective. It reveals Bhasha Co-ordinators giving good guidance and support for the teachers regarding the implementation of Multilingual Education is effective.
- It is responded by 61 per cent of teachers' responded that there is community and parents support in implementation of Multilingual Education in schools is very effective.

(iii) Achievement Levels of the Students in MLE

- The achievement levels of the pupils studying class – 2 and class – 3 in Language; Mathematics; and EVS have been raised by implementing Multilingual Education. The average marks secured by the students in all subjects in half yearly exams (Post-achievement test) are higher than the baseline test marks (Pre-achievement test).The achievement levels of the girls arc higher than the boys in all subjects. When the achievements in Language and Mathematics are compared students achieved better in language than Mathematics. This reveals that Multilingual Education had impact on improving the academic achievement of the students studying at elementary level in the tribal area of Visakhapatnam district.

(iv) Opinions of the Parents towards MLE

- All the parents 100 per cent expressed their interest towards the implementation of Multilingual Education in tribal area of Visakhapatnam district.
- Majority of the parents (92%) expressed that their children are interested in implementation of Multilingual Education in schools and 73 per cent of the parents told that their children are attending the school regularly because of the implementation of Multilingual Education.
- Majority of the parents 89 per cent expressed that their children had reported that they could understand the lessons better in Multilingual Education and 82 per cent of the parents told that their children studying well at home because of the implementation of Multilingual Education in schools.
- It is expressed by 76 per cent of the parents that Multilingual Education text books are good and useful for their children and 58 per cent of the parents expressed that the content in Multilingual Education text-books should be more related to their tribal culture.
- It is expressed by 64 per cent of the parents that multilingual education helps their children understand the lessons better and it also helps to preserve their language and culture. And 78 per cent expressed that the teachers who know their language should be appointed in schools or the teachers may be given training in that particular language. Then only they could teach better to their students.

Opinions of the Students towards MLE

- All the students 100 per cent expressed their interest towards the implementation of Multilingual Education in their schools.
- All the students 100 per cent expressed that they would like to use Multilingual Education text-books supplied to them in schools.

- It is expressed by 94 per cent of the students that they could understand the lessons better in Multilingual Education.
- It is reported by 58 per cent of the students that they have been using the children literature supplied to them in their language as a part of implementation of multilingual education.

Educational Implications

The present Study has great educational significance in Multilingual Education and Tribal Education. It may facilitate the policy makers. Educational administrators, Curriculum developers, Text-book writers and Resource persons by providing information on what is happening at the gross root level *i.e.,* implementation of Multilingual Education in *Konda kuvi, Adivasi Oriya* languages in tribal area. This research study brings the following facts into lime light.

- The Multilingual education had great impact on the Elementary Education in the Tribal areas.
- The teachers need more orientation in implementation of Multilingual Education in tribal areas.
- More Resource material to be prepared and supplied to the schools on Multilingual Education for effective implementation.
- Text-books should be more enriched with Local Tribal culture.
- The school complex/MRC/PMRC/DIET should act as Resource centres for academic support and guidance to the teachers in Multi-lingual education.

Suggestions for Further Research

The study had given very important and useful findings for effective implementation of Multilingual Education in tribal areas. The results had given some avenues for further study relevant to the field concerned. Hence the suggestions for further research are as follows:

- A similar study can be undertaken on implementation of Multilingual Education on other tribal languages.
- A study can be conducted on the Utilisation of Multilingual Text-books.
- Some studies can be under taken on the Classroom process in Multilingual Education.
- It is also suggested to study the impact of Multilingual Education on achievement levels of the tribal students.

Conclusion

Multilingual Education has a great significance in developing quality Elementary Education in the tribal areas. The present study concerned with investigating the facts and effectiveness in implementation of Multilingual Education in the tribal area of Visakhapatnam district .The analysis and interpretation of data collected enabled the investigator to arrive at the following conclusions. It is observed that Multilingual Education text books in *Konda Kuvi Adivasi Oriya* languages are being utilised by the teachers and students for effective teaching learning process in the classrooms.. The teachers' parents and students have positive perceptions towards the implementation of Multilingual Education.. The Enrollment Attendance and Achievement levels of the tribal students have been improved due to the implementation of Multilingual Education.

REFERENCES

Best John.W. (2001), Research in Education Prentice Hall of India Pvt. Ltd. New Delhi.

Cummins, J. (2000), Language, Power, and Pedagogy: Bilingual Children in the Crossfire. Clevedon, England: Multilingual Matters.

Government of India (2001), Census Report. New Delhi.

http://ssa.ap.nic.in

http://unesdoc.unesco.org

Koul. L (1997), Methodology of Educational Research Vikas Publishing House Pvt. Ltd. New Delhi.

MHRD (2011), Working Group Report on Elementary Education for the 12th Five-year Plan, Department of School Education and Literacy MHRD Government of India New Delhi.

Mohanty, A. K. (1990), "Psychological Consequences of Mother Tongue Maintenance and Multilingualism in India". In D. P. Pattanayak (Ed.), Multilingualism in India (pp. 54-66). Clevedon: Multilingual Matters.

NCERT (2005), National Curriculum Frame Work-2005 Position Papers NCERT Aurobindo Marg New Delhi.

NCERT (2009), Multilingual Education in Orissa NCERT New Delhi.

NMRC (2009) Andhra Pradesh – MLE Status Report National Multilingual Resource Centre (NMRC) JNU New Delhi.

NMRC (2010), Resources for Multilingual Education in India National Multilingual Resource Centre (NMRC) JNU New Delhi.

Sujatha. K. (1999), Education of Indian Schedule Tribes A Study of Community Schools in the District of Visakhapatnam I. I. E. P. UNESCO Paris.

UNESCO (2011), Multilingual Education in Nepal A Report UNESCO Paris.

UNESCO (2003), Education in a Multilingual World. Paris, UNESCO.

UNESCO (2007), Advocacy Kit for Promoting Multilingual Education: Including the Excluded. BANGKOK, UNESCO Asia and the Pacific Regional Bureau for Education.

World Bank. (2005), In their Own Language: Education for All. New York: World Bank.

www.nmrc-jnu.org

18

Tribal Education and Government Policies in Kerala

Dr. S. Kandasamy*

INTRODUCTION

Education in the modern society assumes multiple roles ranging from fulfilling the basic needs of human beings to shaping the future of the individuals. Majority of the population depends on education for fulfilling their aspirations and livelihood. At macro-level, education is a tool of nation building and development. As a nation building measure, in India, education being the subject matter of both central and state governments, their share of contribution in allocating the resources for education is also distributed.

But, the development of educational infrastructure, beneficiaries, and outcome is not uniform throughout the territory. There are disparities in the regions, among the group of people and the conditions of masses to acquire the educational facilities. In availing the educational facilities, the most vulnerable group of people are SCs and STs. Even though

* Assistant Professor, M.P Law College, Aurangabad – 431 001. Maharashtra.

the governments established the institutions, they may not be in a position to receive the education because of their socio-economic conditions. The other important question is what type of education the governments are extending to SCs and STs. In the present scenario, parliament made right to education as a fundamental right and enacted a separate enactment also.

Kerala is known for higher human development and a near universal education. Even in Kerala also the opportunity to education and particularly higher education is not uniform. Some groups enjoy a disproportionate advantage over other groups. Private institutions have a focus on rich and only rich are able to get quality higher education easily. In Kerala, the government is poor, whereas people are rich. The government is unable to implement the schemes due to financial constraints. Due to changing political scenario and frequent changes of communist and congress regimes, the government is unable to get stable financial aid from the central government regularly. When the state government frames policies on education with a focus on tribal community, implementation of policy does not reaches the tribals properly due to one or other reasons.

Tribal education is mainly focused on elementary levels. But only elementary education cannot fulfil the aspirations of people or achieve the national development. Higher educational institutions in tribal areas are rare and the enrolment of tribal students in higher education is less. 100 per cent literacy in higher education only can reflect the real achievement. Merely 100 per cent literacy at primary or secondary level or simply ability to read and write cannot be an achievement in education.

Educational Development in Kerala

The prevalence of education was not only restricted to males. In pre-Colonial Kerala, women, especially those belonging to the matrilineal Nair caste, received an education in Sanskrit and other sciences, as well as Kalaripayattu (martial arts). This was unique to Kerala, but was facilitated by the inherent equality shown by Kerala society to females and males, since Kerala society was largely matrilineal, as opposed to the rigid patriarchy in other parts of India.

The rulers of the Princely state of Travancore were at the forefront in the spread of education. A school for girls was established by the Maharaja in 1859, which was an act unprecedented in the Indian subcontinent. In colonial times, Kerala exhibited little defiance against the British Raj. However, they had mass protests for social causes such as rights for 'untouchables' and education for all. Popular protest to hold public officials accountable is a vital part of life in Kerala.

A pilot project began in the Ernakulam region, an area of 3 million people that includes the city of Kochi. In late 1988, 50,000 volunteers fanned out around the district, tracking down 175,000 illiterates between the ages of 5 and 60, two-thirds of them women. Within a year, it was hoped, the illiterates would read Malayalam at 30 words a minute, copy a text at 7 words a minute, count and write from 1 to 100, and add and subtract three-digit numbers. On February 4, 1990, 13 months after the initial canvass, Indian Prime Minister V. P. Singh marked the start of World Literacy Year with a trip to Ernakulam, declaring it the country's first totally literate district. Kerala's literacy rate 91 per cent 3 is almost as high as in China (93%) or Thailand (93.9%).

In 1957 Kerala elected a communist government headed by EMS Namboothiripad, introduced the revolutionary Land Reform Ordinance. The Land reform was implemented by the subsequent government, which had abolished tenancy, benefiting 1.5 million poor households. This achievement was the result of decades of struggle by Kerala's peasant associations. A second communist ministry pushed for the reform again in the late 1967. The land reform initiative abolished tenancy and landlord exploitation; effective public food distribution that provides subsidised rice to low-income households; protective laws for agricultural workers; pensions for retired agricultural labourers; and a high rate of government employment for members of formerly low-caste communities. All these reforms led to educational development in Kerala.

Table 18.1: Literacy rate from 1951 - 2011

Year	Persons	Males	Females
1951	47.18	58.35	36.43
1961	55.08	64.89	45.56
1971	69.75	77.13	62.53
1981	78.85	84.56	73.36
1991	89.81	93.62	86.17
2001	90.92	94.20	87.86
2011	93.91	96.02	91.98

Education Policy in Kerala

In Kerala, fixed grant system was introduced way back in 1899. The Grant in Aid Code was revised several times incorporating new conditions for aid. The main purpose was to improve the efficiency of school education system. The District Municipalities Act and Local Bodies Act were passed in 1920 with a view to transforming all government elementary schools to local bodies. Levy of education cess introduced was a step taken far ahead of time. New schools started from 1926-27 onwards. Labour Department offered a series of scholarships in 1921 to attract students for studies instead of work. Special efforts were made to attract girls, Scheduled Casts and Scheduled Tribes. Labour Department itself started a number of elementary schools for the education of the children from deprived castes and tribes which was a milestone for the improved conditions of education particularly among the deprived castes and tribes.

Missionaries and Social Reform Movements in Kerala

It cannot be denied that there is a significant role of missionaries and Social Reform Movements of Kerala for the development of education among masses and particularly among depressed castes and tribes. The pioneers of English education in the country were Christian Missionaries. There were three missionary societies in Kerala at the beginning of the 19th century namely the London Missionary Society (LMS), the Church Missionary Society (CMS) and the Basel Mission. These missions started their pioneering work in the field of education in their respective areas with the support of local rulers, British residents and officials. The educational activities of these missionaries helped a lot in achieving a quality education without partiality and with a focus to reach the deprived castes and tribes. Sree Narayana Dharma Paripalana Yogam (SNDP) started in 1903 stood for the advancement of Ezhava, a depressed community. Sadhu Jana Paripalana Sabha in 1907 worked for advancement of dalits. Owing to these movements, government threw open all its schools for all castes in 1912. These movements were also started schools on their own.

Educational Attainments of SCs and STs in Kerala

After the formation of the State of Kerala in 1956, several steps were taken by the government to mitigate the regional disparities in educational development. In the allocation of resources and sanction of schools, backward regions and tribal regions received special consideration. Owing to special efforts taken by the government, much of the educational disparities among the regions have almost disappeared.

Reducing educational disparities among the communities received the special attention of all the governments in the post-independence period. Reservation of seats in educational institutions, fee concession, stipend, lump sum grant, free supply of clothes and books etc., were the inducement offered to the children belonging to the SCs and STs. Residential Schools, hostels and coaching classes were also functioning for the benefit of SC/ST students. As a result, SC/ST enrolment in schools increased from 7.6 per cent in 1964-65 to 10.63 per cent in 2000-01. The corresponding figure for ST community is 0.6 per cent and 1.14 per cent. A creditable achievement of Kerala is that the literacy rate of SC/ST population in the State is much higher than that of the general population in India.

Table 18.2: Literacy rates of scheduled castes and scheduled tribes

	General	Scheduled Caste	Scheduled Tribe
Kerala	89.81	79.66	57.22
All India	52.21	37.41	29.60

The shares of SC/ST community in Kerala were 9.9 per cent and 1.1 per cent respectively.

Conclusions

Due to historical reasons, in Kerala private institutions dominate the educational scenario. Due to improved economic conditions people do able to send their children to private educational institutions with the objective of attaining quality and opportunity. Government schools cannot be said as inferior to private schools because of the less facilities available but still they have the high quality man power. Government institutions have a focus to reach the poor and the down trodden and the tribes.

Kerala has already achieved a significant level ahead of national level in education, health and demographic transition. But the thing common is that the scheduled caste and scheduled tribe population in Kerala also lacking behind in the development comparing to the other communities in the State.

It is simply a challenge to the government, but still it is possible to bridge the gap of development.

Kerala government need not stop the development activities, but still there are many things to achieve in the cases of down trodden population.

REFERENCES

Art. 21-A, Constitution of India, 1950.

Census of India, Report 2001.

Census of India, Report 2011.

Economic Review, Government of Kerala, 2001.

Right to Education Act, 2009.

19

Teaching Literacy to Potential Tribal Women and Men Leaders

Dr. P. Viswanadha Gupta*
Prof. Dhananjay Lokhande**
Rupali Suresh Kumbhar***

INTRODUCTION

Laya Resource Centre undertakes 10 days crash literacy programmes with potential tribal women and men leaders in the tribal region of North Andhra.

The main objective of this effort has been to reach out to tribal women and men learners and equip them with basic literacy skills, especially their ability to read in Telugu and numeracy skills in order to facilitate their effective functioning as leaders at the grass roots level.

Background

The idea of undertaking this programme emerged during chance interactions with Dr. Om Shrivastava, Astha, Rajasthan

* Assistant Professor, Department of Adult Continuing Education and Extension, University of Pune. E-mail: drpvgupta@aol.in

** Director and Head, Department of Adult Continuing Education and Extension, University of Pune. E-mail: Lokhande@unipune.ac.in

*** M.Phil Research Scholar, Department of Philosophy, University of Pune. Pune - 411 007.

and Ms. Jaya, Nirantar, New Delhi. Both these organizations have attempted this approach to literacy and their efforts have been successful.

However the medium of literacy for both these organizations was Hindi. Hence we began to look for a Resource organization in Andhra Pradesh. Andhra Pradesh Mahila Samatha Society (APMSS) was suggested to us by Nirantar as an organization with a considerable experience in literacy. Our attempts to interact with APMAS failed. Hence we decided to start from scratch and treat this effort as a meaningful challenge.

Initial Preparations: Identifying a Team of Trainers

The first task was to identify a team of trainers consisting of members of the Laya team as well as young literate tribal enthusiasts who would be willing to be engaged in the process of teaching literacy.

Following the identification of a team we organized a two phased workshop of two days each with the objective of developing a unified perspective within the team, outlining the learning goals, the outcome and the process for the 10 days literacy programme.

Developing Skills and Confidence of Trainers

The first challenge was to develop the skills and confidence of the trainers. This was facilitated by internal reflections on recognising the potential of tribal women learners during intermittent workshops. The following were the insights that emerged during discussions:

- The trainers recognise the rich spoken language of the learners and that they are merely teaching them to read and write. The learners will learn to read and write once they grasp the logic of the Telugu language.
- The inherent motivation of the learners as expressed in staying away from the family for 10 days is a decision made by only those who are eager to become literate.
- The importance of the learning opportunity created by the women being 'captive' as they are away from their home environments.

- The high probability of exposure to some informal learning processes initiated by self, government or NGOs which would facilitate the learning process.
- The underlying grit and determination in motivated tribal learners as positive qualities for learning.
- The capacities of the identified women as potential leaders and hence were likely to be positive learners.

Environment for Learning Literacy

In order to arrive at the meaning of a positive environment for learning literacy we discussed the conditions under which one learns best in any structured learning process. The following was the outcome of the self-reflections:

- When the content of the subject at hand is interesting.
- When the processes of learning-teaching are absorbing.
- When the engagement is perceived to be useful in life situations.
- When the trainer is motivated and committed to teach.
- When learning is fun.

Through this exercise the major insight that emerged was that our challenge was to create these conditions of learning if we have to be successful in our task of teaching literacy.

Approach to Teaching Literacy

- *This is a collective challenge:* The success of the trainees would indicate the success of the trainers.
- We should enjoy the process of training.
- We need clarity in goals and specific outcomes.
- We should develop creative teaching methods.
- We should make the maximum use of time as the learners are 'captive'.
- We should apply the basic principles of learning of moving from the simple to the complex, from known to the unknown.

De-codification of Telugu Language

Since Telugu is a phonetic language and the participants knew spoken Telugu, this made our task hugely easier. The

Telugu language comprises four basic elements: *(i) atchulu, (ii) halulu, (iii) guninthalu* and *(iv) vothulu*. The first two elements must be mastered first before the third and the fourth elements can be learned. Ultimately all have to be mastered for any person to be able to read Telugu. Additionally and simultaneously numeracy skills also need to be learnt because of its importance in everyday use.

Training Methods and Techniques

Methods

- Use a logical approach to learning Telugu.
- Assess the level of each learner through a structured schedule to gauge the level of literacy know-how.
- Divide the learners into homogeneous groups based on their level of literacy capacity.
- Develop specific learning goals for each day.
- Facilitate creative engagement throughout the learning period.
- Use extensive interactional training aids.
- Focus more extensively on reading skills initially and then promote writing skills in the follow-up.
- Introduce numerical skills from Day I around common functions such as money transactions and reading time.

Techniques

- Provide each learner with alphabets of *atchulu* and *hallulu*.
- Create a list of words with *atchulu* and *hallulu* alone before moving from simple to more complex processes of *guninthalu* and *vothulu*.
- Use pictorial presentations.
- Identify games for recognising and remembering alphabets.
- Develop simple stories for reading.
- Organize input sessions introducing key words and their ability to read them.

Programme Experience

Participants

Initially the crash literacy programmes targeted potential women leaders who were members of PRI or other village level people's institutions (PI) such as SHGs, members of tribal community based organizations (TCBO) etc. In selecting the participants we looked for their potential as future leaders in the community.

Subsequently in 2008, we extended this initiative to men farmers as well. The participants so far have been drawn mainly from Visakhapatnam and East Godavari districts of Andhra Pradesh with some outreach to Viizianagaram and Srikakulam districts. They belonged to various tribes such as Konda Reddy, Koya Dora, Gadaba, Bagata, Savara, Jatapus. The age levels were mainly between 20-35 years. This age group has a very large number of illiterates according to our experience because a decade ago the access to formal education in tribal areas was very limited. However it must be noted that quite a large proportion of the women and men in this age group have had some exposure to literacy, usually of an informal nature: through their children or through having participated and dropped out of non-formal education attempts made earlier by the government or voluntary agencies in the region.

Trainers

The trainers comprise mainly those with a tribal background with the assistance of Resource Persons and a Lead Trainer from the Laya team. The tribal trainers are young men and women who have had an opportunity to complete at least Class X. The trainers are also activists in the region and are familiar with the issues in the area.

Duration

The duration of the programme is for 10 days. From experiences of various organizations involved in literacy initiatives '10' days were considered as the minimum in taking learners from a very basic recognition of alphabets to reading skills within this period. Our experience reveals that in order for internalisation of reading and numerical skills to take place a sufficient time period is necessary.

Place

The programmes have been organized so far in the training centres of Laya in Visakhapatnam and East Godavari districts. The trainees are free from the responsibility of managing logistics and hence concentrate on literacy skills throughout the training period.

Motivation

A high level of motivation is demonstrated by a majority of trainees during the training process. This is evident from the degree of self learning that takes place during the period and the kind of effort that the trainees put in.

Selection Process

We have realised that the selection process is the most important aspect of the training process. The trainees must know what to expect especially in terms of the time agreement. The trainees also pay a token registration fee of Rs. 20 to ensure a commitment of their participation.

Results

So far 12 programmes have been organized reaching out to 185 females and 143 males. The results have been satisfying. About 50 per cent of the participants who came for the programme were unable to recognise the Telegu alphabets. The remaining 50 per cent had some rudimentary exposure to the alphabets and a few exceptional ones come with an ability to recognise alphabets properly. By the end of the period about 30 per cent could read and write words, another 30 per cent could read simple sentences and about 15 per cent reached the level of reading simple stories. (The remaining 25 per cent were struggling to master the alphabets and were just about able to recognise words). In the case of numeracy skills (which we introduced more specifically in the last few training programmes), the participants were helped to read and write numbers and do simple calculations.

Impact of the Programme

The impact of the programme has been tangible as it addresses the basic question of confidence among women and men particularly in playing leadership roles in the community. Several of the participants are taking greater initiative in their communities. An exceptional few are already asserting themselves on local issues. Two of the women stood for the local PRI elections and have become ward members of their panchayats.

Conclusions

Initiatives involve creating opportunities for further learning through brief follow-up sessions. We also invite selected participants during the last two days in every literacy camp we organize in order to brush up their literacy skills. To take this process on a movement level we have envisaged the role of learners as motivators for literacy in their villages and we are now discussing. The strategic value of reaching out through village level night literacy programmes. These programmes serve as orientations or follow up to the 10 days crash literacy programmes for the motivated learners.

20

Tribal Development

Programmes and Policies Reviews

Manisha G. Pachpol*
Dr. Vaibhav Jadhav**

INTRODUCTION

Tribal population is the aboriginal inhabitants of India who have been living a life based on the natural environment and have cultural patterns congenial to their physical and social environment. The Concerted efforts for the development of these groups by the Central and State Governments have had only marginal impacts on their socio-economic conditions in spite of the various welfare measures and constitutional protection. This paper attempts an analysis of the development and welfare programmes addressing poverty, land alienation, exploitation, education, health care, employment, social development and in their reach out to these target groups and discussion of policy implications and the strengthening of service delivery. The present paper thus looks to primarily

* Research Scholar, Department of Education and Extension, University of Pune.

** Assistant Professor, Department of Education and Extension, University of Pune. E-mail: vaibhavjadhav07@hotmail.com

examine past researches that have been focused programmes and policies for the development of tribal population in India.

Need of Tribal Development

The need for tribal development in India hardly needs any justification. Their primitive way of life, economic and social backwardness, low level of literacy, hackneyed system of production, absence of value system, sparse physical infrastructure in backward tribal areas and demographic quality of tribal areas coupled together make it imperative for a systematic process of development of tribals and tribal areas. Below are explained some important factors for tribal development in India.

1. *Improvement in the Quality of Life*: One of the long-term needs for tribal development is improvement in their quality of life. Certain basic services like: drinking water, health, housing, nutrition, rural roads etc., need to be provided to them.
2. *Reduction of the Incidence of Poverty*: Reduction of the incidence of poverty of tribals through raising the levels of productivity and off-season employment is also an important factor for tribal development.
3. *Raising the Levels of Productivity*: Raising their productivity in agriculture, horticulture, animal husbandry, forestry, cottage, village and small industries and provision of employment in all seasons will go a long way in reducing the incidence of poverty of Scheduled Tribes. There is, thus, a continued emphasis on raising the levels of productivity and creation of employment opportunities.
4. *Checking Extinction of Lesser Tribes*: There is an urgent need for appropriate and effective development programmes to check extinction of lesser tribes. Presence of non-tribes in tribal areas results in net outflow of resources from the tribal areas leaving them impoverished.
5. *Removal of Illiteracy:* The socio-economic development of Scheduled Tribes depends on educational advancement. Education is more than a mere asset for some tribal

communities; investment in education is, in a way, crucial for their existence.

6. *Elimination of Exploitation:* Elimination of exploitation and enforcement of protective and anti-exploitative measures are the basic needs of tribal development. Exploitation in tribal areas mainly occurs in the fields of liquor vending, land alienation, money-lending, forestry, trade including collection and disposal of minor forest products and labour including forest labour.
7. *Supportive Infrastructure in Tribal Areas:* Another need for tribal development arise from the fact that the tribal areas have sparse physical infrastructure. Adequate infrastructure is required for production, anti-poverty, education and anti-exploitative programmes.
8. *Prevention of Shifting Cultivation:* To check and prevent the shifting cultivation is another need for tribal development. Tribals were perhaps the original settlers of the Indian soil, hence called primitive or and aborigines. (Panda, Nishakar. 2006).

Constitutional Provisions

The Constitution of India has provided many privileges to the scheduled tribes considering their complex problems in terms of geographical isolation, socio-economic backwardness, distinctive culture, poor infrastructure facilities, language and religion, exploitation by various groups. Tribal population is the aboriginal inhabitants of India who have been living a life based on the natural environment and have cultural patterns congenial to their physical and social environment. The term 'scheduled tribe' is primarily an administrative and constitutional concept. 'Tribal folk' is defined as people living in a particular place, who enter into marriage relationships among themselves, who have no specific skills in any work, traditionally or ethnically ruled by an *adivasi* leader who speak their own special language, and have their own beliefs, customs and traditions (Article 342, The Constitution of India).

Concerted efforts were started by the Central and State Governments for the formulation of separate development strategies for the development of the scheduled castes and scheduled tribes during the Fifth Five-year Plan and subsequent plans. It is now explicitly recognised that these attempts have had only marginal impacts on their socio-economic conditions in spite of various welfare measures and constitutional protection (Baiju, K. C., 2011).

According to 1991 census 67.76 per cent of persons belong to Scheduled Tribe (ST) in different States and Union Territories excluding Assam, Jammu and Kashmir. This constitute 8.08 per cent of the total population. The percentage of Scheduled Tribe population has marginally increased from 83 per cent in 1981 to 7.95 per cent in 1991. The Scheduled Tribe population has increased by 25.67 per cent during the decade of 1981-91. The growth rate is high in comparison to the total population of the country (23.79%). This paper gives an insight into the policies, plans and programmes for tribal development in India (Government of India, Census, 1991).

Following are some main constitutional provisions for tribals in India.

(a) Statutory recognition of tribal communities.

(b) Creation of scheduled areas for the thorough development of the tribals.

(c) Special representations in the parliament, in the legislative assemblies and local bodies.

(d) Special privileges in the form of reservation of a certain percentage of posts in government services and seats in educational institutions.

(e) Recognition of the right to use local language for administration and other purposes and to profess one's faith.

In addition to the above, three provisions of the constitution deserve special mention. According to the fifth schedule, Union Executive is given the power of giving direction to the States in matters relating to the administration of scheduled areas. The sixth schedule designates tribal areas in Assam and Meghalaya where autonomous district councils and regional councils have been constituted with powers to make laws for management of land, forests, shifting of cultivation, appointment or succession of chief and headman, inheritance of property, rnaniage and divorce, social customs and matters relating to village or town administration. Article 275 (1) of the constitution provides for grant-in-aid from the Union to the States for promoting the welfare of the Scheduled Tribes or for raising the level of administration of the Scheduled Areas. The constitution also provides for the appointment of a commission for Scheduled.

Tribe's for safeguarding their interests. Thus, tribal development in the true sense and in the present context of India is in fact a post-independence concept and draws the spirit from the constitution itself.

Programmes for Tribal Welfare

A number of employment oriented and developmental programmes for tribals have been introduced by the government of India. The major programmes are Integrated Rural Development Programme (IRDP), Jawahar Rosgar Yojana (JRY), Prime Ministers Rosgar Yojana (PMRY) and Training For Self-Employment For Rural youth (TRYSEM). IRDP scheme is absolutely for rural people those belong to below poverty line and others are for both rural as wellas urban youth. All their schemes are implemented in the state by District Rural Development Agencies (DRDA's) in collaboration with Commercial and Co-operative Banks. PMRY was initiated in October 1993 to tackle the burning problem of educated unemployment. PMRY relates to setting up of self-employment ventures through industries and services. Any unemployed youth who is metric failed/passed or above or IT passed, is eligible for the benefits of the scheme subject to the condition that if he is between the age group of 18 to 35 years and his family income does not exceed Rs. 24,000 per annummz T3 he youth should also be the permanent resident of the areas for at least three years and he should not be defaulter to any bank or financial institution. The scheme envisages 22.5 per cent reservation for Scheduled Caste, Scheduled Tribe and 27 per cent for OBC. A maximum loan of Rs. 1 lakh per candidate is provided under this scheme, at an interest rate of 12.5 per cent to 15.5 per cent. The entrepreneur has to contribute 5 per cent of project cost as margin money. No collateral security guarantee is asked on such loans. Period of repayment starts after a moratorium of six to eighteen months and range over 3 to 7 years. The government provides subsidy to the extent of 15 per cent of the total loan imbursed with a ceiling of Rs. 7,500 per entrepreneur. In case of joint venture each partner may be provided a loan of Rs. 1 lakh subsidy. In such cases the interest is calculated for each partner separately at a rate of 15 per cent of his share in the project cost limited to Rs. 7,500 for each partner. (Varghese, T. 2010).

REFERENCES

Bagai, S., and Nundy, N. (2009), Tribal Education: A Final Balance. Mumbai: Dasra.

Baiju, K.C. (2011), Tribal Development under Decentralised Governance in Kerala: Issues and Challenges, *JOAAG*, Vol. 6. No. 1.

Menon, G.D. (2012), The Adivasi of India: The Politics of Struggle and Silent Languages. Retrievec from UMI Dissertation Publishing, copyright by ProQuest LLC. UMI Number: 1512474.

Varghese, T. (2010), Policies and Programmes for Tribal Development in India (pp. 45-75). Retrieved from *shodhganga.inflibnet.ac.in/bitstream/10603/222/12/12_chapter3.pdf*

Tribes and Development Policy retrieved from www.egyankosh.ac.in/bitstream/123456789/36698/1/unit%2028.pdf

Index

I

J

K

L

M

N

O

P

Q

R

S

❑❑❑